Archaeological Survey of India

REPORT

OF

A TOUR THROUGH THE BENGAL PROVINCES

OF

PATNA GAYA, MONGIR, AND BHAGALPUR ;
THE SANTAL PARGANAS, MANBHUM, SINGHBHUM, AND BIRBHUM ;
BANKURA, RANIGANJ, BARDWAN, AND HUGHLI ;

BY J. D. BEGLAR,

ASSISTANT, ARCHAEOLOGICAE SURVEY.

UNDER THE SUPERINTENDENCE OF

MAJOR-GENERAL A. CUNNINGHAM, C.S.I., C.I.E.,

DIRECTOR-GENERAL, ARCHAEOLOGICAI, SURVEY OF INDIA.

VOLUME VIII.

" What is aimed at is an accurate description, illustratcd by plans, measurements, drawings or photographs, and by copies of inscriptions, of such remains as most deserve notice, with the history of them so far as it may bo traceable, and a record of the traditions that arc preserved according them."— LORD CANNING.

" What the learned world demand of us in India is to bo quite certain of our data, to place the monumental record before them exactly as it now exists, and to interpret it faithfully and literally."— JAMES PRINSEP.

Bengal Asiatic Society's Journal, 1838, p, 227,

GYAN

ISBN: 978-81-212-1388-2(HB)

First Published in 1878
Indian Reprint in 2017

Published by

Gyan Publishing House
5, Ansari Road
Daryaganj, New Delhi-110002
Phone: 9811692060
E-mail: books@gyanbooks.com

Cataloging in Publication Data—DK
Courtesy: D.K. Agencies (P) Ltd. <docinfo@dkagencies.com>

Beglar, J. D., author.
Report of a tour through the Bengal Provinces of Patna, Gaya, Mongir, and Bhagalpur, the Santal Parganas, Manbhum, Singhbhum, and Birbhum, Bankura, Raniganj, Bardwan, and Hughli in 1872-73 / by J.D. Beglar ; under the superintendence of Major-General A. Cunningham.
pages cm. — (Archaeological Survey of India ; volume VIII)
Reprint. Originally published: Calcutta : Office of the Superintendent of Government Printing, 1878.
ISBN 9788121213882 (HB)

1. Bihar (India)—Antiquities. 2. West Bengal (India)—Antiquities. 3. Jharkhand (India)—Antiquities. I. Cunningham, Alexander, Sir, 1814-1893. II. Title. III. Series: Archaeological Survey of India (Series) ; volume VIII.

DS418.B44 2017 DDC 954 23

CONTENTS.

TOUR OF 1872-73 IN THE BENGAL PROVINCES.

LIST OF PLATES.

PREFACE.

MR. BEGLAR began the tour described in the present volume at Patna on the Ganges, where he was led to examine the question of the ancient course of the Son river. This question he has discussed at considerable length, and with much acuteness. I have myself lately gone over all the country to the south of Patna, when I made a searching enquiry into the subject, and the result of my investigation most amply confirms all that Mr. Beglar has advanced. He has clearly established the fact that a large river bed is traceable from Tarârh (near Dâüdnagar) on the Son, *viâ* Râmpur-chai and Kyal to Siddhrâmpur and Sonbhadr on the Pûnpûn river. Now there can be no doubt that Siddhrâmpur is the same place as Siddhâsrampur, which was certainly on the Son; and the name of *Sonbhadr* speaks for itself, as *Sonabhadra* is one of the well-known names of the river at the present day. The lower course of the present Pûnpûn river was therefore the ancient course of the Son, the junction taking place at Sonbhadr. The Murhar river then joined the Son 4 miles to the west of Jahânâbâd. Both sand and boulder stones were found at Nima, on the present course of the Murhar, when digging for the foundations of a bridge between Bânkipur and Jahânâbâd. I made numerous diggings still further to the east, and at Pakaoli, Pathariya Jhil, and Kasba Patna, all to the south of the present city, I found coarse red sand and boulder stones. Similar sand is also said to be found at Chilbil,

4 miles to the south of Phulwâri, and near Maholi on the lower course of the Pûnpûn. Putting all these facts together, it would appear that the Son must formerly have flowed from a point close to Dâüdnagar to Siddhrâmpur, and thence to Sonbhadr on the Pûnpûn, from which it followed the present course of the Pûnpûn and Murhar rivers to Chilbil, south of Phulwâri, where it turned first to the east as far as Panch-Pahâri, and then to the south-east, finally joining the Ganges at Fatuha. The long tract of low ground in this direction is noticed by Buchanan. It is almost destitute of trees, and the inundation waters of the Son, Pûnpûn, and Murhar still find their way down this old bed to the Ganges. This is the old channel to which Buchanan gives the name of *Mar-son*, the "dead or deserted Son." The courses of the Ganges and Son would thus have been nearly parallel for many miles, and in this narrow tract, lying between the two rivers, was situated the famous city of Pâtaliputra or Palibothra, the capital of the Gangetic Provinces. The site was exactly similar to that of Hamirpur in the long narrow strip of land between the Jumna and Betwa rivers.

Connected with Palibothra Mr. Beglar has broached a theory that the Erannoboas of the Greeks was not identical with the Son, because "both Pliny and Arrian mention the Son and Erannoboas as distinct rivers" [p. 4]. But the very same objection holds good as to the Gandak being the other large river, as Pliny mentions the Condochates as well as the Erannoboas. There is another fatal objection to the identification of the Gandak with the Erannoboas, as the *Gaṇḍak* is a female river, while the *Hiranyabâha* (or Erannaboas) is a male river like the Sona, whose wooing of the Narbada river is a well-known legend. I may add that, according to Patanjali, the city of Pâṭaliputra was actually situated on the Son (*Anu Gangam Pâṭaliputram*); and as Mr. Beglar himself has shown in the previous discussion that the old course of the Son flowed past the southern side of the city, then the Son, on which Pâṭaliputra stood, must be the same river as the Erannoboas, on which Palibothra stood.

To the south of Patna Mr. Beglar visited *Telâdha* or *Telâṛa*, a place which Mr. Broadley has described, and which I have identified with the *Ti-lo-tse-kia* of Hwen Thsang. Mr. Fergusson has objected to this identification that I "persist" in calling the monastery *Tilaḍaka*, "though M. Julien calls it *Tilaçakya*.* It is true that M. Julien so names it in two places (I, 139, and II, 439); but in a third place (I, 211) he calls it *Tilaṭaka*, and in his index, at the end of volume III, he gives both readings, *Ti-lo-tse-kia* or *Tiladhaka*, and *Ti-lo-shi-kia* or *Ti-la-ça-kia*. But with regard to this latter reading he adds: "mais peut-etre que dans ce mot, ou *chi* (ça) a le même groupe phonetique que *tse* (dha), it faut reconnaître la transcription fautive de *Tiladhaka*." Here it will be seen that M. Julien himself gives the preference to the reading of *Tiladaka* which I have adopted, and as the Chinese syllable *tse* is the usual representative of the Sanskrit cerebral *d* or *t* (just as we say *nashion* for *nation*), I thought it very probable that it was the same place as the *Tillâra* of our maps. The proper name of this place is *Telâḍha*, the *Tillaṛa* of Mr. Broadley. Here Mr. Beglar found the short inscription which Mr. Broadley describes as illegible, but in which he read the word Samvat. The inscription is on the architrave of the entrance to an old Masjid which is built of Hindu materials. It opens with the words *Sri Telâḍhaka*; and there is no trace whatever of the word Samvat. During the past cold season I paid a visit to *Telâḍha* where I obtained a small Buddhist figure, with an inscription round the head opening with the words—

Telâḍhakya vâstavyam.

With these two ancient evidences of the old name of *Telâḍhaka*, and with the modern spelling of the name as

* Royal Asiatic Society's Journal N. S. VI.—222.

Telâḍha, I believe that my identification of it with Hwen Thsang's monastery of *Tilaḍhaka* is now placed beyond all doubt.

In his account of Râjgir Mr. Beglar has broached a theory regarding the Sattapanni cave, which, in my opinion, is quite untenable. I believe that the only cave in these hills which has any claim to be identified with the famous Sattapani cave is the artificial cave now called *Son-bhândâr*. This is the only one that has been regularly cut and formed with chisel, like those at Barâbar. It bears also on the outside a row of socket holes, for the ends of the wooden beams of an outer apartment, which agrees with the description of the hall prepared by Ajâtasatru for the reception of the 500 monks who formed the first Buddhist Synod. Lastly, this cave is situated in the *south* face of the Baibhâr mountain, exactly as described in the Pali annals of Burma.

A. CUNNINGHAM.

NOTE.

Since the report was written, and while it was in the press, I have, in company with General Cunningham, again visited some portions of Magadha; and although this is not the place to give an account of the places seen, and the results obtained from excavations, a few notes on disputed points will not be out of place.

In page 27 I have spoken of Bhika Pahari as a rocky hill, and have considered it identical with Panj Pahari: in both these statements I am incorrect. Panj Pahari turns out on excavation to consist of brick, and brick alone; it appears from the stratification disclosed in the excavations that the mound had long ago been dug into for bricks, the entire ones being carried off while the broken ones and the rubbish were thrown up on the sides, and mark the occurrence by the distinctly-sloping lines of the layers of rubbish with the well-defined accumulations of the larger pieces of brick-bats at the lower end of the slope, where in the actual course of excavations they would naturally roll down and accumulate; the remains, besides, of *fragments* of walls imbedded in the mass of rubbish point to the same conclusion. Panj Pahari was therefore clearly a brick structure of some kind. General Cunningham proposes to identify it with the hill of Upagupta, and I fully concur in his identification. But I will leave him to marshal his arguments in support of the position himself. Bhika Pahari I now learn, to my surprise, to be one of the wards within the modern city of Patna, so that it is clear my informant, in calling the great mound Bhika Pahari, had misled me. Bhika Pahari is itself a high spot, but has not been examined.

In development and continuation of my views regarding

the old course of the Son, I may mention that the peculiar coarse yellow sand and the rounded Son pebbles were dug up at various and numerous spots this season by General Cunningham, shewing that the river once flowed about half a mile south of Panj Pahari, and ran parallel or nearly so to the Ganges, falling into it at Fatuha. I have, in the body of the report, indicated the course of the Son by the modern villages of Daudnagar and Tararh (about 60 miles above its present junction with the Ganges), past the villages of Rampur-Chai, Kyal, Kojhasa, Chandhos-buzurg, Bihta, into the Murhar, and then *viá* Mohiuddinpur Khera and Fatehpur Kalán into the Ganges at Fatuha; and in addition to my arguments in the body of the report, I can now add that, close to Mohiuddinpur Khera, there is an extensive jhil or lake, evidently the remains of the old bed, and that excavations at Sonmayi, a village 3 miles south-east of Mohiuddinpur Khera, and 1½ miles south of the great jhil, yield coarse yellow sand and pebbles precisely resembling what are well known as the Son sand and pebbles.

Sonmayi is at present an insignificant village, and enjoys no advantages of position—geographical, commercial or political—to render it of any importance; but that it was once an important place is evidenced by the ancient remains in it. The principal of these is a mound about 20 feet high and 150 feet long by 100 feet wide at the base. This mound is evidently the ruin of some large and important temple; it is strewn with brickbats, and near it is a pillar of greyish white stone, 9 feet high and 20 inches square. The capital and base are plain and 18 inches high each. The central portion is ornamented with a flowered band of sculpture about its centre, and by four boldly sculptured female figures round the shaft. There were formerly, an old man says, three other pillars like this one, on the mound, about 15 feet apart, of which about 18 inches were visible above the top of the mound when he was a boy; their positions, as indicated by him, form the three corners of a square of 15 feet side, so that I have no doubt they, with the existing fourth one, formed the pillars of the Maha-mandapa of a Temple.

If we suppose the Son to have flowed as indicated by me, the road from Rajgir to Patna would cross it at Sonmayi, so that we have an intelligible reason for its ancient importance. On the north bank would have stood Mohiuddinpur Khera, a place even now of importance, and whose ancient importance and present decay is attested by its very name, Mohiuddinpur Khera, "Khera" meaning old ruin.

But although it is perfectly clear that this was the course of the Son at a certain period as stated in the body of the report, the excavations of General Cunningham shew that at one time the Son, or a part of it, flowed close to the south of Panj Pahari and Patna, past Manpur Bairia and Mahaoli. General Cunningham has also pointed out to me a statement of Patanjali, that Pataliputra was situated on the Son [*Anu Sonam Pataliputram*], which proves that in his time it certainly flowed down this channel. This is an important link in the chain. I have shewn, I believe conclusively, that the Son flowed down the course I have indicated in the body of the report at the time when the Ramayana was written; that it continued in this course at the period of Buddha's death; and that, at the period of the composition of the Mudra Rakhshasa, it had begun flowing down its present bed. It now appears that at some intermediate and so far undetermined period it began flowing down a channel which has not left many traces, but which I take to have been the channel found by Captain Maxwell from Saidabad past Naubatpur, Bikram, and Phulwari, *and on eastwards past Manpur Bairia and Mahaoli.* That it did not *long* continue in this course is attested not only by the absence of jhils along this line, but by the far more emphatic absence of a single important place of antiquity, and the absence of all remains of antiquity, along it. No great river like the Son can flow long down any channel without unavoidably causing the establishment of places of importance along its banks.

But the Chinese records furnish, most unexpectedly, evidence bearing on the change in the course of the Son (see Journal Asiatic Society, London, 1836, for July and August; also Journal Asiatic Society, Bengal, Vol. VI) :—

"At the close of the years Kan Yuen (about A. D. 750) the bank of the river Holung gave way and disappeared."

The "Holung" General Cunningham justly considers as the Ganges.

At first sight the statement seems to have no bearing on the subject under discussion, nor did I think of it as having any bearing on the subject till General Cunningham pointed it out to me. It is clear that the mere falling-in of the banks of a river, large or small, is a thing of such a common occurrence, and so little import, that it could not, by any stretch of the imagination, be considered as of sufficient importance to be noted down in an epitome of Indian History, written by a nation that was so far and had so little to do with it as China, and accordingly the passage long puzzled me by its apparent want of purpose. But if we remember that the capital of India stood on the banks of the river, and that part of this capital did at some time assuredly fall into the river, the apparent mystery is instantly cleared up, and I think there can remain no reasonable doubt that the solution offered, *viz.*, that it refers to the destruction of the city of Pataliputra by the falling-in of the banks of the Ganges is the correct and only reasonable one that can be suggested.

But river banks are not in the habit of "falling-in" and "disappearing" wholesale without adequate cause: the shifting of the embouchures of the great Son or the Gandak would be the only causes physically competent to produce the catastrophe.

But the embouchure of the Gandak has certainly not

appreciably shifted from Buddha's time to the present day, as Vaisali still stands on the banks as it did then, only 20 miles above the junction; therefore, the only possible cause must have been the shifting of the embouchure of the Son suddenly from Fatuha to Maner. I have already shewn in the body of the report what changes such an event would produce in the course of the Ganges.

It is therefore clear that the change did take place very shortly before A. D. 750, and I feel gratified that my inference regarding the date of the change, based upon other and independent grounds, is thus unexpectedly confirmed.

I must not, however, omit to note that the statement of Patanjali that Patna was situated on the Son, coupled with the statements of the Greeks that it was at the confluence of the Ganges and the Erranoboas, and the actual fact that it is, and always was, on the Ganges, seems to settle the question as to the identity of the Son and the Erranoboas.

I have also visited Rajgir again, and this time with the aid of Hwen Thsang.

Fa Hian says,—"Entering the valley and skirting the mountains along their south-eastern slope for a distance of 15 li, we arrive at the hill called Gridharakonta,"—and he then goes on to describe the cave in which Buddha used to sit in profound meditation, and also Ananda's cave. In the body of my report I have identified these with the Son Bhândâr and the broken cave close to it, Nos. 3 and 4, page 90, text. Now, however, with the aid of Hwen Thsang's writings, of which I could not then avail myself (the books being out of print and not obtainable), but extracts from which have now been kindly supplied me by General Cunningham, I find that those identifications are not tenable. Following Fa Hian and entering the valley, one has to skirt the south-eastern foot of a range of hills; but as the ranges which bound the old city run north-east and south-west, it is clear that one may skirt the south-eastern foot of the northern range, the only range of which the *south-eastern* slopes are within the city, in two ways,—first, by going south-west and skirting the foot of the portion of the range to the west of the northern entrance; second, by going north-east and skirting the toe of the range to the east of the entrance. I followed the first route, and naturally enough identified the Son Bhândâr and the broken cave with Buddha's meditation cave and Ananda's cave: but the extracts from Hwen Thsang shew that I ought to have followed the second route; this I have now done, and am compelled to consider my previous identifications of these two caves incorrect.

My arguments against General Cunningham's identification of the Son Bhândâr with the Sattapanni cave rest on various grounds, not the least important of which are those very identifications which I now not only abandon but consider as hopelessly wrong. So long as my identifications of these two caves with Buddha's meditation cave and Ananda's cave remained unchallenged, my arguments against General Cunningham's identification of the Son Bhândâr cave were absolutely unassailable, for by no possibility could Buddha's meditation cave be identified with the Sattapanni cave. But the moment those identifications are abandoned as untenable, my arguments are at once brought down from the unassailable into an assailable position, and I must leave it to my readers to judge whether the residuum of my arguments against General Cunningham's identification of the Son Bhândár cave with the Sattapanni cave carry conviction or not.

General Cunningham and I separated before entering Rajgir, he going northwards towards Silao and Bihar; but before separating he gave me the extracts from Hwen Thsang bearing on the question, and explained to me his ideas as to the positions of the various remains there noticed near Buddha's meditation cave. How can I adequately shew my worthiness of noble confidence thus placed in an adversary but by unhesitatingly acknowledging my error?

The plate* will shew the positions of some of the various objects discovered.

Going eastward from the Nekpai embankment along the toe of the slope of the Ratnagiri, I soon came upon an embankment R. R. which runs across the valley in a south-easterly direction on the right hand, while on the left it runs up along the slope of the hills in a north-easterly direction. The left-hand portion of the embankment does not go quite across the valley; it goes on to within a short distance of the eastern Banganga rivulet, and stops abruptly; *opposite to it, however, on the slopes of the southern range* of hills are lines of walls, shewing that, even if the wall never did actually run right across the valley, it was at least intended to do so.

The left-hand portion goes up along the side of the hill nearly parallel to its toe and crest, crossing, close to the angle of junction with its south-eastern branch, a small dry water-course which descends from the Ratnagiri; some remains of walls and platform appear to have once existed on the right or west edge of this water-course above the crossing of the ramp R. R., but I cannot say what they represent.

Continuing along the ramp I came at a short distance on a small heap of ruins on the right-hand side of the ramp at its edge, and on the very edge of a tolerably levelled spot on the slope of the hill; the ruins are of brick, and I could trace straight walls in the ruin; this is evidently Mr. Broadley's "small stupa in the very centre of the staircase, about 8 feet square;" the remains may be the remains of a small stupa, and it is evident that Mr. Broadley saw more of it than I did, as he avows having removed numerous figures from near it to Bihar, and possibly dug a little into this mound also in search of figures. I accordingly consider that the 8 feet square plinth is the square basement of a still maller stupa: continuing to ascend, the ramp after some

* Plate XXII.

distance turns due north, and skirts the edge of a deep gorge between the Deva Ghat and Sailagiri hills. Close to the bend is a large platform of brick remains, evidently the place of Mr. Broadley's "second stupa, and a large quantity of images, pillars, &c." I could see nothing to shew that a stupa ever existed here, but, perhaps, Mr. Broadley dug it up, and it has disappeared accordingly: the ramp goes on northwards a short way further on and then all traces of it cease I could not trace it further.

Crossing now the gorge and going north-east, I found a cave near the toe of a high mass of naked rocks which rise up on the main spur from Sailagiri hill.

The cave is a natural cavern of an irregular shape 12 feet long by 10 feet wide; it has two entrances, one facing south-west, the other north-west; it is situated literally in the northern shade of the mass of naked rocks just mentioned, which form a peak subordinate to the great peak of Sailagiri; 20 feet from the north-west entrance of the cave is a large rock 30 feet square and 5 feet thick.

Fifty feet from this cave, to its south-east, and under or within the mass of rocks which rise up in a peak, is another cave, also irregular in shape.

Both these caves were once ornamented with a brick or plaster lining, or rather, I should say, the irregularities appear to have been somewhat reduced by built brick-work and stone-work. Within the first cave are several sculptures—one, a longish stone, and apparently a fragment of a pedestal of a statue, is ornamented below by a line of 4-petalled lotuses, and over it by a line of sculpture representing an elephant standing facing a Dharmma Chakra. On the opposite side sits a human figure, followed by a figure like a lion; this again followed by a female, a man with a stick (?); and, lastly, a horse and rider. There are, besides this sculpture, two others, one representing Buddha seated with attendants on the sides in a fine-grained purple sandstone; on the pedestal were sculptured two lions on the two sides of a Dharmma Chakra The figure has split off, the front portion, including the face, having split bodily off; the style of the sculpture appears to me to be of as early as the Gupta period: the other sculpture appears to have been similar, but is even more mutilated; there is, besides, a fine head of Buddha.

The height of the roof of the cave, which is formed of an overhanging projecting slab of natural rock, is at present 5 feet above its earthen floor; the cave is full of loose fragments of rough stone, but no bricks.

Both these caves have two openings each; the one at the base of the rocky peak has one opening upwards giving access to the plateau above. There cannot be a doubt, I think, that here is the cave mentioned by Hwen Thsang and Fa Hian as Buddha's meditation cave. Fa Hian says (Beal's transl., p. 114), that 30 paces to the north-west of Buddha's meditation cave is the stone cell of Ananda. Buddha's cave, according to him, clearly had two openings. If now we suppose the cave at the foot of the mass of rocks to be Buddha's meditation cave, we have to north-west of it at 50 feet the other cave which contains the sculptures, and about 100 feet off also to north-west the great block of stone mentioned above. The cave is quite far enough to be Ananda's cave, as the loose measurement of 30 paces may mean anything from 50 to 90 feet; but the great stone is, perhaps, the real spot, although it is not a cave, for it does not appear to me quite certain that Ananda's meditation place was a cave. Hwen Thsang calls it simply "a great rock."* But as Fa Hian distinctly calls it "a stone cell," it would appear that the cave which he saw had fallen in before the time of Hwen Thsang's visit.

On the peak, or rather a little below the highest point of the mass of rock, is a small oblong levelled terrace, partly natural and partly artificial. On this terrace undoubtedly

* Julien's translation III, p. 21—"une large pierre."

stood several brick buildings, among which stood a small tope of nearly 8 feet diameter crowning the highest spot. I found enough of regularly cut and wedge-shaped bricks to determine the size with tolerable accuracy; the tope was adorned with mouldings, as I found several curved wedge-shaped bricks with their outer edge cut into simple mouldings, both straight-lined and curved. I could not find a single entire brick to measure; but whatever the lengths may have been, the breadth was $10\frac{1}{2}$ to 11 inches, and the thickness varied from $2\frac{1}{4}$ to $3\frac{1}{2}$ inches.

One curious brick that I found deserves mention; its underside was hollowed into a gentle cup-shaped cavity, while the top side had a square socket hole cut into it, 2 inches square, immediately over the lower cup-shaped hollow.

Descending the ridge on the side opposite to the cave,—*i. e.*, on the east side, to the natural terrace on which the caves before mentioned are,—are the ruins of some sort of building of brick. Proceeding now in a northerly direction along the foot of the rocky crags; at a short distance, on a tolerably level rocky terrace above the lower terrace, are some remains of brick structures, among which I found curved bricks similar to those on the high peak noticed, and from these I ascertained that the diameter of the tope which must have stood here, and to which no doubt they belonged, was also about 8 feet.

These two small topes are accordingly situated to the right and left of a low pass in the craggy ridge through which people coming up the hillside direct must pass to get to the caves which are situated on the other side of the ridge.

This craggy ridge, which crops up along the centre of a spur from the great peak Sailagiri, runs north-east and south-west; it culminates into a distinct high peak at its extreme south-west end, on which, as noticed, one of the topes stood, and at the foot of which is what I call Buddha's meditation cave; about 100 feet off is a lower crag, close to which on a natural terrace is the other tope noticed before. Between these two eminences is the pass which connects the somewhat level surface of the spur itself on the opposite sides of the craggy ridge; the cave which I consider Buddha's meditation cave is accordingly situated in the "northern shade" of this craggy ridge.

From Hwen Thsang's detailed account it does not appear to me that the sloping ramp or wall R.R. was meant as a road to these caves,—as not only did I fail to trace it up to the caves, but it does not appear to go anywhere at all; it stops precisely where the west side of the water-course, along whose edge it runs for the last 300 feet of its length, becomes steep and precipitous; it appears to me accordingly to be a line of defence, especially when I remember that walls in its prolongation exist to this day on the slopes and ridges of the southern range of hills beyond the Banganga valley.

The natural ascent to the caves would be from some point near Q at the south-east foot of the slope of the main spur. Although I could see no signs of a made road, this circumstance ought not to have much weight against the supposition, when we remember that portions of massive walls, several times larger and stronger than this road could ever have been, have effectually disappeared in places in the outer line of fortifications of this very city of Girivraja; and after all, the great road, so much spoken of by the enthusiastic pilgrim, was in all human probability only a track-marked out on either side by lines of boulders.

Assuming, however, that the road did ascend up from near Q, it would necessarily go through the pass, just before reaching which would be the two small stupas to the right and left as described by Hwen Thsang.

Having visited the caves, the pilgrim appears to have gone up towards the peak; in doing so he would necessarily come upon the various other objects which he has described.

Close to the two caves already noticed are five others, all at the foot of the craggy ridge already mentioned. Of these, one certainly enshrined a statue, as at the end of it, in its back wall, exists the remains of a small brick-built niche which had once certainly been ornamented with sculpture and scroll-work in plaster, and from the remains that exist I conclude it had a pointed or circular top, built, however, of overlapping bricks; within this cave appears to have stood a very small stupa also, as I picked up two curved wedge-shaped bricks within the cave.

Along the front of all these caves, and immediately along the edge of the water-course which runs along the north-west toe of the spur, is built a long and massive revetment, and the space in front of the caves and between the revetment and the foot of the craggy ridge appears to have been to some extent artificially levelled.

Going on still further are numerous other caves, of no consequence, and containing nothing. Near these is a long ledge of rock which I take to be the long stone mentioned by Hwen Thsang over which Buddha used to walk. Close to, and almost in the very bed of, the torrent is a huge flattish rock in a sloping position, which I take to be the rock on which he dried his clothes.

I looked in the bed of the torrent for the brick well mentioned by Hwen Thsang, but did not find any. I found, however, a spot where the waters rushing down a miniature fall have worn away the rock below into a deep round cistern.

Near the north-east end of the craggy outcrop and between it and the torrent is a small squarish mound of brick ruin.

Beyond the north-east end of the craggy outcrop, on the top of the spur, and at the foot of the steep ascent of the main peak of Sailagiri, is a flat space which evidently once was the site of some building of stone; there lay lots of convenient-sized broken rubble, but no bricks.

The main peak of Sailagiri is crowned by a heap of bricks, but I could see nothing to shew that a tope stood here; the portion now existing is an oblong running east and west, 20 feet long and 15 wide; the length could have been at some period greater, even up to 30 feet, but the width could never have been an inch more than the 15 feet it is now. To have made it wider would have necessitated the building up of gigantic revetments from an immense distance below, on the side of the hill, which here is so steep that no foundation for a revetment could have been got without going some 30 or 40 feet down where the steepness begins to moderate; that such an immense wall could have disappeared leaving not a trace is highly improbable.

If the building of which the ruins exist on the peak were a Vihar or temple, it must have faced east; the bricks are 11 × 15 × $2\frac{1}{2}$ inches. I found not a single cut stone nor a single curved or wedge-shaped brick, and of moulded and cut bricks I found a very few, and all of the same pattern.

Between this peak and the next peak to its west is a low pass defended by a wall; the wall extends just so far on either side as is necessary for defensive purposes, and is not, as Mr. Broadley supposes, part of "the terrace" which "now becomes more broken, but its traces are visible up to the peak."

ERRATUM.

Plate X, for Scale $\frac{1}{20}$, *read* Scale $\frac{1}{40}$.

ARCHÆOLOGICAL SURVEY OF INDIA.

REPORT OF A TOUR IN THE BENGAL PROVINCES, 1872-73.

The work of this season was spread over a large extent of country, as will be evident from the length of my route, amounting in the aggregate to more than 4,500 miles, of which 1,700 were not by rail, and the rest by railway.

The districts explored more or less were the following :—

Patna, Gaya, Mongir, Bhâgalpur, Sântal Parganas, Mânbhum, Singhbhum and Birbhum, Bânkurah, Rânigànj, Mirzapur, Jaunpur, Allahabad, Bardwân, and Hughli.

Over a hundred and twenty photographs have been taken to illustrate the ancient remains visited, besides the plans and sections which accompany in 21 plates.

PATNA.

This great city was anciently known by the name of *Pâṭaliputrapura*, or *Pushpapura* or *Kusumapura*, and although from Hwen Thsang it would appear that *Pâṭaliputrapura* and *Kusumapura* were distinct, yet they are spoken of as identical in the Mudra Râkshasa. It is perhaps possible that at the time when the Mudra Râkshasa was written (which was probably not far removed from the time when the Muhammadans established themselves in the country) the two had amalgamated into one large city, known indifferently as Pâṭaliputra or Kusumapura.

The origin of the great city is noticed in the Mahâparinibbâna Sutta (Turnour in Journal, Asiatic Society, VII, 992). It is there mentioned that on the last occasion when Buddha was going to Wesâli from Nâlanda, he came to Pâtiligâmo. where the inhabitants had built an "*awasthagaran*" (rest-house) in the middle of the city, as it was on the high road between Vaisâli and Râjgir. At that period two great ministers, Sunidho and Wessakaro, of the Raja of Magadha were building a "Nagaran" (citadel) there. Buddha then predicts that the village Pâtali is to become a great city, and that it is to suffer from fire, water, and treachery. The gate of the city in course of construction, through which he passes, and the ferry where he crosses, obtain the names of the Gotamo gate and Gotamo ferry.

The Barmese account, as given by Bishop Bigandet, is slightly different (Bigandet's Life of Gandama, page 256):—

"Phra summoned again Ananda to his presence, and directed him to tell the Rahans to be ready for a voyage, as he desired to go to the village of Pâtali. When he arrived at that place, the people prepared for him the 'dzeat' or hall which had been erected by the order of Adzatathat. It is in the following year that the same king built the city of Pâtalibot, or Pâṭaliputra, on that same spot. In anticipation of that event, Buddha foretold that the village would become a great city, which would obtain a renowned celebrity among all other cities. Thither countless merchants would resort from all parts of Dżampoodipa. At the same time, he predicted the great calamities that would befall it. Internal discords, fire, and inundation of the Ganges would gradually work out its total destruction."

The date of the building of Pâṭaliputra as thus given in the Barmese version is the year of Buddha's death. Ajâtasatru is there stated to have ascended the throne in the 37th year of Buddha's public ministration, or eight years before his *nirvân*, thus corresponding with Turnour's account in the Mahâwanso (page xlvii). The era, however, used in the Barmese version is called the Eetzana era; this era is there stated to have been established by Eetzana (Anjana), King of Dewaha. As Buddha was born in the 68th year of this era, it is clear that this era was established 67 years before his birth; it began on a Sunday, the 1st of the waxing moon of the month of Tajoo.

The Eetzana (Anjana) era was done away with by King Ajâtasatru in its 148th year, and a new era dating from the *nirvân* of Buddha established. In the third year of this era Vaisâli was conquered by Ajâtasatru.

Ajâtasatru is stated to have reigned 35 years, and died in the year 25 of the religious era; but this statement must be a mistake, for as he ascended the throne in the 37th year of Buddha's ministry, *i. e.*, eight years before his death, and died in the 25th year from Buddha's *nirvân*, he could not have reigned over 32 years, and this corresponds with the number of years assigned to his reign from Ceylonese records, *vide*—Turnour, page xlvii.

Ajâtasatru was succeeded by four other kings of his race, when the people of Pâṭaliputra are stated to have revolted and set up Susinâgo as king in the year 63 of Buddha.

This king removed the capital from Râjagriha to Vaisâli (Bigandet, page 363),—

"That monarch, not unmindful of his mother's origin, re-established the city of Wethali, and fixed in it the royal residence."

His successor Kálasoka is said to have removed the capital to Pâṭaliputra.

From Turnour, page xxix, it appears that for some time at least, if not the entire of Kálasoka's reign, the capital continued to be Vaisâli. Be this as it may, it is certain that the nine Nandas reigned in Pâṭaliputra, and that it continued to be the capital of Magadha for a long but hitherto undetermined period.

In Barmah it appears that two different eras existed besides the religious era dating from Buddha's *nirvâna*. One lasted 1,362 years, the last year of that era being equivalent to A. D. 1156; the other consisted of two eras succeeding and, as it were, replacing each other. The latter of the two is still in use. It began, according to Bishop Bigandet, in 639 A. D.; previous to it, another era had lasted 562 years, but as two years of these two eras overlap, that era may be considered to have virtually lasted only 560 years, making it begin in A. D. 79, and corresponding to the Indian Saka era.

This era was established in the religious year 625, or, deducting the two overlapping years, in the religious year 623, which therefore must correspond with A. D. 79. Hence year 1 A. D.=545th year of the religious era, and year 1 B. C.=544th of the religious era. Consequently the nirvâna of Buddha took place by this calculation in B. C. 544.

Comparing the Ceylon and the Barmese versions, and adopting as correct the Ceylon version of Ajâtasatru having reigned 32 years, instead of the palpably erroneous number 35 of the Barmese account, we find that as Ajâtasatru ascended the throne in the 37th year of Buddha's ministry, *i. e.*, eight years before his nirvân, and consequently in the year 140 of the Eetzana (Anjana) era, and he died in the year 25 of the religious era, it is clear that the total number of years of his reign can be 32, only on the supposition that the 148th year of the Anjaña (Eetzana) era corresponds to the year 1 of the religious era, *i. e.*, that there was no year 0 of the religious era.

Bishop Bigandet has B. C. 543 as the year of Buddha's nirvâna, but as there was no year 0 A. D., I do not see how the year 1 of the religious era, the year of the nirvâna itself, can correspond to any but B. C. 544.

General Cunningham places the nirvâna of Buddha in 477 B. C.; Turnour adopts 543. It were much to be desired that so important a date be submitted to the most rigid scrutiny, and the causes of the discrepancies, if possible, ascertained, or at least indicated, before its final adoption. Further elucidation of this point has since appeared in Volume III of General Cunningham's reports.

The classical accounts of *Pâṭaliputra* are very meagre. Strabo, on the authority of Erastosthenes (Volume III, Falconer's and Hamilton's Translations, page 79), states its distance from the mouths of the Ganges at 6,000 stadia, and that the river flows "past Palibothra, a very large city" (page 80). Further on (page 97), Strabo, describing Pâṭaliputra (it is supposed on the authority of Megasthenes), states that it is situated at the confluence of the Ganges and another river; that it is in length 80 stadia, and in breadth 15. It is in the shape of a parallelogram surrounded by a wooden wall pierced with openings through which arrows may be discharged. In front is a ditch which serves the purpose of defence and of a sewer for the city.

From Pliny it appears that Palibothra was situated 425 Roman miles below the junction of the Ganges and the Jamna.

Pâṭaliputra was situated on the right bank of the Ganges, and at the confluence of a large river with it. "This river was named Erranoboas according to Arrian (who had his intelligence from Megasthenes' Journal), and was of the third degree of magnitude among Indian rivers, and inferior to none but the Ganges and the Indus" (Rennel's Memorandum, 49).

From all these accounts and the close resemblance of name, it is clear that Palibothra and Pâṭaliputra are identical, and indeed at present there is no question about it. But it is by no means quite so clear that the *Erranoboas*, the *Hiranyavaha*, and the *Son* are identical; on the contrary, if the city of Palibothra stood at the confluence of the Ganges and the Erranoboas, and if its site now be correctly represented by Patna, then it would appear that the *Son* and the *Erranoboas* are distinct rivers.

Both Pliny and Arrian mention the Son and the Erranaboas as distinct rivers, and this objection to their identity is so strong that it has been noticed by Professor Wilson (*vide* his Hindu Theatre, Volume II, preface to the Mudra Râkshasa; also in Turnour's Mahâwanso, preface, appendix).

The position of Patna as being on, or at least very near, the site of Pâṭaliputra is too well established to be shaken by this, and against this position the objection is invalid. But as in the vicinity of Patna several rivers join and did join the Ganges, the argument maintains its full force against the identification of the Erranoboas with the Son; had there been but one river joining the Ganges, it would be clear that the two were both names of the same river; as it is, no less than four tributaries join and did join the Ganges not far from Patna, any one of which, except the Sarayu, would fulfil the condition of having its confluence near Patna, but one only of which at this moment rigidly fulfils the condition of having its confluence with the Ganges, not near, but at Patna, and this is the Gandak.

Mr. Ravenshaw (Journal, Asiatic Society, volume XIV, page 137) has attempted to prove by very plausible arguments that the Son and Erranoboas are identical, and the *facts* on which he bases his inferences are perfectly correct. A wide, light sandy expanse, now under cultivation, may be traced from a point near Saidabad *viâ* Bikram to Naubatpur, but from this place the traces on to Phulwâri are not those of a great river like the Son, as Mr. Ravenshaw supposes, but of a small stream; and so far from Bânkipur having once been the bed of the mighty Son, three miles in width, there is the most indubitable evidence of its never having within historical times been the bed of any river even of ordinary magnitude. A short time ago, on the occasion of a well being dug in the Bânkipur Jail, stiff clay and kankar were found down to a depth of 44 feet from the present surface. A second well, sunk at a village named Sipara on the Patna branch road, about one and a half miles south of Bânkipur, and which on reference to the map will be found to be almost in the middle of the so-called bed of the Son, had to be abandoned, as water had not been reached at a depth of about 35 feet.

The site of Bânkipur itself is indeed one of the highest points in the district, and this may be most easily verified by observing the heights of the railway embankments from Patna to the present Son Bridge: so is Dinapur; and this may indeed have been inferred from the very circumstance of these sites having been chosen for the British civil and military stations in the district. Not merely, however, are these two points high, but the whole country between, and also for most part of the distance between Patna and Bânkipur, is remarkably high, as proved by the railway embankments, and not a single bridge of large size occurs in the entire distance between Dinapur and Patna.

Another very strong proof is, that the outfall of the Eastern Son Canal, now in course of excavation, passes between Bânkipur and Dinapur. As this canal is meant for purposes of irrigation, it necessarily goes along the highest ground, thus clearly demonstrating that no large river like the Son could within historical times have flowed between Patna and Dinapur.

The facts on which Mr. Ravenshaw's theory have been built are very slender; one of his bases is Rennell's statement that

> the ancient bed of the Son is yet traceable on the south of Patna, and seems to have led into the Ganges near Fatuha."

This statement of Rennell's is perfectly correct, but Fatuha is nearly 15 miles from Bânkipur lower down the Ganges, and the old bed of the Son which Rennell alludes to is evidently the Punpun river, 7 miles south of Bânkipur. Mr. Ravenshaw further states that Lieutenant Maxwell of the Artillery

> "was successful in clearly tracing the old bed from a point on the Son near Saidâbâd (about 18 miles above Maner, the present junction of the Son and the Ganges) *viâ* Bikram, Naubatpur, Phulwari, and Mithapur to Bânkipur, where it appears to have joined the Ganges about 200 yards west from the Golah."

The Golah referred to is one of the highest spots in Bânkipur, and an examination of the stratification of the river banks, which here frequently stand in high cliffs, shows clearly that no large river joined the Ganges near this point. The evidence of the well in the Bânkipur Jail shows that it could not have been at that spot, so that if ever the Son joined the Ganges at Bânkipur, it must have done so between the Golah and the Jail. It is needless to add that the mighty Son could never have been confined between these limits, especially at its delta.

Having thus disposed of Mr. Ravenshaw's identification, hitherto generally accepted to such an extent that even General Cunningham considers the Son to represent the Greek Erranoboas, it will not be uninteresting if I make some suggestions as to the old course of the Son, so far as I can from my own personal observations, assisted by information and opinions derived from other professional engineers.

To show that my opinion is fairly entitled to some consideration, I may mention that for a year and half I was employed as an engineer in the Patna, Gaya, and Bihar districts, and consequently have had opportunities of making myself acquainted with the engineering features of the country. According to my observations then made, and information from competent authority, I consider that at some remote period the Son flowed in a south-east course from the present village of Tarârh near Dâüdnagar, passing close to the villages of Rámpur-Chai and Kayal, and not far from the great plain (Tanr) of Deokund or Deokurh, as it is indiscriminately pronounced by the people. *Tarârh* or *Tarârah* in Hindustani means the high bank of a river, and the name clearly refers to the village having once been on the high banks of a river. Immediately close to Tarârh and between it and Dâüdnagar, recent excavations and works for the Son Canal have proved the country to have been once the bed of a great river; extensive pieces of water still exist, both at Chai and at Kayal, the remains probably of the old Son. At Deokund an annual fair or *mela* is held. From Kayal I consider it probable that the Son continued in a north-east direction, entering the bed of the present Punpun at the village of Son-Bhadr.

Son-Bhadr is a great place of pilgrimage, and although the village of Son-Bhadr is not now a place of pilgrimage, I have ascertained by long and patient enquiry from various people that Son-Bhadr is the name given to the *ford or ferry where pilgrims to Gaya* (from the west) *have to cross the Son;* the name is now applied to a part of the Son near the present Grand Trunk Road, where pilgrims halt to bathe, and make offerings to the *pitris*, and this offering here is considered the first or initiatory step to the fulfilment of the pilgrimage to Gaya. The present Son-Bhadr is not entered in the best map extant, as it is not now a *mouzah* but merely a *ghât;* but the Son-Bhadr village alluded to above is an actual village situated on the banks of the Punpun.* I cannot give the etymology of the name with certainty, but I think it not improbable that it is derived from the words *Sona* and *Bhadra*, meaning the "auspicious Sona." *Sona* means "red, to become red," and the name may originally have been

* I conclude, therefore, that the village owes its name to having sprung up at the site of the old crossing of the Son, and has naturally retained its name even though the place is no longer the crossing used. The modern crossing having come into use since the existence of the village on its banks, the village naturally retains its old name, and the crossing alone is called Son-Bhadr.

applied to the Son from the circumstance that at some parts of its course the waters of the Son appear to be tinged red. This is the popular belief at this day, and the correctness of this belief has been vouched for by native pilgrim travellers, and has been doubtless handed down by tradition from the earliest times, for we have in the Râmâyana (Griffith's Translation, Vol. IV, Book IV, Canto XL, page 197):—

> "And Sona's waters swift and strong,
> With *ruddy* billows foam along."

Since writing this, I have had an opportunity of testing the correctness of the native tradition. The Son rises in the highlands of Amarkantak, and flows through a country possessing a reddish gravelly soil. In the floods the river necessarily brings down large volumes of the red dust and sand, which it deposits in the deeper pools. In the cold season this deposit, seen through the clear waters, gives a distinct tinge of *red* to the water—see my report for 1873-74.

From Son-Bhadr, the Son in olden times appears to have flowed in what is now the bed of the Punpun as far as Sigori, a small village close to the Punpun near Chandhos Buzurg, where an annual fair is held and offerings to the *pitris* made by numerous pilgrims as at Son-Bhadr and Gaya. From here it, or at least a branch, appears to have taken a course due east, crossing over from the bed of the present Punpun river to the bed of the present Murhar river. The country at and for several miles about this place, and between these two rivers, shows the unmistakeable traces of having once been the bed of a mighty river, much mightier than the Punpun; from here it flowed in the bed of the present Murhar river till it finally joined the Ganges at Fatuha.

In parts of the bed of the Murhar river, and on its banks for some distance inland, are found rounded pebbles, precisely similar to the well-known pebbles of the Son. So close is the resemblance, that it has struck every one who has given any thought to it. Native tradition, unable to account for the appearance of these remarkable pebbles in the Murhar, has placed faith in a silly story, which relates that on a certain occasion, when the marriage procession of a baniya was passing, there were many guests and much pomp, and food consisting of unbaked dough ready rolled into balls and flattish cakes was abundantly provided for the guests, to be baked and distributed at their halting place. A fakir went up and begged as alms a share of it; in reply to his entreaty, they said to him, "None of us have yet eaten; do you want stones to eat?" Thereupon the irate fakir departed, saying, "May all your food turn into stones!" and the pebbles that now occur there and thereabouts are the petrified flour-balls and cakes.

It is possible that a portion of the Son waters crossed over the intervening country at Masouri Buzurg and Sándá, and fell into the bed of the present Dardha. Certain it is that an immense valley of sand stretches on from Masouri across the present road (from Patna to Gaya), and it has been found necessary to provide a great deal of waterway, by numerous and long viaducts, to pass off the spill-water which to this day rushes across this point in the rains.

I close my observations as an engineer on the old course of the Son by an extract of a letter to me from Mr. M. P. B. Duell, the Engineer of the Patna Division, an officer whose knowledge of the engineering features of this portion of the country has been obtained during an active employment of twelve years in charge of the Patna and Gaya Divisions, during which, for the purpose of ascertaining the waterways necessary at various points of the road in construction by him, he has examined the country with great minuteness and attention.

Referring to the Son, he says—

"I believe it wandered from its present channel between Urwul and Dâüdnagar, crossed the Patna branch road north of Masouri, entered the Punpun, and thence flowed partly into the Ganges at Futwah, and partly along the course of the Maithwan nuddy towards Mongir."

When the Râmâyana was composed, the course of the Son must have been as I have suggested, as will presently appear.

When Viswamitra asked Dasaratha and obtained the assistance of his son Râmâ to protect his sacrifices, they journeyed along the Sarayu for two days, crossed it on the third, and the same day Tádaká was killed by Râmâ. On the fourth day they reached Viswamitra's hermitage; from here they went north to Mithila, "and then the mighty saint set forth and took his journey to the north." (Griffith's Râmâyana, I, p. 158.)

At the close of the first day's journey from Viswamitra's hermitage they halted on the banks of the Son; here Viswamitra, addressing Râmâ in reply to his inquiries, says—

"And Vasu bade his city fair,
The name of Girivraja bear.

This fertile spot whereon we stand,
Was once the high-souled Vasu's land.
Behold! as round we turn our eyes,
Five lofty mountain peaks arise." (Griff. Râm., I, p. 160.)

Clearly showing that from the banks of the Son where they rested, the Râjgir mountains were visible. From no part of the banks of the present course of the Son are the Râjgir hills visible; neither are they visible from Patna; but from the point where I have indicated the Son to have entered the bed of the present Murhar river, the mountains of Râjgir are visible and continue visible for a good distance down—certainly down to where the Murhar crosses the Patna branch road.

(Griff. Râm., Vol. I, page 170.) In the morning Râmâ asks,—

"Here fair and deep the Sona flows,
And many an isle its bosom shows.
What way, O saint, will lead us o'er,
And land us on the further shore?"

To which Viswamitra replies,—

"The way I choose,
Is that which pious hermits use."

And crossing the Son, they reach the banks of the Ganges that evening, showing clearly that the road from Viswamitra's hermitage to Vaisâli crossed the Son. Next day crossing the Ganges, they go to Vaisâli.

The point where Râmâ crossed the Ganges to go to Vaisâli and on to Mithila is well known traditionally; it is at the junction of the Ganges and the Gandak, and is known as Râmbhadr; and as the old high road from Vaisâli southwards crossed the Ganges here, as proved by Buddhist writings (see *supra* on the foundation of Patna), the tradition which associates Râmbhadr with Râmâ's journey is countenanced. Râmâ therefore crossed the Ganges at Patna. A glance at the map will show that if the Son flowed then in the course it follows now, Râmâ could not only *not have seen the Râjgir hills from its banks,* but could have got to Patna (then not in existence) without crossing the Son, for, as he with Viswamitra journeyed *northwards* to Vaisâli, they must have started from a point south or nearly south of Patna, and consequently on the eastern banks of the Son, and their route to Vaisâli would not have crossed the Son at all; and even if we adopt Mr. Ravenshaw's line of the old Son, Râmâ not only would have got to Patna without crossing the Son, but could not have seen the Râjgir hills from any point on its banks. The course suggested by me, however, fulfils all the conditions.

It may not be amiss to note that the marches of Râmâ on this occasion, as detailed in the Râmâyana, are such as could easily have been accomplished. The distance from Ayodhya to the junction of the Sarayu and the Ganges is 170 miles taken in a straight line; but there are strong reasons for supposing that, in ancient times, the Sarayu joined the Ganges higher up, which would reduce the distance. However that may be, 170 miles in two days is no impossible or improbable feat, if we suppose, as suppose we must, that the king's son did not *walk on foot* the whole of the way, but rode. Thence to Viswamitra's hermitage is only a day's journey, for though it took Râmâ two days to do it, most part of one day was consumed in fighting with Tádaká, and they reached the place on the second day in time for Viswamitra to begin the initiatory rites that very day. (Griff. Râm., Vol. I, page 152.)

> "Begin, O best of saints, we pray,
> Initiatory rites to-day.
> Then thus addressed the holy man,
> The very glorious sage began
> The high preliminary rite."

On the return journey, however, Râmâ and Viswamitra were accompanied by several of Viswamitra's pupils and holy old anchorites—men who from age or weakness could not be supposed to sustain much fatigue. We find now that on the third day after starting from the hermitage, Râmâ travelled only 26 miles or so, *viz.*, from the Ganges crossing, to Vaisâli, two well-known and fixed points; this is perfectly natural. Assuming now that Râmâ travelled at this rate the two previous days also, and working backwards, we shall obtain for his halting place, on the first day, the very point on the banks of the old Son whence the Râjgir hills first become visible, as I have pointed out before; and for the site of Viswamitra's hermitage, some point 25 miles or 30 miles at most, south, or nearly south, from the first day's halting point on the suggested banks of the old course of the Son. This distance will bring us almost exactly to Deokund or Deokur, a place where, as noticed above, an annual fair or *mela* is held, and which is held in great veneration.

The name of Viswamitra's hermitage I find to have

been *Siddhâsrama,* which Griffith has translated in his Râmâyana as the "perfect hermitage." It is remarkable that close to Deokund, on the banks of the Punpun river, is a village named Siddhrâmpur. So strong a similarity of names, combined with such close identity in position, justifies the inference that this is the position of Viswamitra's hermitage. At all events, the place is clearly somewhere between it and Deokund, where the *mela* is held.

Reverting now to the journey of Râmâ from Ayodhya to the confluence of the Sarayu and the Ganges, we find that, assuming it to have had its junction in those days where it has now, Râmâ travelled about 75 miles daily; but, as stated before, this distance must be diminished if, as is probable, the junction was higher up. The distance from Viswamitra's hermitage at Siddhrâmpur to the Ganges is actually about 70 miles, of which only a small portion was travelled on the first day, when Tádaká was killed in the great forest. It is remarkable that just about 50 miles from Deokund and 20 from the Ganges, near Bihia station, an extensive forest still exists, which may accordingly, with great plausibility, be identified with the Tádaká forest.

The only link wanting to complete the chain of evidence regarding the identifications proposed, is the want of all mention of the crossing of the Son before reaching Viswamitra's hermitage. This may be merely due to there being nothing remarkable about it worth noting or needing mention.

Let us see now what light the Mahábhárata throws on the old course of the Son (Sabha Parva, chap. 20, ver. 24 *et seq.*)—

"They, Krishna, Arjuna and Bhima Sena, departing from *Kurudeça* and passing through *Kurujangala,* arrived at the beautiful *Padmasarovara* (or lotus lake); then passing beyond (or surmounting) Kalakuta, and gradually crossing the everflowing Gandaki, Carkarávartta (stony bedded), and a mountain torrent, proceeded. Crossing the pleasing Sarayu, and seeing the whole of the eastern Koçaladesa, they marched through Mithila and Malla and crossed the Charmanvati river; then crossing the Ganges and the Sona, these three brave men of unwearied courage, clothed in cloth of the Kusa grass, turning eastwards, arrived at the boundary of the Magadha kingdom."

The above extract first states that the Pándava brothers with Krishna crossed the Gandak and the Çarkarávartta and a mountain stream. The next passage states in greater detail what they did. Crossing the Sarayu, they saw Eastern Koçala, then they saw Mithila and Malla. No doubt this is a very roundabout way of going from Indraprastha to Râjagriha, but we must not lose sight of the object with which they went; this was no less than the death of the great Raja Jarâsandha, and it is only reasonable that, instead of going madly to certain destruction, as they would had they gone direct and unsupported, they should first visit the neighbouring princes of East Koçala and Mithila in order to obtain their assistance and support. Hence there is not only nothing improbable in their going *viá* East Koçala and Mithila to Râjagriha, but it was the course indicated by sound policy.

So far we have traced their course to Mithila; next we find them going from Mithila to Râjagriha; in doing so, we see *they cross the Ganges and the Sona. To understand their* route, let us turn to Hwen Thsang's route long years afterwards. He went from Vaisâli near the Gandak to Mithila, then to Lalita Patan, and returned by the same route to Vaisâli in order to go to Patna and Râjagriha. Hwen Thsang's route leads clearly to the inference that the usual road from Mithila to Râjagriha went *viá* Vaisâli and Patna; this is rather a detour, but roads then were neither numerous nor well, if at all, looked after. The Pándavas, then, in going from Mithila to Râjagriha, evidently followed the same route, doubtless for similar reasons. Therefore they crossed the Ganges at Patna, which we certainly know was a well-known crossing as early as the time of Râmâ, and continued so to the time of Buddha, when the city was not in existence, and down to the present day.

Having crossed the Ganges at Patna, they are represented as crossing the Son to go to Râjagriha; this clearly shows that the Son then flowed between Patna and Râjagriha,—that is, in the course I have indicated before.

The mention here of the Charmanvati, usually identified with the Chambal, is very puzzling. It certainly cannot mean the Chambal; and I can only suppose the name to have got in either by mistake, or as being the name of some one of the small streams near Mithila. The absence of all qualifying epithet for it, as in the case of the Gandaki and the Sarayu, tends to favour the last supposition.

While, however, I suggest what appears to me to have been the course of the Son at the time when the Râmâyana and Mahábhárata were written, I must not omit to mention that the shifting of the Son westwards is not what would have been expected considering the general lie or declivity of the country. This declivity appears to be in a north-east direction, for the area extends in length from Patna to Lakhiserai, and in breadth about 30 miles south of and parallel to the Ganges. Within this limit the various rivers, but most especially those in the vicinity of Bihar, have for a long time past shown a decided tendency to work eastwards,—so much so, that artificial cuts, intended for irrigation, taken from the right or east bank of the various rivers, have in almost all cases enlarged beyond control, absorbing the entire discharge during the rains, allowing but a small portion of the flood discharge to pass down the natural old beds. The result of this state of things has in several instances proved doubly disastrous: 1*st*, by depriving the tracts along the west banks of the natural water-courses of their fair supply of water; and, 2*ndly*, sending an excessive volume down the artificial irrigation channels, to the destruction of the crops on their banks and of the banks themselves, thus entailing permanent loss of valuable land. When employed as an engineer in the district, I devoted much attention to the remedying of these evils, but I was too soon removed, and my schemes, approved of then, have not since received attention.

Independent of this tendency of the rivers to work eastwards, the diurnal rotation of the earth must tend to throw the water of all rivers flowing from the equator towards the poles of the earth against the right or east banks, and although the amount of the force thus brought to bear against the right banks is very minute, it is constantly at work. In obedience to both these tendencies, so far from expecting the Son to have worked westwards, we should expect it to work eastwards; but so many different circumstances are capable of producing an opposite result, that it need excite no wonder to find the Son working westwards, and I have no doubt that if sufficient time and attention could be bestowed on the subject, the cause which in the particular instance of the Son did produce the results as they exist could be definitely ascertained.

I must also notice a remarkable fact observed by General Cunningham and communicated to me, that the surface of the country in many parts of the district of Arrah is frequently composed of sand of the Son and not of the Ganges, tending thus to show that at one time the Son had flowed west of its present course. Too little, however, of facts, as regards the determination of this point, has hitherto been observed to warrant any opinions being definitely formed on the subject. I merely notice it as a remarkable fact, which may at a future period prove valuable. In connection with this point, I notice, as suggested by General Cunningham, that the name of the river which now flows immediately west of Arrah is Banás; the Sanscrit Parnâça and Parna Vâha could very well have been converted by the Greeks to Erranoboas.

I notice also, as suggested by General Cunningham, the close connection between the name of the river and of Banâsur, who figures so largely in the legends of Arrah, which General Cunningham has lately proved by ingenious and convincing arguments to be the famous Eka Chakra of the Mahábhárata, and the "Alow" of Buddhist writings. The name Erranoboas, however, as applied to the river whose confluence with the Ganges was at Pâṭaliputra, could not have been applied to any except the Gandak, as will be shown further on.

That a great volume of the waters of Son once flowed down the Banâs appears from the Mahábhárata (Sabha Parva, chap. 9) describing the assembly of Varuna. There we find, among the rivers mentioned, the "Mahanada Sona," and the "Mahanadi Parnáça." The drainage basin of the Banâs being too small, even by any possibility, to procure for the river draining it alone the title of "Mahanadi" or great river, it is clear that it must have derived the great volume of water which, flowing down it, could alone have procured for it the title of great, from the Sona, which to this day communicates with it. A great part of the Son then must, at the time of the Mabábhárata, have flowed down the present Banâs river, though the Son no longer sends any great volume of water down it.

It has been shown that at one period the Son flowed east of its present course down the bed of the Punpun river, joining the Ganges at Fatuha. It has further been shown that this was its course when the Râmâyana was written. It now remains to trace the changes in its course at other different times.

In the Buddhist writings it is stated that the vessel with which the relics of Buddha were measured out, after his cremation, was retained by the Brahman, who erected a stûpa over it on the banks of a river. The Brahman is in the Barmese account named Dauna, but from other sources it appears that the vessel used in the division of the relics was a *Drona* measure, and this is doubtless the correct version of the legend. Be this as it may, a *stûpa* was erected over it by a private individual, and that individual a Brahman. What the Drona measure was exactly, it is now difficult to ascertain, but that it certainly was a very small measure can be seen at once from the Mahábhárata (Adi Parva, 11th section, entitled Chaitraratha, 2nd chapter, 4th couplet), in which the birth of Drona, the son of Bhâradwaja, is detailed. Decency compels me not to insert the passage.

I pause a moment to remark that from this account it appears clear that certainly at this period no great ill-feeling appears to have existed between Brahmans and Buddhists; a great deal has been said regarding the ill-feeling between them; and Brahmans are said to have burned the temples and hunted the Buddhist priests with malignant hatred, and the discovery of charred remains in the course of excavations at Sârnâth has without due consideration been taken as evidence that the work of destruction was perpetrated by Brahmans. But I desire to point out that the very fact of victuals, ready-dressed, and uneaten, found in the Sârnâth ruins, is the strongest proof that the attack on the monasteries was most sudden, and I submit that an attack of such a sudden nature could not have been planned by the Brahmans of the place. Buddhist monasteries are well known to contain usually several hundreds of monks, and such a monastery as that at Sârnâth was least likely to have the fewest number of occupants. To attack and burn it successfully would need a large force well armed, and it would be no easy task for a mob, suddenly roused as in popular tumults, to attack and sack the great monastery. We must therefore look to other agents for the destruction of those monasteries. Those agents are not difficult to ascertain.

I quote Elliott's India, Vol. II, page 113, describing the exploits of Ahmad Nialtigin, General of Masaúd; the author of the Târikha Subuktigin says—

"He crossed the river Ganges and went down the left bank unexpectedly ('nagah'); he arrived at a city which is called Banâras, and which belonged to the territory of Gang. Never had a Muhammadan army reached this place. The city was two parasangs square, and contained plenty of water. The army could only remain from morning to midday prayer, because of the peril. The markets of the drapers, perfumers and jewellers were plundered, but it was impossible to do more. The people of the army became rich, for they all carried off gold, silver, perfumes and jewels, and got back in safety."

This happened in A. D. 1033 (Elliot's India, Vol. II, page 58).

Here then is an account of an attack so daring and unexpected that it is hardly rivalled by the attacks of Bakhtiâr Khilji on Bihâr and Nadiya, at a later period; how Bihâr fared at Muhammadan hands may be inferred from the circumstance that when a Pandit was sought to read the books which were found during the sack of the city, not one could be found, as they had all been killed! Need it be wondered then that in this attack of Banâras as much damage as could possibly have been inflicted on the city was unsparingly inflicted? In such sudden attacks it is the large houses and temples which would be especially sought out, as being likely to yield most wealth with least search. Mahmud's expeditions to India a few years before had taught Muhammadan soldiers where most booty was to be obtained, and they no doubt profited by it in this instance, although the account quoted makes no distinct mention of temples attacked.

Reverting now to the main subject, the changes in the course of the Son, I notice that Hwen Thsang proceeded 100 *li*, or about 17 miles, to the south-east (from the asylum stûpa at Arrah) to another stûpa, which was reputed to have been built by the Brahman Drona over the vessel with which he measured the relics of Buddha.

Remembering that the stûpa was built by a private individual, it could neither have been very large nor magnificent, and the total silence of Hwen Thsang regarding its appearance and size confirms the supposition that there was nothing remarkable about it. As it was built by a Brahman, the name given to it would probably be Brahmanical.

The site of the asylum stûpa has lately been identified by General Cunningham with Arrah, and I refer to his writings for the proofs. Taking measurements and bearings from Arrah as the site of the asylum stûpa, the site of the Drona stûpa falls somewhere in the vicinity of Bhartpura.

If then the Son flowed in the course indicated by me at the time of Buddha's nirvâna, and if Hwen Thsang's bearing and distance be correct, there ought to exist at this day traces of Buddhist remains there or thereabouts. To ascertain this I examined the country about Bhartpura with minute attention, and my labours were soon rewarded by the discovery of a small stûpa at Bhagwânganj, and the remains of temples at other villages in the vicinity.

The stûpa at Bhagwânganj is a low circular mound of

brick, about 35 or 40 feet in diameter, and a maximum height of about 20 feet above the country. It is built entirely of large bricks set in mud; the bricks measure 12 inches by more than 14 inches, are all set in fine mud cement, and are all horizontal. In the centre, at the top of the mound, a square socket-hole appears to have existed, one side of which and part of a second still exist entire. It was about 18 inches square. Close to this mound, and almost touching it, are several others, oblong and round, but smaller; these are also all of brick, but the bricks are not set in solid even layers, as in the principal mound; they are irregular, and the mounds appear to be merely the ruins of structures, temples probably.

The main mound is clearly a stûpa, as evidenced not only by the *even horizontal layers of bricks solidly composing it*, but, as if to obviate all chance of misconception, part of the *socket-hole itself*, where no doubt the *tee*, or umbrella, was set up, *still exists*. From the size of the bricks, and still further from the proportion of height of the stûpa to its diameter, according to the law discovered by General Cunningham, there can be no doubt that it is one of the earliest yet discovered. That the low height as compared with the base is not due to the destruction of the upper courses, is proved by the hole at the summit still existing. I accordingly identify this stûpa with that erected over the vessel with which Buddha's relics were measured.

The name of the village is Bhagwânganj, and remembering that the stûpa was built by a Brahman, this name is very appropriate,—that is, the name is as old as the stûpa. This stûpa accordingly would date to the 6th century before Christ.

Let us now see how the position thus assigned to the Drona stûpa will agree with Hwen Thsang's subsequent route to Vaisâli. He went in a north-east direction, 23 or 25 miles from the stûpa, to Vaisâli (Cunningham, Geog. Anc. Ind., p. 443), and he *crossed the Ganges on the road*. General Cunningham suggests that the Ganges is a mistake for the Gandak, but in going from the asylum as just identified by me to Vaisâli, he must have crossed the Ganges; the direction, too, is correct enough, but the distance is 25 miles to the *Ganges*, and not to *Vaisâli*, and another 25 miles to Vaisâli. I consider, therefore, that the distance given by Hwen Thsang refers to the distance from the *asylum stûpa to the Ganges, which having been crossed*, he proceeded to Vaisâli (another 25 miles).

Since the foregoing was written, General Cunningham has sent me a literal rendering of the passage of Hwen Thsang in question. His words are,—"on parting from this kingdom he crossed the Ganges to the north-east, made from 140 to 150 *li*, and arrived at the kingdom of Vaisâli." Clearly the 140 or 150 *li* refers to the distance of Vaisâli from the Ganges; and so the accordance with my views is perfect.

Not far from the stûpa flows the Punpun river. Along its banks, at about 2 miles from Bhagwânganj, near a small village, are the remains of a stone and brick temple about 40 feet square: only a part of the basement of the temple, marked by a line of moulded stones, exists: the stone is granite roughly dressed into a plain moulding.

A mile or mile and a half further north along the Punpun is a large mound about 45 feet square and 25 feet high. This was once a temple. The bricks in all these are of large size, and the cement used mud; but in the last, along with the large bricks, small ones also are now found, and remains of lime and mortar: the positions of the smaller bricks, however, are such as clearly to show that they did not enter into the construction of the original temple. A few misshapen stones and fragments now occupy the summit of the mound, and are devoutly worshipped by libations of milk and offerings by the Muhammadans of the adjacent village Bihta. (This is not the Bihta on the East Indian Railway which General Cunningham commissioned me to examine, as stated in his Report, Vol. III, but quite another village about 25 miles south of it.)

Tradition ascribes these mounds and others too numerous to detail (all, however, close about this spot) to a Muhammadan saint named Makhdum Sâh; and, absurd as it may appear, the mounds at Bihta and Bhagwânganj are both said to be his tombs or dargâhs, while all the other mounds are his asthâns.

I should have excavated the mound at Bhagwânganj but for the circumstance that the people would not hear of the mound of the dargâh of their saint being dug into, and although I noticed and pointed out holes in the sides of the main mound where bricks had been dug and carried away, it did not in any way make the people more favourable to my designs, and I was forced to be content with noticing the exterior so far as I could, and the portions of interior disclosed by the holes already dug in the sides.

Nothing could be more complete and convincing than the

evidence thus furnished by the existence of this stûpa, of the course of the Son, at the time it was built. Although the Buddhist accounts do not name the river on whose banks the stûpa was built, there can be no doubt it was a large river to deserve mention at all. The Punpun is a small river which discharges a small sluggish stream at all seasons except the rains, when it is swelled to a great size by rain and by the spill-waters of the Son (which breaking through the embanked road now running along its eastern banks, and pouring through the openings left in it, sends part of its spill-waters down its old bed to this day), and would hardly have deserved mention at all in the meagre account (if a bare mention can be so called) which the Buddhist writings furnish of the stûpa over the measuring vessel.

It appears then that from unknown antiquity down to the period of Buddha's nirvâna, the Son flowed in the channel I have indicated, joining the Ganges at Fatuha.

Let us now attempt to trace its subsequent changes.

In A. D. 630 to 640, when Hwen Thsang visited India, he went to the stûpa built over the measuring vessel, which was on the banks of a river. As he does not mention having crossed a river, it appears not unreasonable to infer that no large river intervened between Arrah and the stûpa. Against this supposition, however, is the circumstance that he does not mention crossing any large rivers, except the Lilâjan, on his way from Patna to Gaya, so that his silence leaves the point undecided.

The next mention of the Son is in the Mudra Râkhshasa, Wilson's Hindu Theatre, where the son and successor of the King of the Mountains, leading an army against Pâṭaliputra, says—

> "Then let us march, our mighty elephants
> Shall drink the Son's dark waves, and echo back
> The roaring of its waters; spread through the groves
> That shade its bordering fields intenser gloom
> And faster than the undermining torrent
> Hurl its high banks into the boiling stream.
> Then rolling onwards like a line of clouds
> That girts in rain and thunder Vindhya's peaks
> Environ with portentious storm the city
> And lay its proud walls level with the ground."

From this passage it is clear that the Son then flowed to the west of Patna, and had to be crossed before an invading army from the west or north-west could attack Patna. But beyond this obvious inference there is another very important one. The passage describes the Son as a roaring torrent confined by high banks, which it was undermining by the fierce rapidity of its current—a description which is quite at variance with the character of the Son at the present day. Now, the Son in the cold season, the field season in India, is a very peaceful broad stream, as different from the roaring torrent as it is possible to be; and even in the rains, except in rare floods and at particular parts, it is a mighty stream, but not a roaring and boiling torrent. The description of the Son refers to the month of October or November; for Máḷayá Ketu, the young Mountain King, is represented as giving vent to his hopes and joyful feelings at the apparent quarrel between Chandragupta, the King of Patna, and Chanakya, his minister. This quarrel took place on the day of full moon of autumn, on which for some festival the city had to be decorated. (*Vide* Wilson's Hindu Theatre, II, 191.)

> "Below is Ganga by the *autumn* led
> Fondly impatient to her ocean lord."

And again—

> "What, ho! Warders of the Susanya palace, prepare the apartments for the reception of His Majesty, who is coming hither to view from the lofty turrets, the city decorated as suits the festival of the *autumnal full moon.*"

The only great festival held on a full moon in autumn is in the full moon of Kârtik, which falls in October or November, and at this time neither the Son nor other Indian rivers are in high flood.

The description, therefore, implies that at that time the Son was not flowing tranquil in a wide sandy bed, but in a narrow channel with high banks—circumstances which, taken in connection with the fact of the Son having had a different course before, clearly indicate the channel spoken of having only recently become the bed of the Son.

It might be argued that as the Mudra Râkshasa describes events happening in the reign of Chandragupta, the change in the course of the Son must have taken place shortly before, and consequently that Hwen Thśang must have found the Son running in its present channel. To this the answer is very simple. The leading incidents on which the play has been based were handed down by tradition, or, perhaps, in the form of a brief summary; while the details have all been added by the author of the play, who, as Professor Wilson conjectures, lived about the time of the Muhammadan invasions. Naturally, in composing the details, the author would be guided by the existing features of the country whenever they entered into the plot; precisely as, in ascribing fabulous antiquity to various personages, the Hindus have yet recorded their birth, or some great action of theirs, as having taken place under certain conjunctions and positions of the heavenly bodies which could not have taken place at the time indicated, but which doubtless took place at the time the book describing the event was composed. This furnishes a means of arriving at a rough approximation of the dates of various compositions, and it has ere now been largely made use of by many writers; though not always used with the necessary caution, the method is unexceptionable. In the present instance, had any hint been conveyed in the play, or elsewhere, that it was an adaptation of a written record in existence before, I should have had to examine carefully whether such pre-existing account was or was not likely to describe transactions in such detail as to fix the position of the River Son; but as there is no such hint or mention, and the plot of the play bears on the face of it marks of having been a production of the author's imaginative or inventive powers, such examination, as I have above indicated, becomes needless and indeed impossible. Professor Wilson, on the plot of this play, page 127, Volume II, says "although there is occasionally some want of probability in their execution," clearly showing that in his opinion the details of the play have been produced by the author's ingenuity and imaginative powers.

It is then clear that the change in the course of the Son took place shortly before or at the period of the great Muhammadan invasions, when the author of the Mudra Râkhshasa flourished.

After this the mentions of the Son are frequent, and with it is often mentioned Maner, a small town at its junction with the Ganges. Maner appears to have been founded by the Muhammadans, and was the capital of a parganah named "Maner Sheikh Yahya" (Elliot's India, page 364). His name is clearly Muhammadan, which induces me to suppose that the parganah comprised waste or newly formed lands, which had no name before, not having been in existence. I suppose the circumstances to have been these:

When the Son flowed down its old channel joining the Ganges at Fatuha, the Ganges ran close past Arrah. Indeed, from a passage in the Mahábhárata, where the sojourn of the Pándavas in Ekachakra, now Arrah, is detailed, the Ganges is implied to have been not far of. When, however, the Son began flowing down its new channel, the natural result of the new force brought to bear on the waters of the Ganges at the junction would be to push the Ganges over to the north, thus gradually producing a large tract of newly formed land at the junction of the rivers. That the country now between the Ganges and Arrah was once the bed of the Ganges is sufficiently well established by the nature of its soil.

Contemporaneously with this pushing northwards of the Ganges at Arrah by the force of the Son there newly brought to bear on it, the withdrawal of the force from the Ganges at Fatuha would produce a reaction tending to send the Ganges southwards at that point, for the balance of forces which maintained the Ganges in its original course being destroyed by the withdrawal of the Son current (pushing northwards), the sum of the other forces, *combined with the reflected force of the Son current* from the north or opposite bank of the Ganges facing Dinapur, would cause the Ganges to work southwards. That the Ganges has worked a great space southwards all the way from Patna to Bakhtyarpur, *i. e.*, on both sides of Fatuha as a central point, will be apparent from a glance at the map of the country; the greatest deflection being, as might be expected, just opposite Fatuha. I have not enough of facts to support my theory to the extent that would render it invincible to attacks, but the facts detailed exist beyond all question; and the theory I have propounded offers the simplest and most rational solution and explanation of the phenomena, at the same time fixing the limit of time at which the process of change commenced.

So far then as can now be ascertained, it appears that through some unknown cause the Son abandoned its original bed and took its present course some little time before the Muhammadan conquest, and that contemporaneously with this change a large tract of newly formed land was thrown up between Arrah and the Ganges, while on the other hand a large portion of the south banks of the Ganges from Patna to Fatuha was cut away by the Ganges.

Accordingly, as Pâṭaliputra occupied the south banks of

the Ganges before the change of the course of the Son, all or almost all traces of the ancient city must long since have been swept away by the Ganges.

In strong but in direct corroboration of my supposition, that Pâṭaliputra had been cut away by the Ganges, even so early as Bakhtiâr Khilji's invasions of Bengal, I need only point to the entire silence of the Muhammadan historians regarding it and its immense fort, public buildings, &c. Bakhtiâr Khilji could not possibly have left the great fort of Pâṭaliputra in his rear while advancing on Bihâr, and he certainly did not besiege or take it. What then had become of it? No mention occurs of any fort, great or small, at or near Patna till Shir Shah's period, when he is recorded to have erected the fort of Patna at a small village of that name; and this detailed account (noticed below) does not even allude to a fort or the ruins of one as existing at the village of Patna.

The portions of the old city likely to have escaped would have been the southern outskirts. Modern Patna consequently does not stand on the site of old Pâṭaliputra, but very close to it, the old city having occupied what is now the bed of the Ganges, and perhaps part of the great island between Patna and Hajipur on the opposite side of the river.

I shall subsequently examine and detail the traces of the ancient Pâṭaliputra that still exist, but before doing so I proceed to show that by Erranoboas the Greeks meant the Gandak.

First as to the word itself. Erranoboas has hitherto been considered to represent the Sanskrit Hiranyavaha or Hiranyabâha, while the Gandak has been supposed to have been rendered in Greek into Condochates.

That Hiranyabâha was a name of the Son depends solely on the authority of Amara Kosha, as far as I am aware, and General Cunningham derives the name from the broad yellow sands, and imagines some connection between the names Hiranyabâha, *Sona*, or golden, and the broad yellow sands; but I have already shown that the name Sona refers to the red colour of the waters of the Son, and has nothing to do with gold, whereas Hiranyabâha clearly means gold-bearing. The two names consequently have nothing in common, nor do I remember ever hearing of the Son as in any way connected with gold; but the Gandak river, in Sanskrit "the great Gandaki," appears connected in some way with gold,—see Beal's Catena of Buddhist Scr., page 137, where the Gandak is called the golden river. Mr. Beal, however, in the note appended, confounds the Gandaki or modern Gandak with the Hiranya*vati*, apparently considering them names of the same river; this, however, is not so; the Hiranya*vati* is the modern Hirana or Chhota Gandak river,—see Cunningham's Geog., page 432; and from the Mahábhárat it further appears that the names Hiranyavati and Gandaki did not apply to the same river, as both names occur in the list of rivers, and, to make assurance doubly sure, the Gandak has the qualifying epithet of "great" attached to it; the inference then is that the names Hiranayavati and Gandaki were always applied to distinct rivers.

But if Hiranyavati be a name of the Chhota Gandak (and of this there is no doubt), there appears not only nothing impossible, but the probabilities are strongly in favour of the great Gandaki being named the Hiranyavaha; for if one of the rivers were gold-bearing, the other could not well avoid being gold-bearing also, the smaller river being merely a branch of the latter.

Whether the Chhota Gandak at any time had an independent course to the Ganges is a point that I have not materials to discuss, not is it of much importance for the present investigation; for, whether it had an independent course or not, as it takes its rise in the lower Himalayas or Siwâlik hills, and as the great Gandak flows through and receives tributaries from the same tract only a very few miles off, if the smaller river be gold-bearing, the other must necessarily be so also. The converse of this, however, would not hold, for obvious reasons; but it has been shown that it is to the little river that the name Hiranyavati, or gold-abounding, belongs; therefore if (and I cannot imagine it otherwise) the name gold-abounding were given to the small river for its actually yielding gold, a name of similar meaning would naturally be only the just due of the other and larger river also. I consider then that the names Hiranyavati and Hiranyavaha belong to the two Gandaki rivers, the little and the great. It is worthy of note that Hiranyavati is a feminine name and Hiranyavaha masculine, and if the former were given to the small or Chhota Gandak, the other would very appropriately be applied to the larger Gandak.

Amara in his Kosha, or some one of his commentators or transcribers, appears through some confusion to have placed Hiranyavaha as a synonym of the Son. To this supposition I am led by the circumstance that the names supposed to be synonyms of the Son are immediately followed by the names of several distinct rivers without any attempt at arrangement of any kind.

If then my inference be correct, the name Hiranyavaha and its Greek rendering Erranoboas belong to the Gandak; Condochates would be the name of the Chhota Gandak river.

The physical characteristic of size of the great Gandak agrees with the Greek accounts, which make it the third river in India, inferior only to the Indus and the Ganges. The Gandak is indeed a great river, and, unlike its southern rival, it is not a river that shrivels up in the hot weather. The Son in the dry months is a very small river, or rather discharges a small volume of water, and only becomes mighty for a short time annually; it is not navigable, except in floods; in short, its essential characteristics are those of a mountain torrent, and as such it cannot bear any sort of comparison with the perennially great rivers, the Ganges and the Indus; but the Gandak, independent of its draining a larger basin than the Son, is fed by the eternal snows of the Himalayas, and never even in the driest months dwindles down to insignificance. It is always navigable in the driest seasons as far up as Baggah, or almost to the foot of the Siwâlik hills (see Rennell's memorandum and map of inland navigation), and may justly bear comparison with the Ganges and the Indus.

It thus appears that physically the Son cannot be held to represent the Greek Erranoboas, and whatever weight may attach to my arguments regarding the right of the great Gandak to the name Hiranyavaha, the physical inability of the Son can in no way be bettered by a decision for or against it; so that the Son must be abandoned, whatever other river may be adopted instead, and there is no other river that can fulfil the requirements but the Gandak. To sum up, then, I infer that the Sona of the Greeks is the modern Son; that the Condochates of the Greeks is the modern Chhota Gandak or Gandaki, joining the Ganges a little above Hajipur; and that the Erranoboas is the Hiranyavaha or the great Gandaki river, the modern Gandak.

Hitherto all proofs of the identification of Pâṭaliputra with Patna have been based on historical grounds. Nothing, however, in or about Patna has been discovered which could with certainty be pointed out as a relic of Pâṭaliputra. This last link in the chain of evidence I have been enabled to supply.

In one of his letters, General Cunningham informs me that

according to Hwen Thsang there existed in his time a rocky hill to the south-west of the palace. His words are—

"To the south-west of the old palace there is a small rocky hill, with many dozens of caves, which was made for Asoka by the demons for the use of Upagupta and other arhats."

To the south-west of the present city of Patna, and about one kos from the Patna bazar, and the same distance south-east from Bânkipur, there is a small rocky hill, at the base of which is a small hamlet; the rocky summit of the hill, however, is uninhabited; it is now known as Bhiká Pahári.

In Muhammadan history a Panj Pahári is mentioned as standing just outside of the fortifications of Patna, from the top of which Akbar inspected the fort during the war with Dâud Khan (Stewart's Bengal, page 153). The fort referred to there is the Muhammadan-built fort, as will be shown further on, but the Panj Pahári appears to me to mean no other than the very hill which I have heard named Bhiká Pahári. The name Panj Pahári is no doubt connected with the five stûpas which Hwen Thsang relates were to the south-west of the hill; they must have been at its very foot.

The name of the hill Bhiká Pahári, meaning the hill of the Bhikhus (or mendicant monks), is so clear a record of its ancient purpose, that further comment is needless; it is unquestionably the hill referred to by the pilgrim.

Hwen Thsang says further—"to the south-east of the city was Asoka's Kukkutarâmâ monastery with a stûpa."

To the south-east of Patna there is yet a small brick mound; its name has escaped me, but it is clearly the ruins of Asoka's Kukkutarâmâ monastery, and would probably be worth excavating.

In support, however, of my assertion, that ancient Pâṭaliputra is now under the waters of the Ganges, I mention that, after a very careful and minute examination of modern Patna, I failed to discover a single relic, or any traces of the great edifices, towers, &c., in it. It is hardly possible that all traces of the grandeur of the city should have so completely disappeared, if the city stood where modern Patna now stands; but if the Ganges has swallowed it, the complete disappearance is accounted for.

Greek writers mention that the walls of Palibothra were of wood. It most probably was so then, but the clear evidence of Fa Hian and of the Mudra Râkshasa shows that Pâṭaliputra was not a wooden city in their time.

The vast quantities of stone which must have been employed in the construction of the palaces and other edifices could not disappear so entirely as to leave no trace; for even if used up in modern buildings, we should see more stone in the buildings than can now be seen; a few wrecks, however, exist in the shape of detached blocks, used as sills or steps; two very fine moulded cornice stones of beautifully smooth, polished black basalt, exactly similar to the stone used in the pillars near Lakhisarai (to be described further on), are built into a couple of mean-looking houses in the narrow lane leading to the holy temple of Patain Devi; a few fragments also lie at the door of Patain Devi's temple, now quite worn and mutilated; but on the river face, near the north-east end of Patna, are numerous boulders of stone lying scattered on the banks, and built into the river revetments, showing that on this side, probably, was the old city, with its stone edifices: besides these, no other traces of old Pâṭaliputra exist in modern Patna.

The modern city of Patna dates only to the time of Shir Shah. I quote from Elliot's History of India, Volume IV, page 477—

"Shir Shah on his return from Bengal (in 948 A. H.=1541 A. D.) came to Patna, then a small town, dependent on Bihar, which was the seat of the local Government. He was standing on the bank of the Ganges when, after much solid reflection and sage determination, he said to those who were standing by: 'If a fort were built in this place the waters of the Ganges could never flow far from it, and Patna would become one of the great towns of this country; because this place is situated to the west on the banks of the Ganges which flows from the north. The stiength of the stream is bioken, and it cannot advance towards the north.' He therefore ordered skilful carpenters and bricklayers to make out immediately an estimate for building a fort where he then stood. These experienced workmen submitted an estimate of five lacs, which on the spur of the moment was made over to trustworthy persons. The fort was completed and was considered to be exceedingly strong. Bihar from that time was deserted and fell to ruin, while Patna became one of the largest cities of the province."

Popular tradition confirms this account, and att he present day a masjid in Patna of plain massive construction is pointed out as the masjid built by Shir Shah; it has an inscription. The name of Shir Shah is said to be written in the interior at the neck of the great central dome. There is certainly an inscription there, but so concealed with repeated coats of whitewash as to be hardly legible; from the style of the building I am of opinion that the masjid does date to Shir Shah.

In plan, this masjid is a square of 63 feet internally, within which is a second square marked by pillars with a clear width internally of 27 feet 2 inches. This central hall is covered by a semicircular dome on a low neck, surmounted externally by a small top-knot, like the Kila Kona Masjid in Delhi Purana Kila. The dome is supported underneath by arches, which mark out the central hall. The pillars are 3 feet 8 inches square; there are four on each side, so that the hall has 12 arched openings springing from the 12 pillars; the corner pillars are in no way larger or stronger than the intermediate ones; the dome rests on arched pendentives.

The galleries on the four sides of this hall are roofed by vaulted arches resting on arches. At the four corners, however, the vaults are replaced by four small domes, similar to the large central dome, and similarly surmounted by small top-knots; the principal mehrâb is in the centre of the west wall of the west gallery. Two other mehrâbs, however, occupy the west-end walls of the two north and south galleries. The principal entrance to the masjid is under a great archway, and through a smaller archway; all the entrance archways are equal, but the central one has a projecting great arch for its façade. The smaller archways, both of the principal entrances and of the mehrâbs, are fretted, but the great arch is quite plain, and so are the side arches; the top of the central projecting portion of the front wall, which is pierced by the great arch, is curved. The four faces of the masjid are precisely similar to each other externally and internally, with this exception, that in the west face there are no entrances, but merely false arches panelled into the façade.

The exterior is ornamented by several small niches. The general appearance of the masjid is plain, and its style is not such as to make it imposing, despite its excessive plainness. The masjid is built entirely of brick faced with plaster, and devoutly whitewashed every year. I have thus described it in detail, as it is traditionally and probably actually the oldest masjid in Patna.

Besides this masjid there are two others of interest, of which the one at Chamni Ghat is remarkably fine. It consists of five openings (of which the central one is slightly larger than the side ones), giving entrance into a long hall divided off into five compartments by great archways across from wall to wall resting on square projecting pilasters. The central entrance is relieved by a bold projection pierced by a large archway, and this projecting portion of the front wall is a little higher than the rest of the façade; it is not curved on the top as in Shir Shah's masjid, but is perfectly straight and ornamented with battlements. Over the other entrances are also battlements and slight projections to give them value. The corners are ornamented by octagonal towers.

The roof consists of one large central dome with two smaller domes on each side; the domes are all flattish, without bulge, and are crowned by small foliated caps and gilt spires with numerous gilt discs and balls alternating, as is the usual custom at the present day. The façade has not much play of light and shade, being, with the exception noted at the centre entrance, almost a dead flat, hardly relieved at the four side entrances; but this want of real beauty is in some measure made up for by a profuse use of glazed coloured tiles along the entire front over the archways, the walls below being perfectly plain. This great band of coloured tiles along the top represents leaves, flowers, scroll-work, &c., in a free style. The towers also at the corners are similarly ornamented by glazed tiles all the way up from the level of the glazed tiled band of the masjid face. It is possible that at the towers, if not elsewhere, glazed coloured tile ornamentation extended down to the floor level, but having got broken, has been repaired or rather replaced by plain plaster.

The towers are terminated by small *bulbous* domes, also covered with coloured glazed tiles. The back of the masjid externally is quite plain.

Internally a broad band of glazed coloured tiles run along the walls all round, passing over the mehrâbs. This band contains a long inscription running right through from end to end, but it is much injured. I was not permitted to go in or copy or read them. Besides this band of glazed tiles the mehrâbs are also ornamented with glazed tiles, and the central one is a remarkably fine piece of glazed coloured tile-work, though unfortunately now much injured. At the springing of the southernmost entrance arch, on the jamb an inscription in glazed tile-work reads—

* کسر محمد علي لشمرے عفه الله نوبنر سرکار ابن عمارت *

This inscription apparently, if complete, would have given us the name of the builder and the date; at present it breaks off just as it proceeds to speak of the building.

The pendentives on which the domes rest are corbelled and plastered as in the Khirki Masjid of Delhi, but are not quite plain.

In front of the masjid is a wide pavement, running the entire length of the masjid. It is of brick, but divided into compartments, and bordered by long large blocks of grey, coarse, chiselled granite. The blocks of stone are secured, or rather were once secured, to each other by iron cramps.

The masjid is entirely of brick. It occupies the centre of the west end of a large court-yard which once had long and magnificent ranges of cloisters on the other three sides, and the remainder of the west side not taken up by the masjid proper. This great court-yard had two gates to the east and south.

The cloisters have long ago disappeared, all except a fragment at the north-east corner, from which it appears that the last corner towers were surmounted by flattish round domes; the cloisters, however, appear to have had pyramidal roofs, and three such now exist touching the last tower in the existing fragment of the north-east corner.

The cloisters were all probably more than one storey in height.

The two gateways were very high and ornamented with glazed tiles. Their roofs were surmounted by several small flattish domes, somewhat in the style of the Delhi Jamai Masjid of Shah Jehan. The gates were flanked by little square pavilions with pyramidal roofs covered with glazed coloured tiles. The north face of the quadrangle now consists of small pavilions with pyramidal roofs on projecting towers connected by low railings of stone. Whether cloisters once existed on this side is uncertain; I rather think they did, but having become ruined have been replaced by the present arrangement of open pavilions connected by low railings. This side of the quadrangle overhangs the river, which washes the base of the great massive revetments which rise sheer out of it.

The revetments are very strong and massive, and rise to a great height, as the site on which the masjid is built is comparatively very high. These revetments run on, with various but unimportant interruptions, a long distance, right away to the great revetments and towers of the citadel or *kila* at the end of the city, the ruins of which still frown over the river below in shattered majesty. This citadel or *kila* is now the highest spot within modern Patna, and is a confused mass of ruined houses and brickbat heaps, presenting an aspect of desolation which, far from being relieved, is only aggravated by the existing houses yet inhabited, but mostly in a ruinous condition. No friendly vegetation hides the naked rawness of the ruins there.

The masjid described above is very picturesque (notwithstanding the flatness of its façade) from its position on the edge of the river at such a height as to be a commanding object. The glare of its glazed tiles has been softened down by the hands of time and weather, and presents no harsh contrasts and gaudy colours to offend the eye; the white clean interior seen through the archways contrasts in a pleasing way with the dark time-soiled exterior.

The revetments which confine the river are built of brick and rubble-stone very solidly, and sloping up in the usual way; they are further strengthened with various towers, break-waters, and counterforts; the foot of the revetment is protected by loose large rubble-stone pitched in. It is in this part of Patna alone that stone, rubble and dressed, are to be met with in any quantity, and this, as before noticed, tends to show that the old capital of Magadha with its numerous stone towers and buildings existed on this side, the stone used in the river revetments being the last remnants of the old city which the river had not swallowed up when modern Patna was founded by Shir Shah.

Near Khwâja Kalân's Ghât, a masjid, dargâh, and gateway of some interest exist in a semi-ruinous condition. They date from Aurangzebe's reign, and the tomb is said to be that of Dhum Shah, a local saint of limited fame. It is in form a square with four pillars on each face supporting the roof, which, however, no longer exists entire. The corner supports are groups of four pillars each, of the late Mughal style.

Vertically over the pillars rise arched ribs of sandstone cut to shape; over these were laid transversely slabs of stone, close fitting, in two layers, forming the roof, the arrangement being precisely similar to the way in which the hull of a boat is built,—namely, planks resting against ribs formed to shape. Stone lattices once closed the openings between the pillars, but they have disappeared. On the south a doorway once existed. The pillars are surmounted by double bracket capitals, and are supported on truncated pyramidal bases; the pillars are octagonal and of sandstone, as also the rest of the building; the whole was crowned once by a bold projecting eave.

The gateway leading to the ghat is of brick, faced with stone in the late Mughal style.

The masjid is a plain building well covered with white-wash. It is built of brick and stone. The plainness of the façade is broken by niches, and the front arches are ornamented. Four towers stand at the four corners. The roof is of the flattish vaulted construction; the back wall has the usual projection in the centre marking the mehrâb.

Besides these the only other objects worth mention in Patna of antiquarian interest are four high mounds of brick and earth at the four corners of what once was the Fort of Patnā. These are now known as the asthânas of four local saints; three of these still exist crowned by small white-washed shrines; the north-west one has disappeared in the Ganges.

A plan of the old fortifications of Patna may be seen in Rennell's Indian Atlas, plate XV. The fort was an irregular parallelogram, of which the north side ran along the river. Even in Rennell's time this side of the fort had disappeared to a great extent, notably the north-west portion with its tower; tradition, however, preserves its memory still. The west wall was a curve with the concave side turned outwards. The walls were of earth, and Rennell shows them 32 feet in height at the north end of the west wall. The height now is nowhere 32 feet, and in most places it has quite disappeared. The great road now leading from the railway station towards the dargah of Márú Saheb, at the north-east corner of the city, runs on the crest of the old fort walls.

The moat, however, still exists, but is partially filled up, and in some places so altered by railway excavations that it hardly looks like a moat. The fact, however, of its surrounding the city proves that it is an artificial excavation to defend the city.

The citadel, as noticed before, is a mass of ruin. A plan of it may be seen in Rennell's plan of the Fort of Patna. Its walls were of solid brick masonry, of which a great portion still stands. Rennell gives the height as 32 feet without the parapet, and this height still exists in most parts, but the parapet has quite disappeared, except where abutting houses have necessitated its preservation.

The native legend regarding the first occupation of Patna is very silly; it relates that in ancient times a great magician, Patan Deo, reigned in Patna, who succeeded in destroying by magic all the troops sent to take the place by the Muhammadan emperors. At last, in the reign of Akbar, four saints volunteered to reduce the place; they were accordingly sent, and Patan Deo, finding them proof against his magic, quietly gave up the place and went away. These four brothers then built the four mounds at the four corners and lived there.

They were named—

(1) *Hazrat Pir Mansur Wali Alláh,* after whom the Mohalla *Mansurganj* is named.

(2) *Hazrat Pir Maruf Wali Alláh,* after whom the Mohalla *Maruganj* is named.

(3) *Hazrat Pir Mehdi Wali Alláh,* after whom the Mohalla *Mehdiganj* is named.

(4) *Hazrat Pir Jaffer Wali Alláh,* from whom *Jafferganj* Mohalla derives its name.

The Muhammadan name of Patna is Azimabad, from Prince Azim, son of Akbar (so runs the tradition), who on the conquest of Patna was sent by the king at the request of the four saints. He built several masjids in it, and bestowed on it the name of Azimabad.

From Patna it will be convenient to follow the footsteps of Hwen Thsang, the Chinese traveller.

TILÁDAKA.

From Patna the Chinese pilgrim travelled south-west to the village of Tiládaka. The distances given in the life and in the travels of Hwen Thsang differ considerably; the former making it 7 *yojans*, the latter 100 *li*. The actual distance to *Tillâra*, however, is 25 miles from the south-east end of modern Patna, and 28 miles from what I would consider the south-east end of Pâṭaliputra, and it lies due south instead of south-west of Patna. From Hwen Thsang's itineraries, therefore, it is clear that Tillâra can lay no claim to being the modern representative of Tiládaka, but in this instance there is proof of the most conclusive nature that Tillâra is Tiládaka. An inscription cut on the jamb of the doorway to the present Sangin Masjid at Tillâra distinctly mentions the name Telâḍaka. On submitting the inscription to General Cunningham, he at once read the name as Telâḍaka, and communicated the important discovery to me. Tillâra had been previously identified with Tiládaka by General Cunningham, Geog. Anc. India, page 455; see also J. A. S. for 1872, page 250 *et seq.*

The identification of Telâḍaka is thus established beyond dispute. The modern Tillâra, however, is a small straggling village situated between two branches of the Phalgu river, the Soná and the Katár. The principal objects of interest here are the Sangin Masjid, the dargah of Syad Yusuf, and a high mound near the north-west end of the village. The masjid is a plain hall with flat slabbed roof supported by Hindu pillars. The pillars are of many kinds, and set up without the slightest regard to symmetry or beauty. Most of them are of a coarse kind of granite, but a few are of sandstone. The hall is quite open in front; no arched or front wall appears to have ever existed. It, in short, resembles the masjids built of Hindu materials at Mahobá.

In front of the masjid is a court-yard paved with Hindu pillars, architraves, and other Hindu remains, presenting an appearance of such utter disregard to regularity or arrangement of any kind as is unrivalled in the history even of Muhammadan vandalism.

The side walls of the masjid are prolonged to enclose this court-yard, and a small narrow entrance in the east face of this wall leads through a small chamber to a still narrower and smaller entrance which gives access to the court-yard and masjid. The entrances are so small, especially the inner one, that one has almost to creep in on all-fours.

Close to and outside the masjid is the dargah, remarkable only for its general ugliness. An inscribed stone is in this dargah.

At the north-west end of the village are a few Hindu temples; one contains a fine image of an eighteen-armed female in black basalt. Close to these is an old ruined brick tomb, a square surmounted by a dome; it is very picturesque.

Close to these is a great mound nearly 45 feet high, and another longish one 30 or 35 feet high; the high one is clearly the ruins of a temple, as I traced a portion of the straight walls of the temple; both are crowned by Muhammadan tombs. The path leading from the Sangin Masjid to the Hindu shrines passes over undulating ground; the undulations are not natural, but are the remains of buildings; these undulations cover a space of nearly half a mile in length by about 500 feet in width.

There can be no doubt that Tillâra was at one time a great place, and excavations carried on here would, I doubt not, yield rich results, judging from such remains as can now be seen above ground. See also J. A. S. for 1872, paper by Mr. Broadley.

BARÁBAR.

From Telâḍaka Hwen Thsang proceeded in the direction of his previous bearing 90 *li* (15 miles) to a lofty mountain, from the summit of which Buddha had contemplated the kingdom of Magadha. This mountain General Cunningham, applying his proposed corrections, seeks in the range which runs from Gaya to Girak. But in this part of the pilgrim's route I think no correction is needed. Adopting his bearing and distance, the spot falls in the group of isolated hills now known as the Barâbar hills. In this group the highest peak is named Murali by General Cunningham (Report on Barâbar). On this peak, however, no remains whatever exist, but close to it on the next highest peak overlooking the valley, where the rock-cut caves exist, are the remains of a very old temple. This hill or peak, which General Cunningham in his map (Pl. XVIII, Vol. I, page 40) names Barâbar, was named to me Surajânk; on its summit is a temple extensively repaired, but of which a large portion of the original basement remains entire. Judging from the bold simple style of moulding, this temple must be very ancient.

The temple now contains Brahmanical deities, and is frequented by Hindu pilgrims. Close to it was another, of which only traces of the foundations exist. This was also Brahmanical, judging from a lingam and fragments of statues on the site; and it does not appear to me that these temples were originally Buddhist, as they do not face the east, and because there is in the existing temple a lingam which I was informed by my Hindu servant (I was not allowed to enter) to have been deeply embedded, and apparently in its original position (it is known as Siddheswara). But whether they were originally Buddhist or not, Buddhist temples must at one time have existed in the vicinity, for Buddhist statues are to be found within the precincts of the temple; they are now worshipped as Brahmanical deities.

It is clear, however, that from a remote period Brahmanical temples existed here, as attested by the large life-sized statue of a four-armed Devi, with an inscription in what may be Gupta characters. This statue cannot be Buddhist, as its vâhan is a lion on a pedestal, and the figures on its two sides are Ganesa and Siva, the latter with a serpent round the neck. One right hand of the female is empty and marked with a chakra on the palm; the other holds a rosary and a small Saivic emblem, *i. e.*, a lingam in argha. The two left hands hold, the one a lily or lotus unopened, the other an object which may be meant for a bell or a skull.

In addition to this record of the antiquity of the temple, an inscription (in the Vapiya caves) of the 6th or 7th century records the existence, then, of the lingam now enshrined in this temple, and named "Siddheswara."

The most ancient available records then as to the purpose of the temples here, show that they were Brahmanical; it appears, therefore, that as no other remains of temples exist, the Buddhists at some subsequent period appropriated the temples and were again dispossessed.

Down below on the slope of the hill near the road leading up to it are remains of several statues, both detached and sculptured on the rock, some Hindu, some Buddhist; the Brahmanical ones, however, predominate.

Several natural caverns exist not worth detailed mention. I explored a few, but found nothing; they are now the residences of jogis.

As Hwen Thsang, however, does not describe any Buddhist institutions on the hill he visited, the absence of ancient and Buddhist remains in no way disproves the identification proposed.

But the subsequent route of Hwen Thsang so strongly supports the identification of this hill with the hill of Buddha, that even if Hwen Thsang had described Buddhist temples as existing in his time on the hill whence Buddha contemplated the kingdom of Magadha, their absence now would not invalidate the proposed identification.

DHARÂWAT.

Following him from this hill, it is found that he went 30 *li* north-west to the Gunamati monastery, which was situated on the slope of a hill in a pass.

Adopting his bearing and distance, we get to the village of Dharâwat. The road from the Barâbar hill skirts the eastern foot of the Barâbar hill, and going round the spurs of Murali hill stretches northwards, dividing into two branches; the eastern one goes to the village of Dharâwat with a detour, the western one goes direct over a pass in the Dharâwat hills, and a branch from this again goes over a pass over Ratani hill. At this pass in the Ratani hill, and on either side of it extending westwards more than half a mile, and eastwards a short way, are ruins of brick structures. These ruins consist of mounds and brick terraces, profusely scattered all along the slope and toe of the hill. At the west

Cunningham, *vide* Archæol. Reports, plate XVIII.

end, at about one-third of the height of the hill, there is a great mass of ruined masonry. Here the excavations of the villagers for bricks have disclosed several statues; the smaller ones have gone to adorn the modern shrines in the village, but a colossal figure of Padma-Pâni, with the Buddhist creed engraved round the head in Kutila characters, has been left *in situ*, being probably too heavy to move. The figure is very well executed in black basaltic stone and finely smoothed. A small Buddha is represented seated in Padma-Pâni's hair. This statue appears to be *in situ*, as remains of a straight wall behind and touching its back can yet be traced. I conclude, therefore, that this mound and terrace with its flight of brick-paved approach was a temple. At the foot of the hill is a larger mound, where also images, large and small, have been discovered. A colossal figure, mutilated, lies neglected here.

A few feet off are other terraces and mounds, from which small statues have been exhumed. They were also small temples or chapels, judging from the square cells which have been disclosed in the foundations.

Further on are other terraces and mounds, all of bricks of large size, and each group with a separate approach or paved way leading up to it, with terraces at intervals. The quantity of bricks dug out and yet untouched is incredible; a large quantity has been broken up into road metal, either to metal the Patna branch road which passes a few miles off, or to use as *khoa* for terrace roofs.

To the east of this great collection of ruins the ground at the foot of the hill appears to have been used as a burial-ground; excavations at this end have disclosed numerous human skulls and bones, mostly broken, or so decayed as to crumble under pressure between the fingers, but many yet hard, though devoid of all smell or soluble organic matter.

Near the pass, however, the terraces and mounds, which at other parts go up only to one-third of the height of hill, are found up to two-thirds of its height. No excavations have been made here, but from the results at the west end I am sanguine this part would yield results equally rich.

At the foot of the hill runs a small stream which once was spanned by a small bridge, the foundations of which still exist entire, showing that the road over the pass, now seldom used, was once a much-frequented route.

A few feet from the foot of the hills stretches a fine rectangular piece of water known as the Chandokhar Tal.

The stream just mentioned feeds this tank, and the surplus water passes out at the south-west corner. The tank is bounded on all sides by high earthen embankments. On the western embankment is a Muhammadan brick dargah, and near it a brick mound like a tope.

To the east of the tank is a large piece of high ground, and behind it a smaller tank; the high ground is roughly rectangular, and is known as the "kot," or fortress. Near it are several large mounds containing bricks, fragments of stones, and pottery. An annual fair is held on this spot. The pottery is clearly due to this, but the fragments of bricks and pieces of squared stone and statues which sometimes occur, are ancient. A small stone, much resembling a sati pillar, now stands near the south-east end of the high ground where the fair is held, and is pelted with stones by the village boys and passers-by.

The ancient name of the village is traditionally stated to have been *Dharmmapura*. The legend of its foundation is. that on a certain occasion Raja Chandra Sen came on a hunting excursion to this place, which was then a small village with a good deal of jungal round about. While here, he had occasion to go out to the field with a *lota* of water, but as he set the *lota* down a thirsty cow came and drank up the water. The Raja seeing this, reflected on the great hardship men and animals must be suffering for want of water here, as there were no tanks then, and only a single well; he accordingly ordered his ministers to dig a tank as large as the ground his horse when let loose would circle round. The ministers, apprehensive of the horse making a longer circuit than convenient, selected the north-east corner of the tank (where now a small dilapidated brick temple stands) as the starting point for the horse, turning his head southwards, so that the hills on the south would be the limit of the size of the tank in that direction. The horse, when let loose, went near the hill, up to the nala which, issuing from it, feeds the tank, kept along the nala some distance, then turned north and round to where it started from. The ground thus marked was formed into the Chandokar Tal; numerous costly buildings were soon constructed, and *Dharawat* become a great place.

General Cunningham has described Dharâwat, but it is strange that while describing it, the close coincidence between the remains here and Hwen Thsang's account of the Gunamati monastery did not strike him.

KAUWA-DOL.

From the Gunamati monastery Hwen Thsang went south-west 20 *li* to the Silabhadra monastery, which was situated on an isolated hill. Following the pilgrim's bearing and distance, we get to the vicinity of the isolated *Kauwa-dol* hill. At the foot of this hill, or rather a little way up a low spur at its south-east foot, are the remains of a large temple of stone with tall plain granite pillars. This temple must have been very large and complete, as there are traces of an *arddha mandapa*, a *mandapa*, a *maha mandapa*, an *antarâla*, and the *sanctum*. The few pillars of the temple still standing form a long colonnade leading to the sanctum; the back and portions of side walls of which still exist in a ruinous condition. The cell is occupied by a colossal statue of Buddha seated on a pedestal; on either side are two smaller statues on smaller pedestals; the pedestal of one bears the usual Buddhist creed in Kutila characters.

The walls of this temple were apparently of brick. The floor of the sanctum appears to have been lower than that of the mandapa, &c. The large statue has been described by General Cunningham (Report I, page 41); he also describes the various rock sculptures.

The spot where this temple stood is tolerably level, and could well have contained other structures besides the temple.

Native tradition calls this colossal statue of Buddha an Asur, and considers it to be one of the petrified sentries of Banâsur. Wonderful indeed are the stories current of Banâsur; his gigantic size, the extent of his dominions, and his power. The whole of the ancient ruins found here, in the Barâbar hills, at Dharâwat, at Kispa, at Ner, and indeed all round for miles, are ascribed to him. A curse of some kind has converted his soldiers into stone, but he is not dead; when the course of the curse has been run, he and his people will be restored to life. I could not ascertain when or why or by whom the curse was pronounced; the people have only a vague idea that a curse does hang over him.

From the Silabhadra monastery, which I identify with the Kauwa-dol temple, Hwen Thsang went 40 or 50 *li* south-west to Gaya. The actual distance of the north end of Gaya from here is 12 miles; the bearing is about south-west. The only difficulty is the mention of his crossing the Nairanjana river, which, going from Kauwa-dol to Gaya, he would not have to cross. As, however, the old road to Gaya runs along the *east* bank of the Nairanjana river, it is almost certain the pilgrim travelled by that road from Telâḍaka up to the fork, then he struck westwards to visit the various monasteries detailed before, after which it is difficult to decide whether he struck across country from Silabhadra monastery (Kauwa-dol) to Gaya without any road, or whether he returned to the road he had left. I myself am of opinion that the pilgrim *returned* to the road he had left and followed it to Gaya, thus necessarily crossing the Nairanjana. A careful study of the words of the traveller can alone yield a satisfactory solution of the question as to whether, as I suppose, on leaving the Silabhadra monastery he regained the road from Telâḍaka to Gaya, and whether the recorded distance does not refer to the distance along the main road alone, independent of the excursion.

We know from the inscriptions in the Barâbar caves that they had been excavated long before Hwen Thsang's pilgrimage. They were for a long time famous seats of Buddhist priests; and it is most unlikely that Hwen Thsang passing so close to them should have omitted to visit them. In adopting my identifications, not only are Hwen Thsang's bearings and distances found to be nearly correct, but the anomaly of his passing close and yet omitting to visit these famous places is avoided. The absence of all notice of the caves themselves by Hwen Thsang is, however, strange, and only to be accounted for on the supposition that in his time they had been appropriated by Brahmanists—a supposition confirmed by the inscriptions in them.

Having followed Hwen Thsang from Pâṭaliputra to Gaya, I proceed to notice such remains in the vicinity as are of interest.

The most interesting objects are the rock caves in the Barâbar hills with their inscriptions. These have been so fully described by General Cunningham* as to need no further notice. I will only mention the local legend of Sudâma in connection with his cave.

This saint was once a fellow-student of Siva, who, for some purpose not specified, had come to earth to study. Bye-and-bye, when their course of study was over, they went to their respective homes. Sudâma had contracted a friendship with Siva, whom he had excelled as a student, and when at the close of their studentship he found Siva to be the lord of the three worlds, while he had neither wealth nor power,

* Archæological Survey of India, Vol. I, p. 40.

he retired in disgust to this cave. Here he and his wife lived in great distress for a long time, till at last, through press of hunger and the constant entreaty of his wife, he determined to visit his old friend in the hope of getting help from him in some way. Too proud, however, to go empty-handed to his friend, who had been his inferior at school, yet having nothing to carry as a present, he took some gram, and tying it in a corner of the rag which served him for a *dhoti*, he went to the door of Siva's palace; the guards refused him admittance, and to his statement that Siva was his friend, he only received taunting replies alluding to his naked condition, for in tying the gram to his *dhoti*, so much of the rag had been taken up that enough was not left to cover him decently. Siva, however, heard the noise, and, coming out, was delighted to see his old friend, led him up, and gave him a seat of honour, while he himself, with Pârvati, sat down close to him and began talking. The poor Rishi produced his gram as a present for his friend, and Siva took up and ate a handful, and took up a second handful and ate that also; while in the act of taking a third handful, Pârvati restrained him, saying, "Are you going to give him all three of the Trilokas?" The poor but proud Rishi, after a short stay, took leave and departed, greatly dejected and angry, for he had been too proud to ask Siva for a favour, and Siva had not conferred any on him unasked, though he saw his evident distress, but on the contrary had eaten up his gram, which was all he had. Full of grief he returned towards his cell, when to his astonishment he saw a magnificent place on the spot with many servants, who laid hold of him and carried him in, saying the mistress of the house had called him. From the court-yard he saw a beautiful lady covered with jewels beckoning to him to come up; he replied that he was a poor man who had done no harm and did not know the lady, and begged to be allowed to go. Then the lady at the window repeated a *sloka* to the effect that as wealth had so changed her that her husband could not recognise her, she wanted not the wealth but preferred her poverty. Sudâma then recognised his wife, and they lived happy together, and grateful to Siva for his gifts.

This is the popular version as related on the spot. There is a long legend of Sudâma in Hindu mythology, and also of Lomas Rishi; also a Buddhist legend of a Lomas Kasyapa in Spence Hardy's Manual, but they do not appear to have any connexion with these caves.

The Nâgârjuni cave is traditionally ascribed to Nâgârjuna, the famous Buddhist teacher. Hitherto no confirmation of this tradition has been found, but I find from "Sagas of the far East" a collection of Mongolian and Kalmak traditions that, among them, tradition ascribed to Nâgârjuna a residence in Magadha in this cave. I quote the part (page 2):

"In the kingdom of Magadha there once lived seven brothers who were magicians. At a distance of a mile from their abode lived two brothers, sons of a Khan * * * * * The magicians at once recognised that it was a magic horse, and they said among themselves, 'If our art is to become thus common and everybody can produce a magic horse, no one will come to our market for wonders; we had best buy the horse up and destroy it.' Accordingly they paid the high price required, and took possession of the horse * * * * When the Khan's son, who was transformed into the horse, had learnt what was the intention of the magicians, he said, 'Would that any sort of living being would appear into which I might transfer myself.'

"Hardly had he formed the wish, when a little fish was seen swimming down the stream, into which the Khan transferred himself. The seven magicians knew what had occurred, and immediately transformed themselves into seven larger fish and pursued it. When they were very close to the little fish with their gullets wide open, the Khan said, 'Would that any sort of living being would appear into which I might transform myself.' Immediately a dove was seen flying in the heavens, and the Khan transferred himself into the dove. The seven magicians seeing what was done, transformed themselves into seven hawks, pursuing the dove over hill and dale. Once again they were near overtaking him, when the dove took refuge in the land of Bede. Southward in Bede was a shining mountain and a cave within it called the Giver of Rest. Hither the dove took refuge, even in the very bosom of the great master and teacher, Nâgârjuna."

The cave of Nâgârjuna is here called the "Giver of Rest." Let us see how far this name agrees with the actual name of the cave now known as the cave of Nâgârjuna.

This cave, in its inscription, is named *Gopi-ka-kubha*. The word Gopa means preserver, protector; *Gopi-ka-kubha* can therefore mean the "Cave of the preserver," or the "Cave of rest."

I accordingly consider that the Mongol legend does really refer to this cave, and as both in *their* traditions and in Indian traditions the cave is stated to have been the residence of Nâgârjuna, I think it extremely probable that he really did reside here some time. We know from other sources that Nâgârjuna came to Magadha to study. What more probable than that either during or after his studentship he resided some time in this cave?

JÂRU.

The river Nairanjana divides into two branches a little way above the Nâgârjuna hills. One branch passes close to the hills to its east, the other runs further eastwards, and again divides into two, of which the western branch runs a short way and is lost, and the eastern branch runs past Islâmpur. Of these three branches of the Nairanjan, the westernmost one is the main river; the others are dry, except in the rains. Immediately at the angle of the first fork are the ruins of a masjid. This masjid is built of brick and mortar; stone is also used, but the stone is evidently taken from some Hindu structure. It was once a fine masjid; it stands at one end of a court-yard which was once surrounded by cloisters, the cells having each a small domed roof. The masjid itself is roofed by numerous small domes. Vaults exist underneath. The entrance to the court-yard is through a small chamber with narrow doorways. It is remarkable that old masjids in this district, of which the court-yards and outer entrances still exist, have all small narrow entrances, extremely unlike the superb entrances to the masjids in Delhi and Jaunpur. The masjid here is ascribed, but only on tradition, to Shir Shah's time, and the style of the building bears out this tradition, and tends rather to ascribe to it a higher antiquity. I am myself inclined to adopt the traditional account of its age, for though the small domes point to a period anterior to Shir Shah, the fine lime enamelling used and still to be found in small patches indicates a later period. Colour and inscriptions were liberally used, but the inscriptions are all too far broken to be intelligible, and most of the coloured work has peeled away. It is deserted now, but is still visited on particular festivals.

Close to and behind the masjid is the village of Jâru, and behind the village is a chain of rugged hills, at the foot of which are occasionally to be seen dressed stone and other remnants of old Hindu work. On the summit of the highest peak, which is crowned by a picturesque clump of trees (the rest of the hill being quite bare), is a large lingam, known as *Harihar Nâth Mahâdeva*. The story goes that pilgrims, who on their journey to it do not speak at all, can encircle the lingam completely with their arms and hands. The place is visited by numerous pilgrims, and I have no doubt it was at one time a notable place of Hindu worship.

A few miles south of the fork, on the east side of the Nairanjan or Phalgu river, stands a group of bare rocky hills crowned by the dargah of a Muhammadan saint; it is otherwise devoid of interest.

MIRÁPUR NÂDERÂ.

About 7 miles due east of the fort of the Phalgu at Jâru, at a village called Mirápur Nâderâ, are the ruins of Hindu temples converted or rather used up into masjids. The chief object of interest there is an old dargah, about half a mile east of the village. The dargah is ascribed to Syad Ahmad Shah, locally a very famous saint. In the dargah is a tree to which females for miles round come to tie *chillas* with the object of obtaining children. The *chilla* consists of a small piece of the dress of the wearer which must be torn and tied to one of the branches of the tree; the woman tying the *chilla* must visit the spot quite alone and at night. The practice is common all over the Patna and Gaya districts, and so numerous are the holy spots which, when visited at night alone by females to tie *chillas*, are considered efficacious in procuring children, that one can hardly travel 15 miles in any direction without coming on one of them. Built into the dargah, among other Hindu materials, is a fine sculptured gargoyle serving as a drain outlet.

At the back of the village itself is a stone colonnade, the remains of a masjid consisting of three rows of pillars, six in each row, thus giving five openings. The pillars are plain; the building is now open on all sides, but there is no doubt of the existence once of the usual back wall with the mehrâb, making it a Muhammadan masjid. The roof consists of stone slabs over which is laid a layer of bricks. The material of the pillars and slabs is granite; the bricks are of large size, over 12″ long. The building stands on a mound, the length being north and south; at the south end a sculptured gargoyle representing a hooded snake forming a canopy over a human figure shows that the original building whose materials were used to construct the masjid was Buddhist. The floor of the building is now out of repair.

GOWROR.

About 12 miles east by a little north from Nâderâ and half a mile off the road to Bihâr is the village of Gowror; it contains the ruins of a very lofty mud fort. The fort is said to have been built by Mir Mustafá, Lord of Telâda. No date is assigned either to the fort or to Mir Mustafá, but the people have a vague idea of his having been one of Shir Shah's nobles. This Mir Mustafá must have been a man of some note, as a ghat and ferry of the city of Patna are named after him; and on this ground, as the fort of Patna was built in Shir Shah's time, it is not improbable that Mir Mustafá was one of his nobles. In the village are a number of fragments of Brahmanical statues; one of Durga slaying the Mahesasur; on a pedestal is sculptured a seated Buddha. There are besides other Buddhist fragments showing that it was once a place of note, both with Buddhists and Brahmans.

BATHANI HILL.

A short way south of Gowror is Bathan or Bathani hill and village. The hill is a small conical one and quite isolated; it is about 5 or 6 miles to the west of the entrance of the valley of old Râjagriha. Buddhist legends say that Buddha, travelling from Kapila to Râjgir before attaining the Buddhahood, entered Râjgir by the east gate, and, having collected alms, went to the Banthawa hill to eat the food he had collected. The hill is named Pandhawa (Spence Hardy, p. 163) in the Ceylon records, and Banthawa in the Siamese records (Alabaster, p. 136), both names bearing a close resemblance to the name Bathan of the solitary hill noticed. But against this identification is the distinct statement made in both the Burmese and Siamese versions, that Buddha left the city of Râjgir by the same gate he had entered, *viz.*, the east gate (Spence Hardy does not say anything regarding the gate by which he left the city). If, as stated, Buddha left the city by the east gate, which could only have been the one leading through the long ravine to the Panchâna river, near Gidha Dwâra, Bathan could hardly have been the hill he went to to eat his meal, as it would have been a distance not of 6 but of over 18 miles by that circuitous route. I content myself by simply noting the close similarity of name and the objections to its identification with Bathawa hill.

There is mention in the Mahábhárata, ch. 20, ver. 30, of a hill named Gorath. Bhima, Arjuna, and Krishna, when going to Girivraja to slay Jarâsandha, came, as before noticed, *viá* Vaisâli, and, crossing the Ganges and the Son, arrived in the kingdom of Magadha; then "ascending the Goratha hill, they saw the beautiful capital of the Magadha kingdom." The names "Goratha" and "Bathan" are both connected with cattle, and as there is no hill near enough to Râjgir besides the Bathan hill, the inference is obvious that the hill named Goratha in the Mahábhárata is the same as the present Bathani hill. I accordingly consider that the ancient name of the hill was "Goratha," meaning cattle-car. "Bathan" in Hindi means a cattle-pen, a place where cattle are kept.

ISLÂMPUR.

About 10 miles to north and a little east of Nâderâ is Islâmpur. Here are several remains, but the better preserved sculptures were all removed to Bihâr, and only some large squared stones and fragments now remain; part is used up in modern buildings and huts, and also in some modern Hindu temples, of which there are several in various stages of neglect. The remains of this place had been noticed by Doctor Buchanan Hamilton; but the place is no longer rich in ancient remains.*

A few miles south-west of Islâmpur is a small village named *Lát*, from a huge monolithic pillar now lying there half buried. This had been noticed by Dr. Buchanan, but he does not give any traditional account of it. The traditions of the place assert that it was being floated down to some place, when by some accident it was stranded here; and all subsequent attempts to float it down have proved abortive. Accounts differ as to where it was being carried, and tradition is totally silent as to where it came from; some say it was being carried to Telâda, others say Hilsa, and some even say it was being carried to Bihâr by the Subah. Wherever it may have been going, it is certain that it came from the south, and is not a remnant of the ancient grandeur of either the village of Lát, or of Islâmpur. Possibly it is part of the pillar at Bakror, of which another part is now in Gaya set up as a central mark in the city.† It may possibly be even the Râjgir pillar which once stood near the tope (long since excavated), but of which hitherto no traces have been discovered; this, however, is very unlikely. (See J. A. S. for 1872, paper by Mr. Broadley.)

---

* Martin's East India.
See J. A. S. for 1872, paper by Mr. Broadley.

† Archæological Survey of India, Vol. I, p. 12.

OLD LINES OF ROAD.

The old road from Gaya runs along the east bank of the Nairanjana river from Gaya northwards, passing close to Islâmpur and Telâda, through Hilsa. From Telâda, however, a road must once have gone direct to Patna, as Hwen Thsang travelled by it from Patna. Of this road, however, at present few traces exist; and it certainly is not now a great or even a much-frequented road, but it is still used by numerous pilgrims. From Gaya to Telâda, however, the old road is still not only extensively used, but is the best natural road that could have been laid out between the two places.

The present great road from Gaya to Bânkipur necessarily follows a different line; the shifting of the head-quarters of the district from Patna to Bânkipur made it a necessity to select a new line; but with Patna for the capital, the old great road, though not very pleasant for the portion between Patna and Telâda, was no worse than any other that could have been chosen, while beyond Telâda, following closely as it does the high banks of the Nairanjana or Phalgu river, is the line marked out by Nature herself.

The branch from Telâda, which went past Hilsa (written "Milse Buzurg" in the Indian Atlas sheet), is now the main route for travellers from Fatuha, and is also naturally a good fair-weather road. It is difficult to determine whether the cities of Fatuha and Hilsa were the cause of the existence of this road, or whether the road being in existence caused the rise of Fatuha and Hilsa. I am inclined rather to think that the natural difficulties of the road direct from Patna to Telâda, which in ancient times would have had to cross the Son, which then flowed between the two places, caused the existence, for commercial purposes, of the comparatively easy road from Telâda to Fatuha, just below the embouchure of the ancient Son. This road, therefore, apparently owes its existence to a physical necessity, and it accordingly appears more reasonable to attribute the rise of Hilsa and Fatuha, or at least of Hilsa, to the road. Hilsa is situated just at the point where the road from Telâda to the junction of the old Son and Ganges crosses the main arm of the Nairanjana river, and thus necessarily became a place of some importance, as testified by its traditions and the ancient remains existing there.

The importance of tracing the old great lines of roads may be illustrated in this district. Admitting the great antiquity of Patna, Gaya, Râjgir, Ara, Benares, Nongarh, Mongir, and admitting that roads connected these great cities, it will not be uninteresting to trace the consequences.

The road from Patna to Gaya would be crossed by the following roads:—

By the Benares-Râjgir road at Jâru, at the bank of the Lilâjan.

By the Ara-Râjgir road at Telâḍa.

The Benares-Râjgir road would cross the old Son at Son-Bhadr (*vide* supra). The Murhar at Bishânpur Ghenjan, the Nairanjana at the Nâgârjuni hills, and at Jâru.

It would pass through or very close to Dharâwat, and Mirapur Nâdera.

The Ara-Râjgir road would cross the old Son near the village Bhagwânganj, where the Drona stûpa exists (*vide* supra), the Nairanjana at Telâḍa, and pass through or very close to Islâmpur.

The Patna-Râjgir road would cross the old Son somewhere near Fatehpur Kalân or Mahiuddinpur Khera; it would cross the Nairanjana and the Fatuha branch of the Gaya-Patna road at Hilsa, and pass through Nâlanda and Silao.

The Gaya-Benares road must have struck the Benares-Râjgir road at the Son, for from the life of Buddha we learn that to go from Buddha Gaya to Benares, he went through Gaya, and the name of the Son crossing, the "Son-Bhadr," shows that this was the usual crossing for pilgrims to Gaya; it therefore becomes a branch of the great Râjgir-Benares road, branching out from it at the old Son crossing, and it would pass through Konch, and cross the Murhar opposite Páli, to avoid crossing two branches of the river, which it would have to do if it crossed either above or below.

The Râjgir-Nongarh road would cross the Panchâna at Giryak, the Sakri near Afsar or Parvati hill, and would pass through or very close to Sikandra.

The Râjgir-Mongir road would cross the Panchana somewhere near Ghoserâwan, pass through Titrâwan, cross the Sakri near the Parvati hill, pass through or close to Shekpura, and cross the Kiyul river at Rajjhâna or Hasanpur.

The Gaya-Râjgir road, it is needless to mention, passes through a whole chain of old places.

Of the places mentioned above, all except Fatehpur Kalân, Mahiuddinpur Khera, and Sikandra, are known to possess ancient remains. These places have not been examined, but I have heard that Sikandra possesses a famous old dargah, which may safely be taken as a sign that some Hindu or Buddhist structure existed here ready made to allow of being converted into a dargah. Of the other two places I have no account.

It thus appears that, given a series of important points, we can with tolerable accuracy fix upon the sites of other secondary points, provided we take into consideration the physical features of the intervening country.

This process is applicable, I believe, on a very extended scale. So far I have taken only a part of Magadha as an illustration; let the process now be extended, and let us take Tamluk, the ancient Tamralipti, into consideration.

Roads would naturally lead up from Tamluk to Patna, to Mongir, and elsewhere.

There would be a choice of several routes to Patna; the most direct route would be through Bishânpur, Bahulâra, Sonatapan, Ekteswar (where the Darikeswar river would be crossed), Chatna, Raghunâthpur, Telkuppi, Jhâria, Rajauli, and Râjgir. It would cross the Salay river near or at Ghátál, the Darikeswar between Bahulâra and Ekteswar, the Damuda at Telkuppi, the Barâkar close to Palgunjo, the range of hills near Rajauli, and pass into Râjgir by the great south gate and out by the north on to Patna. This road would be a great thoroughfare, and we see that, at every great obstacle, large cities sprang up, as attested by the remains about Ghatal, about Bishanpur, at Telkuppi, about Pâlganj, and near Rajauli. There are, besides these, ruins at Chatna and at Jhâria. Of these, Chatná is the point whence a road, yet in existence and use, branched off, going close past Pachaet through Pándrá, Kharakdihá, between the rivers Sakri and Khuri (where there are ancient remains still on the Sakri near Maháwar hill), through Nowádá to Râjgir. Jhâria appears to have been the capital of the country which anciently was called Jhârkhand.

After crossing the Darikeswar, a branch probably started from near Ekteswar to Mongir, passing close toRânigan j, crossing the Ajay at or near Bhimgarh, where remains yet exist on both banks of the river, then through or close past Nagore, where exists a place of pilgrimage known as Bakeswar, close past Bhaskinath, Mandar hill, Kherhi, to Mongir.

Of the places mentioned, *all* except Rânigan j contain ancient remains.

Another great road would go to Benares; this road would

naturally go past Pakbirrá and Buddhpur, through or close past Barabhum, through or close to Dulmi (which I shall subsequently show to be Hwen Thsang's Kirana Suvarna), there crossing the Suvarna Riksha, close past Rânchi, Palâmow, across the Son to Benares. There are remains about Palâmow and Rânchi (see notices in Journal, Asiatic Society), and there are extensive remains at Pakbirrá and Buddhpur. Their occurrence is well explained by the circumstance that the cross road connecting the two great roads from Tumluk to Patna and to Benares started from Pâlgunj, going through Katrás, Chechgáongarh, Pârá, and Chorrá, and striking the great Benares road at Pakbirrá and Buddhpur. Kâtras was once a place of importance and succeeded Jhâria as the capital of Jhârkhand; Chechgáongarh is at the crossing of the Damuda; Pâra is at the intersection of this cross road with the road between Dulmi and Jhâria; Chorrá alone enjoys no particular advantage of location, but nevertheless possesses ancient remains, and is therefore an anomaly.

Thus we may trace the great old roads, and by their aid fix upon the sites or lines which on examination would be likely to yield any return. It appears to me quite a mistake to imagine that districts like Mânbhum, Palâmow, the Sântal Parganas, Jhârkhand, &c., could ever have been extensively cultivated and peopled densely like the plains of Magadha or the valleys of the Jamna and the Ganges; the occurrence of ruins among the wilds of Chutia Nagpur can *only* be due to cities having from some generally intelligible natural cause sprung up at points along a great road; and by no means to the whole district, or even a considerable portion of the district, having been in a flourishing condition, densely peopled and highly cultivated. The contrast between the profusion of remains scattered broadcast in the fertile and known densely-peopled plains of Magadha and the isolated remains in the wilder districts is too great to be explained away by any amount of imaginary dilapidations and destruction from any causes; indeed, so far as destruction goes, built remains, in the civilised tracts, are generally in a far more advanced stage of decay (even when they have not absolutely disappeared as structures, leaving only the materials as witnesses) than those in the wilder places.

List of old places.—The following is a list of places known to possess ancient remains, or otherwise of archæological interest, in the districts of Gaya and Patna. For facility of reference I divide them into groups.

1.—Along the right bank of the present Son—

Maner—Near the junction of the Son and the Ganges—see *ante*.

Dâudnagar—Possesses a Muhammadan tomb of no interest or great antiquity.

On the Punpun.

Bihta,
Deoriya,
Bhagwânganj,
Son-Bhadr,
Deokund,
Sidhrâmpur, } see *ante*.

Between the Rivers Punpun and Murhar.

Kispa.
Barawang.
Konch.
Pâli.
Sibari.
Deokut, on the Dháwá nala.
Manda Hills.
Bhuraha.
Gunarya.
Umga.
Deo.

On the Murhar.

Bishenpur Ghenjan.
Pái Bighá.
Mátka Hill.
Chillor.
Murhar.
Sherghâti.

Between the River Murhar and the main branch of the Lilajan.

Hasanpur kako.
Dharâwat (see *ante*).
Ner Mushakrat.
Kauwa-dol Hill (see *ante*).
Barâbar Hills (see *ante*).
Belá.

On the main branch of the Lilajan.

Hilsa.
Telâḍa (see *ante*).
The Nâgârjuni Hills (see *ante*).
Jâru (see *ante*).
The Hariharnáth Hill (see *ante*).
Gaya.
Ram Gaya.
Buddha Gaya.
Mora Pahar.
Bakror.

On other branches of the Lilajan.

Sheonogar.
Islampur (see *ante*).
Dapthu.
Lát (see *ante*).

Between the River Lilajan and the Panchana.

Shâhpur Átmá.
Baragaon.
Jagadispur.
Jáfara.
Silao.
Nâdera (see *ante*).
Gowror (see *ante*).
Râjgir.
Jethian.
Kurkihâr.
Punâwa.
Bishanpur Tandwa.
Sitamarhi.

To the east of the Panchana.

Ghosrâwan.
Titarâwan.
Parvati.
Afsand.
Roh.
Satgaon.
Ektârah.
Shekpura.
Sikandra.
Premaya.
Naulakagarh.

On the Kiyul River, and near it.

Balagudar.
Rajhâna.
Raghogarh.
Lakhisarai.
Jaynagar.
Brindâban.
Hasanpur.
Nongarh.
Indpa, *near* Jamui.

Of these places, such as have already been noticed have a note "see *ante*;" the others I now proceed to describe.

Kispa is a large village about twelve miles to the west of the Barâbar hills, and four miles west of the Murhar river. It stands on the banks of a deep narrow branch of the Murhar, and is now famed for possessing a temple of Târâ Devi, to which people for miles round flock with sacrificial he-goats. This temple, which is at the west end of the village, is a small rude brick building of modern date, built on a high stone platform, approached by stone steps. Numerous cut stone blocks lie about, and there is not the least doubt that the platform now supporting the modern brick temple is the basement of an ancient large temple.

Several lingams are lying scattered outside, and various sculptures. One of these is of Vishnu Chaturbhuj; another is a stone sculptured on four sides, and therefore evidently meant to be a pinnacle to some structure; besides a statue of Vishnu on Garud and several fragments. On the sides of the entrance to the temple two statues of Hara-Gauri are let in. The great object of worship in the temple is a life-size standing statue, clothed in a yellow sári, and known as Târâ Devi. There are several smaller statues besides the principal one.

In the village are numerous fragments, Brahmanical as well as Buddhist, most of them mutilated; two of these are life-size standing statues of Buddha, with the "*Ye Dharmma Hetu*" creed over the halo round the head of one of them. This statue is a really fine one in very fair preservation, of exceptionally good execution, and deserving of preservation.

The general appearance of this statue so strongly resembled in size and shape that known as Târâ Devi in the temple, that I was induced to go back to the temple; and as the ministering Brahmans had loudly resented my attempt to go up even the steps of the platform to the temple, I sent up my Hindu servant. He was allowed to go up and enter the temple, and examining according to my directions the halo round the head, he found the usual *Ye Dharmma* inscription (at least I guess it to have been the Buddhist creed from his description—that it was exactly like the other inscription on the statue in the village). Thus satisfied in his own mind that the statue was not an object of orthodox worship, he ventured to peep in behind the sári, and discovered the statue to be a male and not a female one. The ministering Brahmans now became as abjectly submissive as they had before been defiant, but I thought it unwise to take advantage of their offer now to let me enter the temple, as I was quite satisfied the statue was Buddhist, and there was nothing of any interest to induce me to enter then.

There are in the village several fragments of pillars and capitals, but most of the stones that could have been used up have been appropriated by the villagers and used either as door-steps or as foundations to their huts. There are now few remains, but these are enough to show that the place was one of importance. The character of the inscription, which is Kutila, induces me, in conjunction with the superior style of art in the sculpture, to ascribe the remains to the end of the 9th or early part of the 10th century.

Barawang, or Jylepoor Barawan, as it is spelt in the map (Indian Atlas), is situated between Konch and Goh, close to the road from Gaya to Dâudnagar; the place is noticed by Buchanan (Montgomery Martin's compilation), but I found no time to visit it.

Konch is a large village about 18 miles from Gaya on the Dâudnagar road; there are numerous remains here, but the principal one is a temple of brick in good preservation at the north of the village. The temple as it stands consists solely of the sanctum, with its tower roof; it is a square externally of about 28 feet each way, and $11\frac{1}{4}$ feet internally. A lingam is the object of worship inside, which is partially filled in with earth and rubbish. The bricks used in the temple are properly shaped, well-burnt bricks, the largest measuring $11 \times 5\frac{1}{2} \times 2\frac{3}{4}$ inches, but there are many measuring only $9 \times 4\frac{3}{4} \times 2\frac{3}{4}$ inches, and some $13 \times 7\frac{1}{2} \times 2\frac{3}{4}$ inches. This variety in the sizes of the bricks used induces me to suppose that the temple has undergone extensive repair since it was first built, if indeed it be not only a restoration of an ancient temple; in the latter case, however, the restoration must have taken place so long ago that it is ancient even as a restoration.

The sanctum is roofed internally by tunnel vaults, not semicircular, but of arcs meeting at the crown in a ridge; the arch sheeting is entirely of brick cut to shape in the lowest course of bricks; in the arch sheeting, at the springing, the bricks are placed, not as usual with their beds horizontal, but on their edges with the beds vertical; over this row of vertical bricks are 8 or 10 courses of bricks, with their beds horizontal, or rather with their beds slightly inclined to the horizon, as they should properly be in a true arch. Beyond this the bricks are all on edge, with their beds vertical; this construction, however faulty in an arch of small depth transversely, as in walls, is of great strength when built of *bricks cut to shape* and of great depth *transversely*. With stone, especially sedimentary stone which has widely different strengths along and across the layers or plane of cleavage, a mode of construction which brings the line of pressures to bear not perpendicularly, but along the planes of cleavage, it is undoubtedly faulty; but in brick which is homogeneous, the construction of an arch of bricks edge to edge is positively an advantage, as the number of joints of compressible mortar is lessened by the arrangement; the only drawback, lateral weakness, does not come into calculation in long *tunnel* vaults, which in this direction have more strength than they need.

A cornice runs along three sides of the interior of the sanctum at the springing of the tunnel vaults, but there is no cornice in the back wall; further, the side walls of the chamber are each a little over 8 feet thick, while the fourth wall is 10 feet thick, and the back wall only 6¼ feet; these circumstances, combined with the fact that bricks of three different varieties occur in the temple, show that the tunnel vault is a subsequent addition; for if we, without altering the external dimensions of the temple, make the thickness of the walls all round 6¼ feet, by enlarging the chamber inside, we shall get a square chamber 15 feet square, placed centrically as it ought to be.

The absence of a cornice, too, on the back wall internally, shows that the original building was not cut up into two storeys by the interposition of the vaulted or any roof. It is clear, therefore, that the temple, as originally built, consisted of a chamber 15 feet square, with walls 6¼ feet thick all round; subsequently the vault was added by increasing internally the thickness of the side walls by 1¾ feet nearly, and thickening the front wall by additions internally to 10 feet, thus leaving a square chamber no longer 15 feet, but only 11¼ feet square, and *eccentrically* placed within the structure.

The walls of the temple internally are ornamented by niches, three on each side, doubtless meant to hold lamps.

The entrance is as usual represented by a great rent or opening in the face of the tower, consisting of vertical sides, spanned by an arch of overlapping bricks; the necessities of construction from the small size of bricks have caused this arch to assume the form of a tall isosceles triangle with indented sides.

This opening or entrance is divided into two portions by a stone let in right across a lower rectangular one, and an upper rectangle surmounted by the triangular opening; the lower rectangular entrance giving admission into the sanctum, the upper opening into the present, and, as I have shown, subsequently-built upper chamber.

It is an interesting question to determine when this division of the entrance into two was made. At first sight it appears only natural to suppose it to date only to the period when the vault was added, but from examples elsewhere, where, in the absence of the upper chamber, the architrave nevertheless exists, I am of opinion that it was a feature in the original temple; constructively, too, a little reflection will show that it was necessary, if the sanctum had the usual mandapa in front, and the remains here show that some sort of mandapa once existed in front of the sanctum of this temple.

The annexed diagram will help to illustrate what I say.

ADCB represents the front wall of the sanctum (the parts shaded being in section), BDEFGH the mandapa in front, which must have been roofed in; constructively, if the block CD do not exist, the rain from the roof of the mandapa will find its way straight into the sanctum, but by having the block CD the water is prevented from coming into the sanctum.

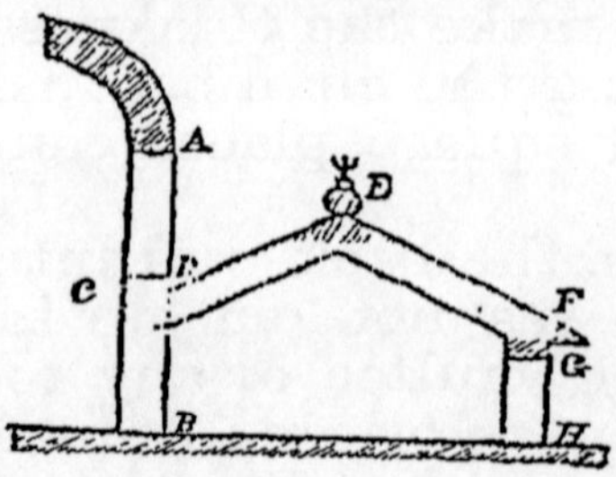

But it is not constructively alone that CD is needed; æsthetically it is even a greater necessity. The votary entering the temple does not see the great rent above CD, nor can he see it even when he is beyond the entrance of the mandapa GH, by reason of the height of the roof DEF, which effectually hides the rent above CD on the outside, so that he is unaware of its existence, and is naturally surprised at the strong and very effective light which this rent, of which he is not aware by reason of the interposed block CD, throws direct on the object of worship at the further end of the sanctum; and as the votary is not allowed to go beyond the threshold of the entrance, he completes his devotions much mystified by the to him inexplicable illumination of the statue, which he probably ascribes to supernatural causes.

Priestcraft has been as much an inherent feature of Buddhism as of every other religion.

The vault now would of course prevent this illumination of the object of worship in the cell, and at present the cell is dark.

The vault is only one brick deep at the crown, but as the bricks are disposed vertically it has great strength. There is or was a thick coating of mortar terrace over it. The upper chamber resting on the vault is $11\frac{1}{2}$ feet square, but the wall is only 7 feet thick in front; this is due partly to dilapidation and partly to a very slight taper in the wall itself.

The chamber is roofed by slightly overlapping courses of bricks; thus the great height of the tower roof is a constructive necessity.

The external shape of the tower, however, differs from that of the great Buddha Gaya temple in being a curved and not a straight-sided pyramid; it is consequently more graceful than the temple at Buddha Gaya. The ornamentation externally consists of a great oval on each face, at a point nearly in the middle of the total height of the tower proper, and of various mouldings and indentations rather sparingly used; the whole of the ornamentation is of brick cut to shape, and it is evident from the way the ornaments are distributed that the whole of it was cut on the external faces of the tower after it had been built up plain. The labour required may easily be imagined; to this is due the fact that the face of the brick-work is so even; for I do not think it possible, without subsequent laborious rubbing down, that any amount of care in setting the bricks, and in the preservation of the shape and sharpness of edges of the brick during manufacture, could produce the wonderfully smooth even face that the work has to this day, notwithstanding the ravages of time.

The temple does not appear to have been originally covered with plaster, but portions of it are now covered with plaster, the remains, no doubt, of a coat put on at some subsequent period.

The tower is, or was, surmounted by a cylindric pinnacle like the temple of Buddha Gaya. This sort of pinnacle is very remarkable, and its form resembling a lingam may be more than a mere accident of construction. Constructively, it was evidently impossible to form in brick the amalaka which invariably surmounts temples of stone, itself again surmounted by either urns or tapering discs ending in a spire. But whether the cylinder with a hemispherical top bears a not merely accidental resemblance to a lingam, or whether it is intended to represent a chaitya or stûpa which, originally hemispherical, became gradually elongated till it resembled nothing so much as a lingam, is a point deserving of inquiry. The temple of Konch appears to have been Buddhist, if we assume, as is sometimes done by high authority, that the Buddhists alone adopted the effective mode of lighting up the object of worship in the manner explained before, while the Brahmanists were rather disposed to hide their gods in the gloom of a dark sanctum; but this is a view not only not supported by any evidence, but is contradicted by examples elsewhere; in the brick temples of the Central Provinces, notably in the example at Sirpur, which proves that the Brahmanists as early as, perhaps, the 5th century, did not hide their gods in the gloom of a dark sanctum, but actually adopted precisely the same mode of lighting the object of worship as is supposed to have been adopted by the Buddhists alone. This circumstance shows that on this ground alone the temple at Konch cannot be considered Buddhist, but there is other evidence more conclusive as to its Brahmanical character. The spout for letting out water used in libations by Brahmanists, but not by Buddhists, still exists buried under accumulations of rubbish at the centre of the north side of the temple, and the sculptures lying about are all Brahmanical, so that I conclude that the temple was originally a Brahmanical shrine and not a Buddhist one; the cylinder, therefore, which crowned it could not have been intended as the representation of a Buddhist chaitya.

But this is not all. General Cunningham ascribes the construction of the present Buddha Gaya temple to the 1st century after Christ. His arguments are very ingenious, but by no means conclusive;* and especially so, as he gives no argument to show that the temple was *not* built, as is expressly stated in the "Amara Devâ" inscription, by Amara Devâ, one of the nine gems in the Court of Vikramâditya, and

* General Cunningham has since informed me that there is strong reason for considering the Amara Devâ inscription a forgery.

therefore identical with Amara Sinha, who lived about or after A. D. 500. (Report, Vol. I, p. 7.)

The existence of the cylindric pinnacle on the top of the temple may now be added as another argument against the construction of the temple so early as the 1st century A. D., if it be supposed to be a representatation of the Buddhist chaitya, for the Buddhist chaityas of the period were far from being the tall cylinder that is here represented; if, however, the temple be ascribed to A. D. 500, there is no difficulty on this score.

But I am not disposed to attach much weight to this argument, as I do not consider it likely that it represents a Buddhist chaitya. The story of Hwen Thsang about the temple having been built by a Brahman by order of Mahâdeva tends to show that the emblem is really a Saivic one. Nothing is more natural than that a Brahman building a temple to Buddha, by order of Mahâdeva, should place the symbol of that deity as the crowning ornament of the temple, and the occurrence of the same finial in other and indisputably Brahmanical Saivic temples tends to show that it really is meant to represent the symbol of Mahâdeva, and that its occurrence in the Buddhist temple of Buddha Gaya is not only not reason for supposing the temple at Konch to have been Buddhist, but is, on the contrary, an evidence in support of the tradition that the Buddhist temple at Gaya (in which it occurs) was built by a worshipper of Brahmanical deities.

In this view, therefore, I do not consider that the age of the Buddha Gaya temple can be even approximately inferred from the existence of this pinnacle on its top; that question must be decided on other grounds; and although I have taken the liberty of pointing out the weak point in General Cunningham's argument, I am not disposed to dispute his finding, as it does not appear to me that there is sufficient evidence for or against, and therefore I bow to his superior experience and authority.

But whether the 1st or the 6th century be finally fixed upon, when sufficient evidence is forthcoming, as the date of the temple, it is clear from the existence of this pinnacle, and quite independent of the coincidence of the features of the existing temple with Hwen Thsang's description, that this temple was built by a Brahman; and as there is record of a Brahman having built the temple but once, whether it be in the 1st or the 6th century A. D., the opinion of Mr.

Fergusson, that its "external form" belongs to the 14th century, must, notwithstanding his high authority, be unhesitatingly set aside.

Reverting now to the Konch temple, I have remarked that the statues lying about are all Brahmanical; these, besides the lingam inside and the statues of Haragauri, which are not scarce, consist of the Ashta Saktis, and the Das avatârs. Buddha avatâr is represented by a standing figure holding a staff diagonally across; the Kâlki avatâr is represented by a man and woman beside a horse, the man with his arm round the woman; the fish incarnation is represented by a fish standing vertically on its tail; the tortoise incarnation bears a close resemblance to the Saivic emblem of the argha and lingam, with the sole addition of a couple of human figures on the sides holding a string which is wound round the lingam, which does duty for Mount Mandar. It is needless here to point more than cursorily to the unmistakable Phallic features of these two Vaishnavic sculptures.

The temple, I conclude from the lingam inside, apparently undisturbed, and from the other Saivic statues, to have been Saivic; the existence of Vaishnavic statues is no objection, as it is not uncommon to see temples where all three—Brahma, Vishnu, and Siva—are sculptured, but of whom one alone is considered pre-eminent and assigned the place of honour.

There lie outside several pillars of granite, of which four are entire ones, five pilasters, and some fragments; besides these, the remains of eight pillars in the shape of eight capitals are now ranged along the steps leading up to the temple. The four pillars I take to represent the four central pillars of the maha mandapa; there must have been more than five pilasters, but only five now exist. The pillars are of granite, very short and massive, and evidently very old.* They taper somewhat, being 1 foot 4 inches square at the base and 1 foot 2 inches at top; the total height of the shaft, including the lowest plain square portion, is 5 feet 6 inches, so that they are little more than only 4 diameters in height. They must have stood on bases, but none are now to be seen; the capitals were plain and massive, with little drops at the four corners; the capitals were not cruciform, though a cruciform capital may have surmounted the square one,

* See plate XII.

as is not unfrequently the case; the pillars are ornamented by a single lotus carved on each of the faces in the lowest square portion of the pillar.

I can find no clue as to the precise date of the temple, but the massiveness of the pillars shows that it must have been built at a very early period; tradition, as noticed by Captain Kittoe, assigns it to Bhairab Indra, and says it was dedicated to Sûrya, but I could hear nothing of this at Konch itself. The following lines are all I could get in the way of tradition regarding Konch:—

> "Konch basé sab soch mité
> Durj Raj pasend Mahámun gyán
> Bed Puránan ki charchá
> Tánhá punjat hai ád Bhawáni,
> Sáh, Saráf, haráf chhab jiwan par bin bakháni
> Jatenhi Tatenhi Thun Mathun ki jánhá det
> Abhay bar Sewsimbh Bhawasü

which, as far as I can make out, means—

> "Konch was established, all troubles ceased, Durj Raj chose a wise Mahámuni (as chief?), and discourse of Vedas and Purânas spread. There is worshipped Bhawâni; merchants, good men, evil men, all life (heard of) the fame; on going (there) the gift of fearlessness and virile strength is bestowed by Siva and Bhawâni."

But many of the words are obsolete, and people disagree as to their meanings.

On the other side of the village road, *i. e.*, to the south, is a mound, the ruins of another temple; the bricks are being carted away to Tikâri; two pillars are lying on the site. This temple, and also the one previously described, are assigned to the Kol Rajas.

A few miles east of Konch on the road to Gaya is the small village of *Páli*. There are, to the east of the village, the remains of two or three temples; but all that now remains are the ruins level with the ground of a large Saivic temple, of which a few pillars alone are standing. The pillars are plain tall shafts with corbelled cruciform capitals; details are given in the plate.

The temple appears to have been a very large one, consisting of a *sanctum* enshrining a large lingam, an *antarala*, a *maha mandapa*, and probably also a *mandapa* and portico. The temple was built of bricks picked with stone. It stood at the north-west corner of a tank. The lingam measures 5 feet 7 inches in circumference, and is 2 feet high at the apex; the argha extends 1 foot 10 inches beyond it all round; there is on the mound a fourteen-armed statue in black basalt, and a second similar one mutilated.

On the other side of the village are two statues of Devi (Parvati). There is also a mound said to have been once larger, and the remains of a temple near the road, which was dedicated to Mahâdeva; but a tree has completely enveloped the argha and lingam, and has split the stone of the pedestal.

There are a few other nondescript fragments lying about; the existing remains, except the statues, are all modern.

Utrain is a small village near Páli. To the west of the village is a small mound with lingam, and fragments of statues scattered about; there is also a fine carved black stone door-jamb.

A small mound adjacent is known as Himmat Khan's garh. It is an inclosure on a mound of earth, and contains six graves; close to it is a small mound which contains bricks and the remains of two graves. The great mound is 25 feet above the level of the country, and is doubtless the site of an old temple; it is 300 feet long and 200 feet wide. The entrance to the dargah, if dargah it be, is on the south; the entrance has two jambs and an architrave of rough granite; the lower sill is a rough pillar set flat.

To the east of the village, near a tope of trees, is a small mound with numerous fragments; among them are several of Ganeça, Haragauri, Nandi, &c., all Saivic. In a room on the mound, whose walls have half tumbled down, and which is 14¾ feet square, is a great lingam 5 feet 9 inches in circumference, 1 foot 10 inches high to the round part, and 2 feet 3 inches high to the apex; the argha extends 1 foot 9 inches all round beyond the lingam.

The room was once roofed by a vault, as fragments of it exist on the ground to this day; the bricks used measure 11 inches × 8 inches, and 9 inches × 6 inches.

The remains doubtless represent a modern shrine built on the site of an older temple.

Sihári is a small village 8 miles to the west of Konch; here is a comparatively modern temple and some fragments. I have not visited the place, but I believe Mr. Peppe took photographs of the remains here.

Deokut is a small village on the Dháwá, a small stream flowing from the Murhar into the Punpun. I have heard that it contains remains of statues, &c., but have not seen the place myself.

The *Mándá hills* are situated about 12 miles west of

Phahrá, a large village on the Murhar, and south of Deokut, near the Dháwá river; the remains here consistsimply of statues, and have been noticed by Kittoe, J. A. S., 1847, page 278. I did not see the place.

Bhuráhá is a small village 2 miles east of the Mándá hills. It is noticed by Kittoe in J. A. S., 1847, page 277. I did not see the place. There were, he says, several chaityas and vihâras here, and here are also some springs of mineral waters, to which no doubt the place owes its ancient importance.

Gunaria is situated 3 miles south-east of the Mándá hills; its ancient name Captain Kittoe discovered to have been Sri Guncharita, and it was the site of a large vihara and town; here are also the remains of numerous lingam temples. (J. A. S., Bengal, 1847, page 278.)

Umgá and *Deo* are two interesting places on and near the Grand Trunk Road from Sherghàti to Benares; the description of the remains in these places is too long to be extracted. (I refer to the original papers in J. A. S., Bengal, 1847, page 656 *et seq.* and 1221 *et seq.*) I must add that since Kittoe's time several additions to the list of remains in and about Deo have been made by Mr. Peppe, who has, I believe, taken photographs of the more interesting remains. At *Cheon*, eight miles north-east of Umgá, are old temples; to the east of the village, to the south of these, and to the east of a little hill, are mounds with statues; 300 yards west on another hill called Pachhár is a cave with a figure of Maya Devi inside; the cave faces south. A mile to the south is another cluster of hills within the boundary of the village Deokili, where there are numerous small caves. I did not visit any of these places.

Bishanpur Ghenjan is a considerable village about two miles north-east of Kispa, on the Murhar; here are several mounds and a few statues; the place was visited and photographs taken by Mr. Peppe. Two inscribed statues exist; one of these inscriptions is merely the Buddhist creed—*Ye Dharmma*, &c.; the other is a single word incomplete—[*Ma*] *hasramana*, the last word in the Buddhist creed.

Pai Bigha is a considerable village on the Dardhá river close to the point where it separates from the Murhar, and above 2 miles to the south-east of Bishanpur Ghenjan; there are several square granite pillars roughly dressed. One was clearly a pilaster; the temples they belonged to must have been Saivic, as they are all marked with a deeply cut trisul;

they are now set upright in front of the village; besides these there are some remains of statues.

The place was visited by Mr. Peppe, who has, I believe, taken photographs of what was interesting here, but I saw nothing of any particular interest myself.

Mátká Hill, *Chillor*, *Murhar*, and *Sherghâti*, all contain interesting remains, chiefly statues. They are noticed by Kittoe in J. A. S., Bengal, 1847, p. 78 *et seq.* and p. 277 *et seq.* I did not visit these places.

Hasanpur Káko is a largish straggling village situated near a large lake into which a branch of the Jamna empties; the country about is flooded during the rains, and in November I had to wade through a long stretch of water to get to the place. The principal remains of interest here are a dargah and some statues.

The dargah is an unpretentious brick building in a state of decay, situated on a high raised mound on the banks of the tank or lake; there is an outer court-yard where numerous slabs of stone, rough and sculptured, lie about; these are evidently taken from some Hindu shrines. The outer court-yard gives admission through a large gateway to a crooked passage and thence into an inner court-yard, whence a third doorway gives entrance into the innermost court-yard in front of the dargah itself. Into this sacred court I was not permitted to enter. The second outer gateway is battlemented, and has a long inscription in Persian or Arabic in five compartments; the inscription is cut in brick and has suffered greatly from the weather. At one corner of the inner enclosure to which this gate gives admission is a tower similar to the towers in the Begampur masjid in Patna, and I infer the other corners, or at least one other corresponding corner, had a corresponding tower; the enclosure walls have, however, notwithstanding extensive repairs, become greatly dilapidated. In the inner court-yard is an inscription on a long trapezoidal piece of bluish-black stone; the inscription is in four compartments of three lines each, and one long line running the whole length; the stone on which the inscription exists has split down the middle longitudinally. When I saw it, it was thickly covered with a most tenacious coat of dirt consisting of indurated layers of milk, ghee, curds, and lamp-black, the offerings of pious pilgrims. I was allowed to clean it, but not without sundry warnings of the risk I ran of incurring the displeasure of the saint.

The dargah contains the tomb of a local saint who, tradition says, came from Delhi and settled down here for a long time. At last he determined to return to his native country, but did not intend to take his wife with him; he set out and walked a good distance till overtaken by night, when he slept, but in the morning he found himself back at his house. Again he set out, but only to find himself back at his house next morning. A third time he tried, with the same result. He then gave up the attempt, and settled down here permanently with his wife, the efficacy of whose prayers had worked the miracles. She is said to have been so saintly that the water used by her for her ablutions would cure any disease.

Outside the dargâh, and to its east on a mound under a *bat* tree, is a large collection of statues in various stages of mutilation; they are mostly of no very ancient date, to judge from the execution. Among the fragments are those of Ganeça, Lakshmi, several lingams, a badly executed slab representing the Nava-graha, Hara Gauri, &c. The village of Hasanpur Kâko is situated on a high mound.

Ner is a small village to the west of the road from Jahânâbâd to Gaya, and about a mile from the Jamna river. Here is a large pillared hall, evidently the maha mandapa of a temple. In the centre of one end of this hall, which has a wall running partly round it, is a doorway with a lingam sculptured over the entrance, giving access to a small chamber (the sanctum of the temple) with a lingam in its centre; the walls of this chamber, as, indeed, all the walls, appear to have been of brick picked with stone.

There is nothing of special interest here; the pillars are roughly dressed, and are not elegant, either for proportion or sculpture, of which, indeed, there is no trace; the hall is roofed by flat slabs of stone. The place was, I believe, visited by Mr. Peppe and a photograph secured.

Near *Belá* are several remains, about a mile and a half east of the dâk bungalow; these consist of various statues, mostly Brahmanical, but some Buddhist also; and of a lingam and argha, which are fabled to have resisted all attempts at dislodgment for conveyance elsewhere. A fragment of a halo round the head of a Buddha with the beginning of the Buddhist creed was found by me in one of the recently set up earthen lingams. In the vicinity are other temples, none of any antiquity, and containing nothing of interest. One temple contains a statue of the skeleton goddess *Kâli* in black stone.

HILSÁ.

Hilsá is a considerable village on the banks of the Kathar, or principal branch of the Lilâjan or Phalgu river. It is at the point where the old road from Gya to Fatuhá and the roads from Râjgir to Patna cross the river, and it must naturally have early risen to importance. The principal object of interest here is the masjid. This is avowedly built on the site of a Hindu temple, and under the great flooring slabs in the centre of the central arch is buried, so says tradition, the mighty Hilsa Deo, sealed down with the sacred seal of a local saint. Hilsá Deo was a powerful magician, and was overcome with difficulty. It is possible that the principal statue of the temple is buried here to be "trodden daily under foot by the faithful," but of course it is quite out of the question to try and ascertain this by actual excavation. There are a few statues in various parts of the city, but nothing else of any importance or interest.

BUDDHA GAYA.

Gaya has already been so carefully described by General Cunningham, and by various other writers, that I need add nothing to the information already given by them. I note, however, the existence of rude stone circles near the foot of the Pretsila hill; these are traditionally ascribed to Kols.

Râm Gaya and Mora Pahâr have been noticed in General Cunningham's reports, and I need only refer to them.

Buddha Gaya has been dwelt upon at some length by General Cunningham in his reports, and has also found mention in the writings of numerous observers and incidentally in this report also, but it appears desirable to notice various points which appear not to have been fully noticed before.

The vault over the sanctum of the great temple, so far as can now be judged from the coating of plaster that covers it, but which, having fallen off in places, discloses the bricks inside, is composed entirely of radiating bricks, set edge to edge, and not bed to bed as usual in the present day. All the bricks appear cut to shape, and there is no appearance of mortar having been used between the bricks; the cementing material appears to be mud. I have already pointed out that, under the peculiar condition of a tunnel vault incapable of being subjected to a lateral strain, the mode of using bricks edge to edge is not only not weaker than the form of arch we now use, but is positively stronger, as giving fewer joints between the voussoirs; and where the cementing material is mud, which does not set hard, but remains always compressible, the advantage of having as few joints as possible of the compressible material between the voussoirs is obvious.

In the sanctum thus covered by the vault, the pedestal of the statue extends right across, and is even partially embedded on both sides within the walls. Apart from the very unusual nature of this arrangement, the fact of the Singhâsan being *embedded at the ends in the side walls is a very* strong circumstance in favour of the supposition that the sanctum was originally larger, within which the throne stood, detached at the ends from the walls.

The all but universal custom in temple-building appears to have been to make the sanctum square and to place it in the centre of the great tower. There are indeed instances, few and far between, where this rule is departed from, notably in the very interesting instance of the great temple at Pathâri in Central India, and also at Gyâraspur; but these temples are of stone. In brick temples I have not come upon a single instance where this rule has been departed from, with the single exception of the temple at Konch; and there the very exception has served most emphatically to confirm the rule. As I have proved almost to demonstration that the apparent anomaly is due to *subsequent* alteration, let us now apply this law to the great Buddha Gaya temple. Here the sanctum is an oblong 20 feet in length. By increasing the width on either side, the immediate consequence is that the side walls, which now are thicker than the back, become at once reduced in thickness, and are made equal to the back wall. Further than this, the Singhâsan now no longer runs anomalously right across the sanctum, but occupies, as it should, a detached position abutting against the back wall. It is clear, therefore, that the thickening of the side walls and the consequent narrowing of the sanctum is due to alterations and additions carried out since the building of the temple. This is the opinion arrived at by General Cunningham, although one of his reasons for so thinking—*viz.*, that there is no recorded instance of the use of the true arch by Hindus at a very early period—is no longer tenable, as will be seen further on. The conclusion he has arrived at, that the vault is a subsequent addition, appears unassailable.

It now remains to determine the period of the addition of the vault. To do this satisfactorily, it is necessary I should refer cursorily to some of the laws which governed the construction of Hindu temples.

On *à priori* grounds, we should naturally suppose that the first datum in the construction of a temple was the size of the sanctum.

The size of the sanctum here is, or rather was originally, a square of 20 feet 4 inches (General Cunningham's measurements); from this, the entire temple has to be deduced according to fixed laws.

Following a law which holds good in numerous temples within very narrow variations, the proportion of width of sanctum to thickness of walls is very nearly as 1·5 to 1 (the actual limits vary from 1·4 to 1·5). We have therefore for the thickness of the walls of the Buddh a Gaya temple 20′ 4″ ÷ 1·5, or 13 feet 4 inches; the actual thickness of the back wall is 13 feet 5 inches at this day.

From this law, therefore, it is seen at once that the original temple had walls 13 feet 6 inches thick, and therefore the extra thickness of the side walls is due to subsequent addition.

We have next to determine the width of entrance and its height.

The widths of entrances in various temples are much more various than the thickness of walls. When referred to the sanctum as a datum, they range from 2·0 to 2·9. Taking the average, 2·5 nearly, we find that the width of opening ought to be 8 feet 2 inches. The actual width of opening is, however, only 6 feet 6 inches. We must, however, remember that the opening is vaulted over like the sanctum, and a thickness of at least 10 inches must have been cut off from either side by building up walls to carry the vault. Adding then twice 10 inches or 1 feet 8 inches to the present width of opening between the jambs, we get 8 feet 2 inches as we should.

The width being now found, the height has to be deduced.

There are two classes of temples—one consisting simply of a cell, the other of a cell with other chambers in front. The Buddha Gaya temple clearly belonged to the latter class, and therefore the opening in the front wall of the sanctum was cut up into two divisions—one forming the doorway proper, the other what may be called the illuminating window. Temples in brick of this class are very rare. The essential requisites to be sought for in temples, with which to compare this and deduce the law applicable to it, are that it should possess a tall triangular overlapping opening divided into two parts, *viz*, the entrance and the window.

I can call to mind but three temples of this class which are now available for comparison—the temple at Sirpur in the Central Provinces, the temple at Konch, and the temple at Katras. In all these, the proportion of height of rectangular part of the opening is $3\frac{1}{2}$ times the width. Using, then, this proportion, we get for the height of the rectangular opening 28 feet 7 inches. For the triangular portion there are numerous examples; and from these it appears that the height of the triangular portion was $1\frac{3}{4}$ times the span, or just half the height of the rectangular portion. The total height, then, of the opening amounts to $3\frac{1}{2} + 1\frac{3}{4}$, or $5\frac{1}{4}$ times the width; hence the total height of the opening in the great temple under examination ought by this rule to be nearly 43 feet.

My approximate measurements agree in making the height to be not very different. I took it at 45 feet.

It may not be here out of place to glance at the difficulties in the way of accurate measurements. The laws deduced from examples and applied to this temple here show that these ancient structures were all constructed on definite principles, and in accordance with definite laws. So far the number of laws and proportions discovered bear a very small proportion to the whole of the great code of laws of ancient Indian art, and it would be very desirable to obtain more of them; but the discovery of the laws depends entirely on detailed and accurate measurements of a great number of buildings, and these measurements necessarily demand time. It is quite wrong, I venture to conceive, to lay down at this stage of our knowledge of Indian art what are the measurements that can and what those that cannot be neglected; for the very fact of being able to draw such a line presupposes a knowledge which we do not yet possess of the laws governing the disposition of parts. To render my meaning clearer, I need merely allude to the laws that I have in a previous paper shown as governing the structures at the Kutab in Delhi. Few, I venture to consider, would have imagined that the accurate measurements of the few ornamental bands, not of the great Minar, but of a dilapidated gateway, would have led to the discovery of the law that governs the whole; yet so it is, for the measurements of the Minar would have failed signally to give any clue to the law, for the simple reason that the law which governs it is a complicated law, derived from and based upon the apparently trifling distances of a few lines (not very prominent or remarkable ones) that adorn the ruined and to all appearance unimportant gateway. It was solely because I thought I could trace a definite interdependence between the various lines on the gateway that I proceeded to measure minutely other apparently unimportant details, and finding the law hold throughout, I then alone ventured to take in hand measurements of the distances of the ornamental bands of the great Minar, and to apply to them the proportion already discovered, but for some time in vain, owing to the complicated nature of the law that there holds sway. Thus, then, it is impossible at starting to point to any particular series of measurements as useless; but if this be so, all possible measurements have to be made with rigid accuracy, and this is a work of time. Let us take the Buddha Gaya temple. In the first instance, I have to reach the place; then extensive scaffolding has to be put up, and it is only after this that the series of measurements can begin at all. I need, therefore, materials and workmen; for these, in a place where I go for a few days, and necessarily possess no acquaintance with the men or resources obtainable, I have to pay for heavily either in time or in money, or in both. It is therefore impossible that half a province can be explored in a single season by a single individual with the care and minuteness necessary to obtain materials for deducing the principles that govern the structures visited.

But although the structures visited cannot be measured with the accuracy and minuteness necessary, it becomes possible to judge, even in a rapid tour, *which* are the buildings most likely to yield results of value to detailed measurements; and these alone need at a subsequent period to be re-visited, measured in detail, and carefully examined. The rapid and extensive tour accordingly becomes, as it were, a preliminary survey, but I wish it to be distinctly understood that, if results of solid value are to be obtained, this preliminary survey must be followed up by a detailed examination of particular portions of the country and of particular structures.

It must, accordingly, be evident that a critical essay on Indian art, or even on a particular temple, cannot now be written. A few, a very few, laws alone have as yet been determined, and even those have not yet been subjected to the crucial test of being used to predict results, which alone would entitle them to complete confidence. I shall therefore not attempt to discuss the architecture except incidentally, but will content myself with describing what I have seen. A discussion of the architecture must be postponed to a future period.

Reverting now to the Buddha Gaya temple, I have proved by the substantial agreement of certain main features, with those deduced from theory, the correctness of General Cunningham's inference, that the temple, as we now see it, is substantially not different from the original temple, whether we assume it to have been built in Vikramâditya's epoch, or in the 1st century after Christ; and that the opinion of Mr. Fergusson, notwithstanding the weight of his name in all questions as to style of architecture, is really erroneous, when he ascribes the "external form" to the 14th century, for if there is one thing untouched in the temple by later repairers, it is the broad features of the external form, all changes having been more internal than external. It now remains to determine the epochs of the various changes.

From the interesting story mentioned by Hwen Thsang, in connection with King Ṣasângka's attempted destruction or removal of the statue of Buddha (Arch. Rep., III, p. 83), it is clear that the minister did not remove the statue, but merely built up a wall to screen it in front. Let us now trace the consequences of doing so, remembering that any evident departure from the easily recognised features of temple architecture would have been certainly detected, and would have brought destruction on that minister.

By building up the wall hiding Buddha's statue, he reduced the square sanctum to an oblong. Such an easily perceptible departure from accepted practice could not pass muster; he would therefore be compelled to form it into a square by cutting off portions from the sides also. The walls which carry the inner vault are made just thick enough to do this, and no more, and this is the only reason I can see which can be assigned for making the walls, carrying the vault, of the thickness they actually are. This done, the sanctum becomes at once again a square, and as a crucial proof that the change which has been imagined was actually made at this time, is the circumstance that the lingam now in the temple, and which doubtless is the one set up by the orders of King Ṣasângka, occupies the exact centre, as it should do, of the *reduced square*. The square thus formed did not, it is true, occupy the centre of the tower, but this was a circumstance that could only have been perceived by making careful measurements, and not being obvious, was not likely to attract notice or suspicion.

But to the chamber so reduced the broad original entrance was obviously inappropriate; it had to be reduced also, and it has accordingly been reduced in nearly the same proportionate extent; so that at first sight there should be nothing to excite suspicion and consequent minute enquiry.

But the tall opening thus reduced in width would wear a very suspicious look; accordingly, we find the opening broken up into compartments, and thus lessening the apparent height.

Internally, however, the now narrowed chamber would have been quite out of keeping with the great height to which the apex of the pyramidal roof rose internally, and a lining of the requisite thickness could not, for obvious reasons, be applied to the interior of the pyramidal roof; hence the expedient of the vault, which effectually cut off the suspicious tallness of the roof internally.

Here then we have all the conditions added that were necessary to carry out the minister's intention of deceiving his king; and I conclude, therefore, that the additions enumerated were made by the minister of Ṣasângka about A. D. 600.

No other supposition that occurs to me can adequately explain the *reason* of these changes; they clearly do not add either to the strength or to the grandeur of the temple.

I have abstained from assigning the original building of the temple to any age, for reasons already given; but I do not hesitate to ascribe the vaulting, &c., to the period of King *Ṣasângka*, about A. D. 600. This assignment will fall in with either of the possible dates of the building of the temple, *viz.*, the first century A. D. as General Cunningham has it, or A. D. 500 according to the Amara Devâ inscription. The occurrence of vaulted arches with radiating voussoirs is no objection, for, as will subsequently be seen, the Indians knew the use of it long before this period.

Regarding the subsequent additions there is no question, and as General Cunningham has already written about them, I refer to his account.

The entrance or doorway to the sanctum is of stone; the doorway to the chamber above the sanctum appears, however, to have been an arched opening without a doorway or lintels of stone. The third chamber is now quite inaccessible.

The *mandapa* in front of the sanctum had a true vaulted roof; it is not now possible to tell whether the four curves springing from the four sides met in a point or in a ridge. Looking at it from the light derived from other temples, I am in favour of their having met in a point. One fact is beyond dispute, that it was *not* a tunnel vault, as bits of the corner curves of intersection of the four arches exist to this day.

The chamber over this, built, as Hwen Thsang tells us, subsequently, had last a tunnel vault of the Barmese pattern, but whether this vault was the one seen by Hwen Thsang, or whether the one seen by him had since been replaced by the later Barmese when they repaired it, I am unable to determine. Of this vault enough alone exists to show that it was of the Barmese pattern; the bricks used are thinner also than the usual run.

This chamber is clearly an after-thought, and the marks of its having been added subsequently are numerous and convincing.

Most of the figures of Buddha that now adorn the niches in the temple appear to me to be later restorations. To this conclusion I am led by observing that, in two niches of the central line over the front opening of the temple, the statues are not of brick plastered over, but of stone.

Externally, I note that all projections and corners not protected by stone facings are laid in cement, the body of the temple being built of bricks set in mud, even the arches being in the case of the old ones set in mud.

Under the Bo tree is a small statue resembling the too common statues known as "Hara Gauri." This statue has four lines of inscription on its pedestal in Barmese characters.

Within the sanctum a square portion immediately round the lingam is slabbed in a way different to the rest of the floor; this portion begins immediately in front of the Singhâsan, and measures 13 feet long and 5 feet 7 inches wide.

I here close my notice of Buddha Gaya. For further information, I refer to papers by various people in the Journal, Asiatic Society; the Asiatic Researches, &c.; and to General Cunningham's reports.

BAKROR.

Bakror is a place of some importance, at the fork or junction of the Lilâjan and the Mohâna rivers, and nearly opposite to Buddha Gaya. The remains here are not numerous, and are noticed in General Cunningham's reports.

SHEONAGAR.

Sheonagar is a small village on the branch of the Lilâjan which flows past Biswak, and about 6 miles below it. The place is said to possess ancient remains, and from the circumstance of its being situated at the point where, in all probability, the old road from Râjgir to Patna past Hilsa crossed the stream, I think it likely to contain ancient remains; the place has not, however, been visited by me nor by any of the various investigators of the antiquities of Magadha.

ONGARI.

Ongari is a small village between Sheonagar and Biswak. The place contains some fragments of ancient statues, &c., and was reported to possess an inscribed slab also; but of this last I could not ascertain the exact locality, if it exists at all. (See also J. A. S. for 1872, page 253.)

DÁPTHU.

Dápthu is a small village not far from Islampur, and contains some ancient remains in the shape of ruined temples and statues, &c. Photographs of the interesting remains here were, I believe, taken by Mr. Peppe, and the place is noticed in detail in Buchanan's work (Martin's compilation), and in Mr. Broadley's papers in J. A. S. for 1872.

BIHÁR.

Bihár is the chief city in the important sub-district of Bihár, and still retains something of its ancient importance. The remains here are numerous, but the place has been described and the remains examined by so many zealous inquirers, that it is only necessary for me to supplement the information already available. The papers that may be consulted regarding Bihár are to be found in various volumes of the Journal, Asiatic Society, the last and most interesting being Mr. Broadley's paper in the volume for 1872. General

Cunningham's reports also furnish a condensed mass of accurate and valuable information.

Among the various writers on Bihár, it is remarkable that no one has noticed its ancient name of Dandpur. Tradition states that before the Muhammadan invasion Bihár used to be called *Bihár Dandi* or *Dand* Bihár, an obvious contraction of Dandpur Bihár. If now we remember that Bihár is not a proper name, but means merely a monastery, being only the corrupted form of "Vihâra," it will be clear that the proper name of the town was Dandpura, and tradition has even preserved the memory of the origin of this name, explaining it by asserting that it was called Dandpur from the great collection of dandis (religious mendicants) who made this their head-quarters.

It is therefore clear that previous to, and at the time of, the Muhammadan invasion, Bihár was really named Dandpur, and being at the same time the seat of a well-known monastery, it naturally was known as Dand Bihár; and tradition further states that when the Muhammadans conquered the place, the Governor caused by proclamation the name of Dand Bihár to be changed into Subah Bihár, the name current at this day.

I must now mention that the ancient name of Silao was Vikramasila, and I will subsequently show why.

These being premised, we now turn to Târanâth's Tibet, where we learn that the monasteries of *Otantapura* and *Vikramasila* were burned down. The mention of these two places together shows that the two were close to each other.

Now, I must allude to the inscription which mentions *Udandapura Desa*, showing that the name *Udandapura* or *Otantapura* or *Dandpura* was not only the name of a city, but of a district. (Rep., III, 118.)

The place, therefore, which imposed its name on a district, or *vice versâ*, must have been the chief city of that district. Further, we know that the place was near Nalanda. (Reports, III, 129.)

General Cunningham has hazarded the conjecture that the name Udandapura may refer to Bishanpur Tandwa, but Bishanpur Tandwa never was a place of the importance thus implied, and General Cunningham was evidently unaware of the tradition which makes the ancient name of Bihár Dandpur Bihár.

From the whole of the above but one conclusion can be drawn, that Bihár was anciently named *Udandapura*.

General Cunningham also suggests that the ancient name of Bihár may have been *Yasovarmmapura.* The following legend may help to throw some light on this question.

The *Kahár* caste is divided into various clans, of which the *Ramáni* is the acknowledged head. The name Ramáni is said to have been derived from Ramanpura, a place near Râjgir, where the chief of the Kahârs used to reside before the caste became split up into clans. It happened that at a certain time very long ago the then chief of the Kahârs married two wives, but the two women were constantly quarrelling and gave their husband no peace, so the man removed one of them to *Jaspur*, and her descendants are known to this day as *Jaswâr* Kahârs.

What connects *Jaspur* with Bihár is the circumstance that the Kahârs about Bihár are mostly *Jaswâr Kahârs*, while those about Giriyak are *Ramánis*.

So that it is not improbable that Bihár, or some place not far from it, was named Jaspur, which is only the spoken form of Yasovarmmapura.

I conclude my notice of Bihár with a legend which accounts for the toleration which Hindus are said to have enjoyed in Bihár *after* the Muhammadan conquest.

When the Muhammadans took Bihár they destroyed all Hindu shrines, and for a long time Hindus were out allowed to go into the city (fort ?). At last, after many years, a jogi named Mani Râm contrived to get in and establish himself, and when the Muhammadans heard of it, they at once proceeded to turn him out ; but he was a great magican, and they could not prevail against him, and allowed him to remain. This man naturally used to blow the sankh, as is customary with Hindus in performing their religious ceremonies. One day the sound happened to reach the ears of Aulia Makhdum Sah, who lived on the hill, and he having ascertained the particulars regarding the jogi and the vain attempt to turn him out, determined to destroy his caste by artifice. He accordingly prepared tasty dishes of cooked beef and sent them with a polite message to the jogi. On the arrival of the presents and the polite message, the jogi desired the dishes to be at once carried back, saying, "In intention I thankfully accept the *pir's* present, and send these back now in return." These dishes on being brought back unopened to the pir were found to contain, not beef, but sweetmeats. The pir now felt much respect for the jogi, and proceeded to visit him in person, seated on a tiger. When the jogi saw the pir approach, he happened to be seated on a wall brushing his teeth with the usual native tooth-brush; he stuck this in the ground and said to the wall he was seated on, "Don't you see the pir coming? Why do you not advance and receive him with due respect?" The wall thereupon advanced with the jogi on it towards the pir; they met in a friendly spirit, and the pir, acknowledging the power of the jogi, agreed that thenceforth they should live in peace with each other, the Hindus consenting to hear the Muazzin's call to prayer, and the Muhammadans the sound of the shell, without offence, and thenceforth there has been peace between the followers of the two religions. The tooth-brush stuck in the ground grew up to a *nim* tree, and an old nim tree is now pointed out as the identical one that grew out of the jogi's tooth-brush.

SOH.

There is a temple at *Soh* close to Bihár which is partly built of the materials of an old temple.

PÁWÁPURI.

Páwápuri is a small village close to and about 3 miles north of Giriyak, and is a great place of pilgrimage for the Jains, who have here two temples, one in the middle of the tank and connected with the land by a long causeway, the other in the village. Both of these are of very recent date; the one in the village appears, however, to stand on the site of an old temple. When I first saw it, it had not been quite finished, but it has since been completed. The statues may be ancient. There certainly are some ancient statues here, and I saw several about the temple in the village. These were slightly defective and consequently not worshipped; but I was not allowed to see the ones that are worshipped. (Captain Kittoe has noticed this place in Journal, Asiatic Society, Bengal, for 1847, p. 955.) This is said to have been the place where Mahâvira died. On the banks of the tank in which stands the temple is a round chaubutra with smaller chaubutras rising up in steps in its centre; a pillar occupies the centre of the whole. I could not ascertain what it was meant to represent, and I was not allowed to go up and see for myself. In the map which accompanied Mr. Broadley's paper in the Journal, Asiatic Society, for 1872, Páwápuri is wrongly placed to the west of the road from Giriyak to Bihár; it is just to the east of the road.

CHANDIMAU.

Chandimau is a small village on the west bank of the Panchâna river, and about 2 miles north-west of Giriyak; there are some few remains here. (See Broadley's paper, J. A. S., for 1872.)

Giriyak has been noticed by numerous writers and by General Cunningham in his report, to which I refer. The controversy between Mr. Broadley and General Cunningham regarding the mountain visited by Fa-hian ultimately resolves itself into the question, Is or is not Fa-hian's *Siao-kou-shy-shan* the same as Hwen Thsang's *Indra-Sila* mountain? Fa-hian's account of the legend attached to his rock is not only substantially the same as Hwen Thsang's, but the existence of a cell facing the south is distinctly recorded by Fa-hian in his mountain. Now, although he places this cell on the top of the hill, I think there cannot be a doubt that the cave referred to is the *Giddha-dwár* cave which faces south, and is at the top, not of the mountain, but of the pass, between the two ranges of hills which converge and meet at Giriyak.

In addition to the *Giddhadwár* cave, there is a cave near the foot of the hill on the north side; it is a natural cavern of no interest, but is said by the people to communicate with the *Giddhadwár* cave; it is named the Shekbir cave. Close to it is a great boulder worshipped by the Musahars of the neighbourhood as *Hathiya Deo.*

SHAPUR-ATMA.

Shahpur-Atma is a small village on a branch of the Pewar; it is said to contain some remains.

BARAGAON.

Baragaon, Jagdispur, and Jâfara are three small villages near each other. Jagdispur is remarkable chiefly for a large statue of Buddha, which stands on a mound near it, and is worshipped as Ambikâ Devi, although it must be evident to the most obtuse that the statue is not that of a female. This statue is said to be the identical one worshipped by Rukmini.

The following verses are said to have been sung by her:—

"Parbhuji kahan na parbhutá kari
Jagnakpur me jag Thaneo
Síá jhunkhut khari
Gaye pina ke Raghúnath Tureo
Sakal se jay kari
Parbhuji," &c.

"Bipin bán marich máreo
Bál se chhal kari
Jal madh se Gaj Raj kareo
Nar Gotam Tari
Parbhuji, se," &c.

"Sisiskál sispal áen
Sodh ke sab ghari
Súsúk páti likhat Rukmin
Bikr ke kár dhari
Parbhu," &c.

"Parbhu bilamb kánhá kije
Parbhu áiye ai ghari
Abki beri kát meri
Japo narki hari
Parbhu," &c.

"Garud char ke Gopála áen
Garud punjat nari
Abki beri kát meri
Japo narki kari
Parbhu," &c.

From this it is seen that the ancient name of Jagdispur is supposed to have been Jagnakpur.

Baragaon is said to have been anciently called Kundilpur. These suppositions, as General Cunningham has observed, are all based on the error of confounding Vidarbha with Bihár instead of Berar.

Near the north end of the north mound at Baragaon is a headless statue, the head of which is said to be lying at Jáfara. There is a curious legend regarding it which I give:—

There was once a man named Seodhar, who, for reasons which had best remain untold here, was condemned by Pârvati to lose all desire. He had been married in infancy, before Pârvati cursed him, and in due course, when his wife, Chandáin, became of age, the ceremony of *gauná*, which consists in bringing the bride from the father's to the husband's house, was performed, and Seodhar brought his wife home; but as all desire was destroyed in Seodhar, his wife soon found her position very uncomfortable, and she formed an attachment with one of her villagers, named Lori, and eloped with him. Seodhar pursued and overtook them, but his wife refused to return, telling him, with unmeasured contempt, that as he had neglected her when she lived with him, it was now too late to run after her. But Seodhar would not listen; he and Lori fought, and he was overpowered, and Lori and Chandáin then went leisurely on. On the road near Baragaon, where the headless statue now lies, they met the chief of the juwaris or gamblers, named Mahapatia, a Dosâd by caste from Juafar. Lori wanted to play a game with him, and the two sat down and played till Lori lost everything he had, including Chandáin. Mahapatia now got up to seize her, but she said, I have indeed been staked and lost, but the jewels on my person were not staked, so play one game more with the jewels for a stake. The gambler sat down to play, and Chandáin went behind her lover Lori, and stood facing the gambler, apparently watching the game. She pretended to be so absorbed in the game, that, as it were unconsciously, she gathered up her petticoat into her hand, exposing her person. The gambler overcome by her beauty and by lust, could not take his eyes off her, and he began losing, till Lori had not only won back all he had lost, but also all that the gambler had, who at last ceased playing. Now Chandáin came forward and told Lori what she had done, and how the man had greedily looked on her. "Kill this infamous man, that he may not boast of having seen me exposed," she said. Lori was a very powerful man; his sword weighed two maunds, and was named *Bijádhar*. With one stroke of it he sent the gambler's head flying to Juafar, while his body fell where he was seated, and both have since turned to stone. Lori was the son of a Gwâla named Budhkithai; he had been married to a girl in the village Agori, now Rajauli, on the road from Hâzaribagh to Bihár, but his wife Satmanain was not of age, and the *gauná* had not yet been performed. She had a sister named Lûrki. Lori had a brother, Semru, who, being an orphan, had been brought up by Lori's father as a son. He lived near Agori, at a village which, from the circumstance of his having been brought up as an adopted son, "pâlak," was named Pâli; the place is said to be a few miles north of Rajauli.

Lori and Chandáin now went on to Hardui, a place said to be two days' march (*manzils*) from Mongir on the north. Here they fought with and defeated the Raja and conquered the country. The expelled Raja sued for aid at the Court of the Raja of Kalinga, and succeeded with his aid in capturing

Lori, who was forthwith placed in a cell with his hands and feet stretched out to their fullest extent and nailed down to the floor. A heavy load was also placed on his chest, and in this state he lay for a long time, till at last, through the favour of Durgâ, to whom he devoutly addressed himself, he was freed from confinement. He again fought with and defeated the Raja, re-conquered Hardui, and was re-united to Chandáin. They had a son born here, and lived a long time, but at last a desire to re-visit their native country prevailed, and laden with wealth they reached Páli.

Meanwhile his brother by adoption, Semru, had been killed by the Kols, and all his cattle and property had been plundered. He left a son, and the family was in great distress. Lori's wife also had now grown up to be a handsome woman, but still lived in her father's house, and in great distress. Lori on arrival caused it to be known that a Raja from a distant country had arrived. Time had so changed him that no one recognised him, and having thus secured his incognito, he determined to ascertain whether his wife had been faithful during his absence. Accordingly, when he had ascertained that his wife was among the women who came daily to sell milk in his camp, and had recognised her, though she failed to recognise him, he caused a *dhoti* to be placed across the entrance to his camp, so that no one could come in without striding across it. Next morning, when the women came, he instructed Chandáin to call them in quick, judging that if his wife, in her hurry, should step across the *dhoti*, and thus show that she was not very particular as to a trifle, she was not likely to have been particularly careful of her virtue. Satmanain, hurried by Chandáin, came on fast till she came to the *dhoti* there, and though others stepped over it, she stood, and finding no means of advance without striding across the *dhoti*, she requested the *dhoti* to be removed. Lori was pleased at this, and when she had disposed of her milk and wanted payment (payments being usually made in rice) Lori filled her basket with jewels and covered them with rice, so that she unsuspectingly took them home. Her sister on emptying the basket saw the wealth below, and surmising that her sister had obtained it through dishonour, taxed her with it. She denied all knowledge of the jewels, and the girls agreed that they would next day go together to have the suspicion cleared. Meanwhile the son of Lori's adopted brother, hearing of the suspicion against his aunt, took up arms, and prepared to attack Lori, not knowing that he was Satmanain's husband. The two women went as agreed, and Lûrki then recognised Lori, and the mystery was cleared up, to the happiness of all concerned. But Lori had to undergo a severe lecture for his unnatural behaviour in neglecting his young wife so long, and living in happiness with a mistress. Matters, however, were so arranged as not to deprive Lori of his mistress.

On the other hand, the nephew, not having any knowledge of these transactions, and finding Lûrki and Satmanain both absent from home, attacked Lori furiously; the fight raged for a long time, Lori was overpowered, and was on the point of losing his life, when Lûrki and Satmanain rushed into the fight and explained matters; thereupon there were great rejoicings, and they all settled down comfortably.

Lori ruled his subjects with justice, and was such an earnest encourager of agriculture, that in a short time he turned the wilds about Rajauli to a highly cultivated country, where, so completely was the land brought under cultivation, that even insects found no secure resting place; so the whole body of birds, beasts, and insects went up and complained to Indra, who, taking counsel with Durgâ, saw that Lori ruled his country with such justice, and was so blameless in his private life, that he was beyond the power of harm, and could not be touched, unless he committed some crime. To entice him into crime, Durgâ assumed the form of his mistress, and went to him with his food, which was the usual custom of Chandáin. Lori, ignorant of the trap laid for him, and inflamed by the beauty of his supposed mistress, who on this day seemed to him more beautiful than she had ever been, neglected his food and amorously sought to embrace his beautiful Chandáin. Hardly had he touched her, when Durgâ, knowing that his invulnerability was lost, administered a slap, which twisted his face completely round, and disappeared. Overcome with grief and shame, Lori determined to go and die at Kasi, but his relatives loved him too well to lose him, and they all went to Kasi, where they now all sleep the sleep of magic at the Manikarnika Ghat, having been turned into stone.

The legend is very interesting, as it gives us an insight into the customs which prevailed in ancient times, and we see that there has been but little change to this day. Now, as before, we see the great importance attached to scrupulous observance of a morbid delicacy in the conduct of females coupled with a shameless indecency; the exposure of her person by Chandáin is not considered a very heinous offence against propriety, but the idea of the man living to trumpet it forth to the world is insupportable. And, again, the dwelling together of the wife and the mistress under the same roof is not considered an impropriety, while for the woman to stride over a man's *dhoti* is considered very indelicate, if not actually a crime. In connexion with this idea, I may allude to a custom prevalent in Northern India, for the husband, when going away from his home for a long time, to leave his trousers with his wife, in order that when desirous of having children, she may, by putting them on, obtain her wishes. I may also allude to the legend, to be given further on, where the smelling of a saint's *langoti* was found efficacious in obtaining a child. I may further allude to the custom of tying *chillas* with a like intent at various holy spots. The idea that underlies those customs is evident, and need not be put in plain words; but the unmeasurable distance between modern Western ideas of propriety and Indian ideas, even of the present day, is evident: the one tries to provide against the awakening of even a passing impure thought by an unguarded word or gesture, the other not only does not attempt to preserve purity of thought, but does not even guard sufficiently against purity of conduct. In short, the circumstances alluded to bear out the conclusion one would naturally draw from Hindu sculptures, that female morality during the Hindu period was of a very low standard.

It is interesting to note also that gambling as a *profession* is not a modern institution; the village Jüafar is said to have been so named from having been the head-quarters of professional gamblers.

SILÁO.

Siláo is a large village about 3 miles from Baragaon. It is at the present day noted for a kind of native sweetmeat, and for its parched rice, and from personal knowledge I can bear out in regard to these items the fame it enjoys. It is, however, not devoid of objects of interest, as there are two tombs and a masjid with numerous inscriptions in Persian and Arabic characters. The masjid is of the ordinary kind, without cloisters attached; it is built of stone and mortar, and the floor in front is paved with stone. The whole of the stone was derived from Hindu buildings. The pavement is indeed one mass of imbedded pillars, and proves that the buildings destroyed to furnish the profusion of materials must have been numerous and extensive. Most of these, however, are plain, and there are very few sculptured stones to be seen in Siláo.

Tradition ascribes the building of the masjid to a very early period, making it contemporary with the masjid and dargah at Bihár. There is a silly legend related of a herdsman having once, to avoid the destruction of his calves by disease, vowed to make an offering of the entire milk of his flock to the local saint. This was done in the same way as the offering of the rice and milk to Buddha at Buddha Gaya, by feeding a certain number of cows on the milk of the whole, and on their produce feeding a fewer number, till at last only one cow was fed on the concentrated essence of the milk of all the cows, and of her milk *khír* was duly cooked; but the poor Muhammadan saint did not get off as satisfactorily as Buddha, for the herdsman having in his hurry begun reciting the necessary prayers while the *khír* was still boiling hot, the unfortunate saint found himself sorely punished, for the boiling compost at once miraculously transferred itself to the mouth of the saint, I have no doubt to his great astonishment.

The foundation of Siláo is ascribed to Vikramâditya even by the Muhammadans of the place (two of these volunteered to be my guides to the masjid and tombs), and the excellence of the sweets and of the parched rice is ascribed to consummate halwais settled here by him, whose descendants now carry on the trade. I was inclined at first to look upon the tradition as absurd, but General Cunningham's surmise communicated to me, while at Simla, that Siláo might be found to be a contraction of Vikramasila, recurred to my memory, and I at once perceived the signification of the tradition. This place then is the ancient Vikramasila, and people naturally soon contrived a tradition to account for the name. At present, when the "Vikrama" portion of the name is forgotten, the tradition naturally appears quite unintelligible.

BARAGAON.

I cannot take leave of Baragaon and its vicinity without alluding to Mr. Broadley's excavations at, and his account of, Nâlanda. While giving him credit for zeal and exertion, I cannot but feel that the excavation of this temple, which General Cunningham assigns to the 1st century A. D., was not a work which Mr. Broadley should have undertaken without professional assistance. From a perusal of his account, it is impossible to make out with any degree of certainty, or even lucidity, the details of the temple which he has excavated and destroyed, for the pillars, doorway, &c., have long ago been by him removed to Bihár. He has indeed ventured to give a restored elevation of the great temple; but though this makes a very effective *plate*, and his description is good enough for a "popular account," they are next to worthless for all scientific purposes; and in the interest of true archæology, I venture to enter a strong protest against acts which destroy such interesting ruins without preserving detailed and minute measurements of what is thus destroyed. In exposing ancient ruins buried under ground, destruction of parts, and often wholesale destruction, is sometimes inevitable; but there is no reason why careful and detailed measurements should not be preserved before the work of destruction is proceeded with. These measurements should in fact be made with even more than ordinary care and in most minute detail, for the simple reason that future reference and verification is impossible. I trust my feeble voice will have some effect in adding that discretion to the laudable zeal of explorers, without which they risk destroying for ever that which is of solid and enduring interest.

RÂJGIR.

Râjgir, the ancient Girivraja, is one of the oldest cities in India, and has deservedly obtained a prominent place in the writings of all who have treated of the antiquities of Magadha. My task is therefore greatly lightened, for it is unnecessary for me to do more than refer to the writings of General Cunningham, which contains, as it were, a summary of all that had been discovered and published till his visit last year, and to the later discoveries embodied in Mr. Broadley's paper. A few points alone, which either have not received the requisite attention, or wherein I differ from the writers named, need be considered in detail.

Among the new discoveries are two inscriptions obtained from an old well at the side of the path leading through old Râjgir from the north entrance to the Báwan Gangá defile. The well is situated in the southern portion of the fort outside the long south ramparts of the inner town. These inscriptions are both in brick, and are much mutilated from the effects of weather and saline efflorescence. They are imbedded within the well ring at some distance below the mouth of the well; one is dated in Samvat 1007, the legible portion giving the name "Sri Râma Dharmin," who probably dug the well. The rest is illegible, being too far worn to give even two consecutive letters entire.

Besides these inscriptions I wish to invite attention to the long rambling inscription on the flat rock, over which the present path from the north to the Báwan Gangá defile passes. Kittoe conjectured, and conjectured rightly, that the curious marks are letters. I am quite satisfied that it is a long inscription, written in the curious shell characters which have hitherto to a great extent defied the acuteness of antiquarians. The inscription is not in good order, partly from the nature of the rock on which it is cut, but chiefly from having been to a great extent rubbed away beneath the tread of passengers and cattle for a thousand years; but enough yet remains perhaps to show what it was about, and whether in its loss we are not to deplore the loss of a valuable record. The curious characters have long attracted the attention of the people of the place, who suppose them to be the marks of the hands and feet and nails of the combatants Bhima and Jarâsandha. The place is known as Ranbhûm.

There is, however, another spot equally called Ranbhûm; this is properly not Ranbhûm, but Rangbhûm, being the spoken form of "Ranga Bhûmi," "the coloured earth," from the deep red colour of the earth there found. Tradition ascribes the colour to the blood of Jarâsandha, who was killed by Bhim after having fought with him at the Ranbhûm described before. This spot is situated on the western or main branch of the Saraswati at the point where it enters the western ramparts of the inner town.

My attention was especially directed by General Cunningham to the exploration of the long defile which stretches away between the Baibhár and Sonar hills to the west of the old city. I tried to carry out my instructions, and twice attempted to penetrate the pathless jangal which literally chokes up the valley, but on both occasions without success, having in both cases returned after losing my way and wandering about to no purpose in the jangal. The importance of a thorough exploration of the valley will be evident when it is remembered that Hwen Thsang describes the existence of a great cave (natural probably) at the foot of the northern mountain, and of a tope near Jaktiban, close to a small isolated hill. Hwen Thsang's description is perfectly accurate;

for although I failed to penetrate the valley from below, I could nevertheless look down into it from the heights of Baibhárgiri. The two ranges of Baibhár and Sona are thus seen to approach each other, but without meeting. At the point where the distance is least is a high hill close to, but isolated from, the Baibhár range; a short way to the south-west of it is a small detached hill close to Sonagiri; close to this I could see a small tumulus having precisely the appearance of an old stûpa. The position corresponds accurately with Hwen Thsang's description, and I have no doubt in my own mind that it is the long and vainly-looked for stûpa; but all my attempts to get to it were vain, for on descending the hill only a short way, the dense jangal hides the smaller hill and the stûpa, and from the valley through the pathless jangal I found it impracticable to get to it.

There is a large cave, but quite inaccessible, on the side of Baibhárgiri, near the source of the northern tributary which joins the Saraswati before it enters the inner city. The cave appears to be natural, but from its position it appears too far east to coincide with Hwen Thsang's Asur's cave. A second small cave, and equally inaccessible, exists further east, also on the southern slope of Baibhárgiri.

If, however, the necessary time could be spared to cut down a portion of the jangal in the valley, I have no hesitation in saying that the stûpa described by Hwen Thsang could be got at. Of its existence I had ocular proof, and I think it very unlikely that I could have mistaken a natural mound or hill for a stûpa, the more so as I carefully looked at it with a powerful binocular.

Beyond this, but quite invisible even from the top of the Baibhár hill, are the hot springs of Tapoban; a thin vapour over the spot where they exist declare their position. I did not see them. The outer wall of the great fort, beginning at the north entrance and going eastwards, ascends the Vipulagiri to its summit, then descends down a spur in a southern direction and ascends Ratnagiri. From the summit of this hill two branches diverge; one descends southwards, merging into the Nekpai embankment across the eastern defile leading to Giriyak, and emerging on the opposite side it ascends Udayagiri. The other branch stretches away towards Giriyak; and tradition says it goes right up to, and embraces within its circuit, the Giriyak hill. Whether it stretched unbroken right through or not I have not been able to ascertain, but certain it is that a line of walls stretches westwards from

Giriyak along the crest of the long range of hills. On the summit of Udayagiri the wall on ascending also divides into two; one descending westwards to the Báwan Gangá defile, the other stretching away towards Giriyak, and said to extend, or to have originally extended, unbroken till it met the branch which, as already noticed, runs in the same direction from the summit of Ratnagiri. The two ranges of walls thus extended along the converging crests of the two ranges of hills which enclose on the north and the south the *eastern* Báwan Gangá defile; the spot where the walls cross the defile to complete the circuit being just above the Gidhadwar cave, where Nature has so disposed the spurs of the two ranges that they meet, and the stream rushes down the steep barrier in cascades and rapids to join the Pamchana. Art has taken advantage of the natural features to construct a dam or rather to carry the wall across here, forming, as it were, a dam. (Plates 41, 44, Vol. III, Archæological Report.)

The branch that descends the western spur of the Udayagiri is taken up across the defile by a similar line of walls running up the spur up the Sonar to its nearest peak; here it divides into two, one running down northwards, and merging into the west ramparts of the inner city; the other stretching away towards Tapoban. I have been told by the people that it stretches away right up to Tapoban, where it descends the hill, but cannot speak of it from personal observation.

From the summit or peak stretch out three long arms;—the one west carries the main chain of hills onwards to the west; the south or south-east one slopes down to the south gate or Báwan Gangá defile; the eastern one, however, juts out into the interior of the outer fort, and divides the southern portion of the space between it and the inner ramparts into two portions. The valley between this spur and the south-east one is watered by a rivulet with broad sandy bed. This rivulet, before its junction with the Báwan Gangá stream, receives a tributary from the north; near the point where the tributary joins it, the two main spurs spoken of send out minor spurs towards each other, and the space between was once shut in by a massive wall, through which the river has burst its way. Within this little triangular space are the ruins of two temples, one of which appears to have been Brahmanical; they are of brick. Besides these there are remains of a third, larger than either of the others, but they do not appear to be of any special interest. One of the small ones appears a later restoration, and is perched on a mound which itself was the ruin of a temple, as the straight walls are still traceable where the rain and floods have washed away the debris, and excavation may yield objects of interest.

The main line of walls of the outer fort according to the people is the one stretching away towards Tapoban, then descending and re-ascending Baibhár hill and running along it to the Saraswati rivulet; but this portion of the outer walls, if it really exist, has not yet been explored; the inner western ramparts which cross the Saraswati stream at Rangbhum having alone been explored, and the portion from the crest of Baibhár eastwards down to the rivulet at the north entrance into the valley.

It will thus be seen that the great fort consisted of an outer fort with walls running along the crests of the surrounding hills, and an inner fort consisting of ramparts in the valley on all sides, except the west, where alone, from the outer walls not having been explored, it is not possible to speak with certainty; but I am inclined to accept the statements of the people, who assert the existence of outer walls here also, because without it this side would not correspond in main features with the other sides.

There are several caves in and about Râjgir. Of these the following have distinct names, and are connected with various legends :—

1.—The Asur's cave or palace of the Asuras, mentioned by Hwen Thsang as somewhere near Yashti Vana; it has not yet been found (see *ante*).

2.—A cave close to it (see Geogr. Anc. India by Cunningham, p. 462).

3.—The cave in which Buddha used to sit in profound meditation.

4.—The cave of Ananda.

5.—Devadatta's cell.

6.—The Pippal cave or palace of the Asurs.

7.—The Sattapanni cave.

Of these four have been discovered, but three alone described by General Cunningham. One of these is the Pippal cave behind Jarâsandha's Baithak, *i. e.*, No. 6 of the list.

Of the remaining two, one is called by him the Sattapanni cave; the other is a small broken cave close to it.

As I differ *in toto* from General Cunningham's identifications here,—identifications adopted also by Mr. Broadley,—it is necessary to discuss the subject in detail.

Before doing so, it is best to dispose of those that I do not contest. Nos. 1 and 2 have not yet been found.

No. 6 is the Pippal cave discovered by General Cunningham during his last visit.

No. 5 is the cave discovered by General Cunningham, but strangely enough omitted from his report. During my visit to Râjgir the people told me that General Cunningham had seen it, and from the original manuscript map of Râjgir drawn by himself from his own surveys, which he kindly permitted me to use, and of which I have at this moment before me a tracing executed by myself, I see the position of the cave distinctly marked as a cave, so that I feel that, although he has omitted to notice it, this discovery is his by right. This cave is situated on the slope of Vipula, and is indeed marked in plate 41, 3rd volume reports, with the letter M, which on reference to the explanatory column attached is seen to be Devadatta's house, but there is no allusion to it in the text. This cave is thus noticed by Fa-hian: "Leaving the old city and going north-east 3 *li*, we arrived at the stone cell of Devadatta, fifty paces from which there is a great square black stone". The cave is also noticed by Hwen Thsang. This cave, therefore, may be appropriately called Devadatta's cave.

It now remains for me to discuss the identity of the three caves, Nos. 3, 4, and 7.

I must, however, show that our authorities prove the existence of three distinct caves; for this purpose I quote Fa-hian:—

"Entering the valley and skirting the mountains along their *south-eastern slope* for a distance of fifteen *li*, we arrive at the hill called *Gridhra Kuta*. Three *li* from the top is a stone cavern facing the south. Buddha used in this place to sit in profound meditation (dhyâna). *Thirty paces* to the north-west is another stone cell, in which Ananda practised meditation (dhyâna). The hall in which Buddha delivered the law has been overturned and destroyed; the foundations of the brick walls exist however.

"Returning towards the new city after passing through the old town, and going more than 300 paces to the north, on the west side of the road we arrive at the Kalanda Venouvana Vihara (the chapel in the bamboo garden of Kalanda). This chapel still exists, and a congregation of priests sweep and water it. Two or three *li* to the north of the chapel is the Shi-mo-she-na (Samasana), which signifies the field of tombs for laying the dead.

"Skirting the southern hill and proceeding westward 300 paces, there is a stone cell called the Pippal cave, where Buddha was accustomed to sit in deep meditation (dhyâna) after his midday meal. *Going still in a westerly direction, five or six li,* there is a stone cave situated in the *northern shade of the mountain* and called *cheti.* This is the place where 500 Rahats assembled after the nirvan of Buddha to arrange the collection of sacred books.

"Leaving the old city and going north-east three *li,* we arrive at the stone cell of Devadatta."

The italics are all mine.

From the first quotation we learn of two caves close together, in the south-eastern slope of the Baibhár mountain, one of which, that in which Buddha used to sit in profound meditation, faced the south.

From the next quotation we learn of the existence of two other caves in the Baibhár hill also, one of which is the Pippal's cave, and the other the Sattapanni cave; this last situated to the west of the former and in the northern shade of the mountain.

From quotation 3 we learn of a cave in Vipulagiri.

Of these five distinct caves, two have been identified,—the Pippala and Devadatta's caves.

There still remain three to search for and identify.

We have, however, only two hitherto described caves to dispose of; these are situated close together, and one of them faces the south (I quote General Cunningham's own words), "in front of which the rock has been cut away to form a level terrace 90 feet in length by upwards of 30 in breadth. Two caves have been excavated out of the solid rock behind; that to the west now called the Son Bhândâr or treasury of gold, being 34 feet long by 17 feet broad; and that to the east perhaps somewhat less in length, but of the same breadth." (Arch. Rep., Vol. I, pp. 24 & 25.)

Referring to plate 41, Vol. III, we see at once that "entering the valley and skirting the mountains along their south-eastern slope for a distance of 15 *li,*" we arrive at these two caves; further, the caves face nearly south. Is it possible to resist the conviction that these two caves are the two caves referred to by Fa-hian in the first quotation?

But neither of these two is the Sattapanni cave; of these one is Buddha's cave, the other is Ananda's cave according to Fa-hian.

General Cunningham alludes to the socket-holes in front of what I may now venture to say he erroneously calls the Sattapanni cave, as in some way confirming his identification; but Fa-hian distinctly tells us that "the hall where Buddha delivered the law" was overturned and destroyed in his time;

we thus have clear proof that Buddha's cave was adorned with a hall in front, so that the circumstance of the socket-holes does not affect the question in any way.

General Cunningham also ingeniously tries to make out that, because the range of the Baibhár runs north-east and south-west, and the cave is situated near the northern end, that it may therefore be considered as being in the northern *shade*. I disallow his position entirely; the cave is indeed in the northern end of the mountain, but instead of being in the northern shade, it is precisely in the opposite predicament, being in the southern glare of the hill, and the sun from sunrise to about 2 P. M. blazes furiously into the cave.

Having now disposed of the two caves in hand, there remains to find out the true Sattapanni cave.

Following Fa-hian's direction, we come from the plain between old and new Rajagriha to the Baibhár hill. We do not enter the valley of old Rajagriha at all; 300 paces west from the extreme east toe of the Baibhár hill is the Pippal cave. I appeal to Plate 41, Vol. III, Reports, to show that the Pippal cave is not within the valley; it is on the ridge which forms the boundary of the valley. Now, as this ridge runs not west or north-west, but south-west, it is clear that going due west from the Pippal cave we cannot possibly enter the valley, but travel along the northern toe and in the *northern shade* of the Baibhár hill. Going 5 or 6 *li* or about a mile west from here, in the northern shade of the hill is the famed Sattapanni cave. I travelled as Fa-hian directs. I went even 2 miles, but without seeing any cave that could have served the purposes of the synod. I turned back hopeless, when straight in front of me on the side of the hill was the cave sought for! I had passed it unnoticed. It is so situated that, going from east to west, it is not seen, but is seen distinctly coming from west to east; it is situated rather less than a mile from the Pippal cave, and to west of it; a diagram will illustrate how it escapes notice in going from east to west.

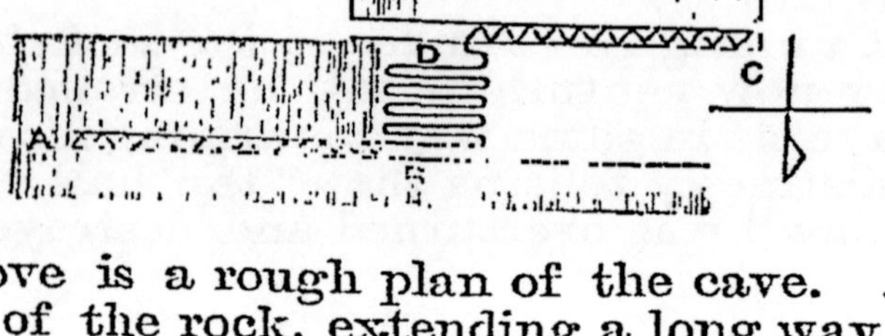

The above is a rough plan of the cave. A B is a steep scarped face of the rock, extending a long way. D. C. is also a steep scarped face of the rock extending a long way on both sides, the hill here appearing to rise in ledges over each other; the entrances of the caves or cave face west, so that going from east to west no cave is seen at all.

In position, the cave corresponds to Fa-hian's Cheti cave. I have now to establish its identity with the Sattapanni cave.

For this purpose I quote various writers :—

(1) First, from "the sacred and historical books of Ceylon" we learn that the true name of the cave was "Sapta Parnna."

(2) From the Mahâwanso, page 12 :—

"On the completion of the repairs of the sacred edifices they thus addressed the monarch: 'Now we will hold the convocation on religion.' To him (the king) who inquired what is requisite, they replied a session hall; the monarch inquiring 'where,' in the place named by them, by the *side of the Webhára* mountain at the extrance of the Sattapanni cave, he speedily caused to be built a splendid hall like unto that of the devas.

"Having in all respects perfected this hall, he had invaluable carpets spread there corresponding to the number of the priests, in order that being seated on the north side the south might be faced; the inestimable pre-eminent throne of the high priest was placed there. In the centre of that hall facing the east the exalted preaching pulpit fit for the deity himself of felicitous advent was erected."

(3) Spence Hardy, Eastern Monachism, p. 175 :—

"One of their first acts was to request a suitable place for the holding of the convocation from the monarch of that city, Ajasat, now in the 8th year of his reign, who appointed for this purpose the cave Saptaparni near the rock Webhára. This cave was painted in a beautiful manner, representations of various kinds of flowers and creepers appearing upon its sides, whilst many parts were inlaid with gold and silver and gems. The floor was sprinkled with perfumes, and curtains of many colours were hung round. There were 500 seats covered with cloth for the priests, and in the centre, looking towards the east, a throne for the person who recited the bana, with an ivory fan placed near it."

(4) Bigandet's Gandama, p. 354 :—

"Adzatathat joyfully assented to the proposal and demands of the Buddhists' Patriarch. He gave full liberty for the holding of the council, saying: 'my power and that of the law are now at your command.' He gave immediate order for putting in perfect order the dwelling place of the Rahans. On the southern face of Mount Webhára there was a cave, which had been a favorite place of resort with Buddha during the season that he spent at Radzagio in the Weloowon or bamboo grove monastery. That spot was fixed upon as the fittest for the holding of the assembly. Adzatathat summoned in his presence the most skilful workmen, and commanded them to exert all their skill and talents in erecting a hall, worthy of the members of the assembly that was to meet within its precincts. The ground was at first encircled with a fence. A fine *flight of steps* made with the utmost care led from the bottom of the hill to the spot where was built the magnificent hall. The seat of the president was placed opposite in the northern part. In the centre, but facing the east, a seat resembling a pulpit was raised ; upon it was laid a beautiful fan made of ivory."

(5) Page 356 :—

"On the 5th of the waxing moon of Wakhaong, the 499 venerable members attired with their cloak and carrying the mendicant's pot assembled in the hall at the entrance of the Webhára cave."

The words of Hwen Thsang are (I quote in second hand from J. A. S., 1872, p. 242, the original not being within my reach) :—

(6) "Au Nord d une Montagne Situe au midi au Melieu d'une vaste bois de bambous il y a une grande Maison en pierre."

The question to be discussed is a complex one : first, we have to ascertain the name of the cave where the assembly was held ; and secondly to fix its position.

The Ceylonese records, quotations 1, 2, and 3, clearly give the name as Sattapanni or correctly as Saptaparnna cave. Mr. Alabaster, in the eighth note at page 167 of the Siamese life of Buddha, calls it the Sattapanni cave, but I am unaware of the source of his information.

But if we turn to the Barmese version, we find from 5 that the cave is named the Webhára cave and from Fa-hian we find it to be named Cheti.

But this is not all. The Ceylonese record describes the seats of the Rahans as being placed facing the south, and that of the president opposite ; it is clear, therefore, that the Rahans were seated at the north end or side facing south, while the president's chair was at the south end or side facing north. The Barmese version, however, says exactly the reverse. They, however, agree in making the preaching pulpit face east. Referring then the description to this common point, and remembering that the Barmese version distinctly states that the cave was on the southern slope of the hill, we find that according to this version the president was to the left and the congregation to the right of the pulpit ; but this Barmese version exactly inverts the arrangement as given in the Ceylon records. The arrangement, according to the Ceylon records, referred also to the pulpit, shows the president's chair on the right and the congregation on the left of the pulpit.

It is now clear that the Barmese version is incorrect; for the seat of the president could not have been placed in the inferior position to the left of the pulpit. I accordingly consider that by some strange mistake the Barmese version has just inverted the position of the president and of the congregation, and as a necessary consequence the distinct statement that the cave was on the southern slope of hill should be corrected and made to state that it was on the northern slope of the mountain.

Making this correction, the Barmese version tallies in every particular with the accounts from the Ceylon records, and with the statement of two independent visitors of the cave, Hwen Thsang and Fa-hian.

In saying that after the proposed correction the Barmese record agrees with Fa-hian and Hwen Thsang's statements, I consider that the expression, "in the northern shade," necessarily places the cave on the northern slope of the hill. I have already combated General Cunningham's ingenious attempt to make out this expression as meaning that the cave faced the south.

The substantial agreement of all the accounts regarding the cave where the synod was held being thus obtained, it is easy to consider that the names Sattapanni, Cheti, and Webhára are all names of the same cave.

The name Webhára is clearly derived from the hill Baibhár, so is Cheti from Chhata, the name of the highest peak in the Baibhár range; the third name, Sattapanni, is derived, Turnour says in his index, from the Sattapanni plant. In accepting his derivation, we necessarily assume that there was some legend or tradition or circumstance connecting the cave with the plant. The assumption, though perfectly possible, is purely gratuitous, and if we can find any derivation for the name which does not involve a gratuitous assumption, it is evidently entitled to more consideration.

Saptaparnna means seven-leaved, and indeed the plant Saptaparnna is so named from its leaf; a cave that was divided into seven sapta by any means would not inaptly be called the Saptaparnna cave.

The cave I now propose as the Saptaparnna cave fulfils this condition. It is a large natural cavern which has been untouched by art, and portions of it have fallen in and over. The cavern is divided by natural septa of rock into compartments, six of which I counted, and there was space between the last one I counted and the vertical face of the ledge above it for a seventh compartment, but the jangal was too dense to allow me to penetrate to it and establish its existence by actual sight. At the time I explored Râjgir I was not aware of the important connection between the name Sattapanni and seven compartments,—in fact, I had not attempted to trace the meaning of the name, but as soon as I mentioned the discovery to a friend of mine, a Sanskrit scholar, and said that I regarded it as the Sattapanni cave, he at once told me that the very fact of the seven compartments gave the cave a right to the name Saptaparnna, which he said was doubtless the original of the Pali Sattapanni. Subsequently, when at the close of the field season I could procure the necessary books bearing on the subject, I found the surmise of my friend verified, as Spence Hardy and the sacred and historical books distinctly give its name as Sapta Parnna.

It is now a matter of regret to me that, although quite satisfied in my own mind of the existence of a seventh compartment, I did not actually wait at Râjgir till men could be sent up first to clear a path for themselves (I ascended alone at the sacrifice of my thick woollen clothes), and then to clear out the cave.

The cave may now be described in detail; the sketch shows its general plan. A series of chambers separated by natural walls of rock running east and west; I counted six chambers, and there was room between the south wall of the last chamber and the steep side of the hill for a seventh. The accompanying is a section through the hill-side just in front of the cave looking east; the various chambers are neither regularly shaped nor equal in size, they are in fact natural fissures in the rock. Some are very narrow; one especially is only 4 feet wide, others are 6, 8, and 10 feet wide; they are not of equal lengths, but they all narrow towards the interior, till at some distance, which ranges from 6 to 12 feet in various chambers, they become mere clefts; the larger chambers are more square or round-shaped at the inner end; the floors of the caves are not also all at the same level, and the smaller ones are very uneven.

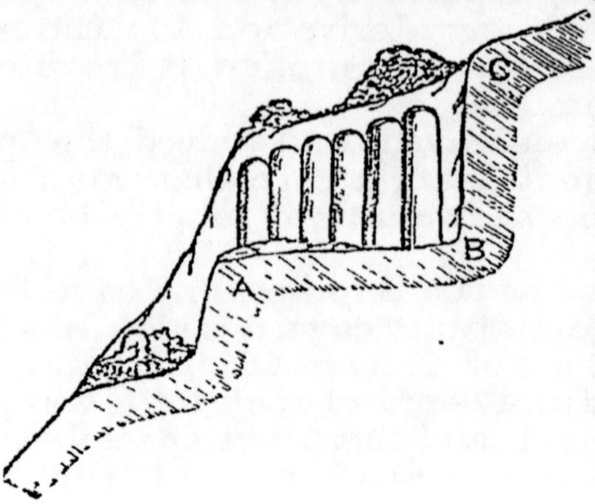

In front of the caves runs a long narrow flat ledge of rock which is tolerably even, and 25 or 30 feet wide; the outer edge of it has partially fallen. I did not examine the vertical face B C; it was not easily to be got at on account of dense undergrowth and overhanging branches, and creepers and lichen completely hide the face of the rock from view; but had I at the time I explored the cave been aware of the importance of a thorough examination of this wall rock, I should have waited and cleared it all out. The ledge runs on in a direction nearly due west from the mouth of the cave for about 150 feet; there is then a large natural boulder beyond which the ledge continues, but the distance from the cave to the boulder is greater than the distance on the other side, so far as I could judge, actual measurement being impossible through the dense jangal.

The cave is situated in the middle third of the hill; there is about one-third of the hill above the cave, and two-thirds or somewhat less below; it is quite inaccessible from the top.

A long winding path led up from the bottom of the hill to a point near the great isolated boulder on the ledge; the path had three turns; it was once paved with brick throughout, but the path which running obliquely up the hill was necessarily formed by cutting into the side of the hill, has long ago become the water-course, and no portion of the pavement exists entire, although the entire distance along this line is marked by brickbats of various sizes from pieces 6 inches square to the size of coarse gravel. At the centre bend in the path was a platform about 15 feet square, remains of which still exist; possibly a chaitya once existed here, but no remains of it are to be found, and I only infer its existence from the roughness of the middle portion compared to the evenness of the edge portions.* Of course a good deal of the platform has crumbled down, but enough exists to distinctly show that it was meant to be a sort of half-way resting place, and is not an accidental adjunct to the steps.

I infer the road that led up the hill to have been in steps, from the circumstance of bricks alone having been used, the smallness of whose dimensions and weakness would have made them less suitable for a ramp than for evenly-laid steps.

* General Cunningham tells me that Hwen Thsang states distinctly the existence of a tope situated to westward of the cave and close to it. The position of the chaitya, which I here notice, occupies the precise position required by Hwen Thsang's account.

There are traces of two paths from the bottom of the hill converging to the platform, both paved or rather stepped with brick. I examined both; the one which is shorter and steeper appears to have been far narrower than the other, but the fragments of bricks lie thicker in it than in the longer and broader one; this is strange. The whole of the toe of the hill here is covered with brickbats and rolled brick gravel, not thickly but sparsely; it is no doubt possible that many fragments have got buried beneath the soil.

Let us now compare the cave and its adjuncts described above with existing accounts of the Saptaparnna cave.

First, as to position. It corresponds with the position assigned to it minutely by both Fa-hian and Hwen Thsang, and generally with other accounts, except the Barmese one, with which also it agrees after making the correction suggested before.

Its features sufficiently explain the reason of the name Saptaparnna assigned to it.

It was approached by a flight of steps, and is situated on the side of the hill high enough to make the flight of steps a necessity.

A great natural boulder is placed, not indeed in the exact middle of the flattish space in front of the cave, but nearly so, and this boulder may reasonably be identified with the preaching pulpit facing east described in the accounts.

The length of the platform being east and west, the hearers had naturally to sit facing north and south.

The president's throne to face north would have had to be erected against the vertical rock bounding the ledge on the side of the hill, and the congregation would sit on the outer side, facing the blank rock in front and the president's throne; further, the president would be to the right and the congregation to the left of the preaching pulpit.

There is ample space for the 500 Rahats, and the allowance for each need not be cut down to 7 square feet, leaving not a bit of clear space between the president's throne and the congregation; on the contrary, a clear lane could be left straight in front of the pulpit separating the president's throne from the Rahats' seats.

The position of the cave on the northern side of the hill and outside the city is a more likely one (independently of all accounts we have), from its seclusion, for the purposes of a solemn religious assembly, than any possible position that could have been selected on the south face, and within the distance of 1 mile from the Pippal cave, as the whole of this south face of the hill was within the limits of the old city.

The Barmese account implies that the cave selected was in the bamboo forest; Hwen Thsang's account does the same. The cave I have suggested is in the bamboo forest, but no cave in any part of the south face of the hill could be considered as being within the Venouvana or bamboo forest.

I here close the discussion.

There are numerous small natural caves on the north slope of Baibhárgiri. I examined two which, from their regularity, appeared at a distance to have been improved by art, but I found them natural caves with nothing of interest about them.

I should not pass Râjgir without some notice of what Mr. Broadley calls the "older type" of Buddhist temple. Comparing his own accounts of it, pages 222 and 241, J. A. S. for 1872, with his own plan of it, nothing can be clearer than that this "older type" of Buddhist temple is a clumsy modern restoration of an ancient temple. No sane architect or workman, I venture to assert, would go and chisel smooth four sides of a pillar three of which were to be "embedded" in brick-work; for, apart from the waste of labour, the smoothing of imbedded faces is the very reverse of what should be done to secure the adherence of the pilasters to the brick-work. Further comment is needless.

Leaving Râjgir by the road which, skirting the northern slope of the range of hills, goes to Giriyak, there is seen on the right, between the road and the foot of the hills, a large lake or marsh. The road in fact runs on the crest of the embankment of this sheet of water, and its artificial origin is abundantly attested by the numerous large stones with which it is lined, and of which it is built; this long embankment is named the Asraenbandh or Asurenbandh, and although the purpose of the embankment is obviously to obtain a store of water for irrigation, tradition connects it with a curious legend which I relate.

When Jarâsandha was king, he built the tower on the Giriyak hill as his bythak; here he would sit and lave his feet in the waters of the Panchana below. Close to his bythak was Bhagavân's garden, which in a year of unusual drought was nearly destroyed. Bhagavân accordingly, after fruitless efforts to keep it flourishing, caused it to be proclaimed that he would grant his daughter and half his Raj to him who should succeed in saving his garden from the effects of the drought by watering it plentifully during a single night with Ganges water.

The chief of the Kahârs, Chandrawat, at once came forward and undertook the task; first he built the great embankment to bring the waters of the Báwan Gangá rivulet to the foot of the hill below the garden, and then began lifting it up to successive stages by means of the common native *chanr* (swing basket) and ropes. It is necessary here to remark that the Báwan Gangá is considered to be a part of the Ganges and to equal in holiness the united sanctity of Ganges waters from the Báwan Tirthas, or fifty-two places of pilgrimage (the belief is based on a legend which I will narrate below). The Kahârs who were to labour at the work were provided with cakes of bread and balls of rice; with these for sustenance the sturdy Kahârs (still the hardiest and sturdiest tribe in Magadha) laboured all night and succeeded in watering the garden; but when Bhagavân saw their success, unwilling to ally his daughter with a Kahâr, he looked about for means to cheat the Kahâr chief of his fairly earned reward. Now the Pipar came forward and offered his services to Bhagavân, proposing to assume the form of a cock and crow, while Bhagavân was to urge the Kahârs to hasten the operations, as the garden was not yet sufficiently watered.

This ruse succeeded completely. The Kahârs, hearing the cock crow simultaneously with Bhagavân's urging them to hasten, concluded that all was lost, as the garden had not been, they thought, sufficiently watered before the crowing of the cock, the signal for morning, so, afraid of their lives for their presumption in venturing to seek Bhagavân's daughter as the bride of their chief, they all fled and lay exhausted on the banks of the Ganges at Mokáma, where the railway station now is.

When day fairly broke, Bhagavân ordered the Kahârs to be brought that he might give them their wages; for though he said they had been unsuccessful in winning his daughter and half his Raj, they had nevertheless laboured hard and were deserving of some consideration, but not a Kahâr was to be found. At last news reached the Kahârs at Mokáma, and a few came up to receive their wages. Bhagavân gave each man 3½ seers of anáj (food-grain), and ever since that period 3½ seers of anáj has been the legitimate wages for a day's work to Kahârs. To this day the Kahârs can legally claim, and as a matter of fact actually receive, the value of 3½ seers of food-grain in current coin as a day's wages. Subsequently, thus re-assured that their lives were not in danger, they returned to their villages and lived in peace. The bread cakes and rice balls they had abandoned in their flight from the hill still exist turned to stone.

MOKÁMA.

Mokáma Tanr is mentioned in another very popular legend, the legend of Chuhar Mal. As it does not appear to possess any archæological value, I give a brief summary of it, suppressing, however, no essentials or names.

The hero of the legend is Chuhar Mal; his father was Behari Mal, his uncle Bandi Mal, his brother Dukha Mal. Chuhar Mal was born when his father was away ploughing in the field; no midwife or assistance was near; he, however, sat up, and when his father came and was followed by the midwife, he would not allow the midwife to approach him. When he became a few years old, he prevailed on his father to remove him to the village of Turki Kainjni, because at Mokáma his house was close to the Kachari, and the females of his home were subject to annoyance by the officials. Budhwa was the cowherd of his father's flocks; he induced him to carry him to the akhâda (gymnasium) of Daljit. Daljit was the cowherd of his uncle, and would not allow Budhwa to pasture Chuhar Mal's cattle near his, and Chuhar Mal went to fight with him, but on second consideration he sent Budhwa to his uncle to represent matters, and solicit orders on Daljit to let him pasture his nephew's cattle at the place. Budhwa went to Chuhar Mal's uncle, Bandi Mal, but he declined to interfere; he was living in Mara Mokáma (old Mokáma). Finding that his uncle would not interfere, Chuhar Mal went to Daljit's akhâda again, fought with him and slew him and carried off the cattle to their owner, his uncle, telling him what he had done. Then followed great fights, &c., which, however, as no names and localities are mentioned, I omit. I could not get the entire legend; it is sung, but few people have sufficiently strong memories to remember the whole song. It is exceedingly long, and is said to take three or four nights to be sung through to the end.

MÁRI.

Close to Fatuha, or rather Bykatpur, is a small village named Mári, where the dhol (drum) is not beaten. The reason, they say, is that a fakir cursed the place. He came thirsty and asked one of the village maidens who was filling water at a well to give him water to drink; the girl contemptuously refused. Next came a wife, and she very gladly gave him water to drink; so the man cursed the place, saying "*Beti ranr, Bahu sohagin,*" *i. e.*, (may the) daughters (of the village) be husbandless and the daughters-in-law fortunate; hence people do not marry the daughters of the village, and if they do, they are sure to die soon; and when any one does venture to take one of the daughters of the village, it is done without music or processions of any kind, but in a thievish sort of way. The village girls are so anxious to get husbands, that it is said they run away with any-one who, by venturing to play on any musical instrument in the village, shows that he is ignorant of the traditional curse that hangs over the place.

BÁWAN GANGÁ.

The following is the legend of the Báwan Gangá rivulet:

There was a Dosâd living in Râjgir whose daughter used to take the household pigs out in the field to feed. It happened that as she was so engaged on the day of the full moon of a certain great festival, she saw a Brahman walking on very rapidly. On questioning him, he replied he was going to bathe in the Ganges on the full moon. The girl replied, "You can't possibly reach the Ganges in time; but if you believe me and your mind be full of faith, this is the exact moment of the full moon and here is a pool (in which her pigs were wallowing); dip into it and you will realise the full fruits of bathing in the Ganges at this auspicious moment." The Brahman did as desired, and when he was in the pool she said, "Now is the exact moment; dive in and see what you get." The Brahman did as desired, and found the bottom full of valuable gems, of which he clutched a handful and came up. "Dive again," said the girl. He dived again, and found only mud at the bottom. "You see," said the girl, "that I told you only the truth, when I said you will be too late if you go to the Ganges, for at the moment of your first diving the moon was at its exact full and you got your reward." The Brahman was astonished, and, seeing her as lovely as she was wise, proposed marriage. She referred him to her father, who refused, saying he could not presume to ally his daughter of low caste to a high caste Brahman. The Brahman thereupon threatened to kill himself, and the Dosâd, fearful of incurring the guilt of Brahmahatya, consented after consulting his friends; the marriage was duly solemnised, and the girl then taught her husband to ask no dowry of her father except a particular cow, a particular pig, and a particular parrot. The Dosâd, on bidding his daughter good-bye and God speed when they were departing, desired his son-in-law to ask for any gift he chose. The Brahman refused, but being pressed, he bound the Dosâd by a promise to grant his request, and then asked for the pig, the cow, and the parrot, as he had been taught. The Dosâd was taken aback, but, bound by his promise, was obliged to give them up. With these the bridegroom and his bride departed. The parrot was an extraordinary one, as he would go daily to Indra's court and bring the news of what took place there to his mistress; the pig was the leader of all the pigs in the country; and the cow was no other than the famous "Surabhi." One day the parrot told his mistress that Indra had given orders that, during the approaching rainy season, it should rain nowhere in the district except on the sterile hills and stony valleys of Râjgir. The girl, hearing this, immediately called her pig and directed him to dig up the whole of the stony valleys and hill slopes of Râjgir; the pig, with the aid of his subject pigs, did as desired. She then directed her husband to go and scatter paddy in all these dug-up places, explaining the object to her husband. He did as desired. When it rained, the paddy seed sprouted and the whole of stony Râjgir was full of paddy, while outside not a blade of paddy was to be found, owing to want of rain. It being reported to Indra that within Râjgir enough paddy had been grown to stave off famine, he ordered an army of mice and rats to be sent to destroy the crops; but the girl informed of this order by her parrot, got her husband to procure an army of cats as guard; when it was reported to Indra that this plan of destroying the crop had failed, he directed that when cut, each load of the paddy sheaves should produce only 1¼ seer of clean paddy; the girl informed by her parrot of this order, directed her husband to make bundles of only two stalks of paddy each tied end to end; the order of Indra having already gone forth and therefore irrevocable, each bundle consisting of two stalks of paddy produced 1¼ seers of paddy; Indra informed of this and seeing himself outwitted, ordered a furious storm to blow and scatter all the paddy which had been threshed out ready for storing; the girl informed of this, and aware that no wattle and daub would resist the storm, should she for safety build such to store her paddy in, directed her husband to dig the deep moat now seen in Râjgir round the wall near the foot of the hills; when the storm came, it naturally blew all the paddy down the slopes into these trenches, where they lay snug until the storm had blown over, and thus was the country saved from famine through the talents of this girl, in memory of whom, the pool where her pigs used to wallow in the southern defile at the south gate of the hill-girt city, was named Báwan Gangá.

Jethian, Kurkihâr and Punâwa have been noticed by General Cunningham in his reports, by Captain Kittoe and by Mr. Broadley. As I can add nothing to their information, I refer to their writings.

HASRA.

About a mile to the south-east of Punâwa are two small isolated ranges of low hills close to each other; the valley or pass between them is known as the Kol, and the place itself is known as Hasra. It appears that there was once a village named Hasra here, though none now exists. The entire space between these hills is thickly studded with remains.

The two ranges are each only about ¼ mile long. The southern range is higher and less bare than the northern, and the valley between the toes of the ranges varies from 200 feet to 400 feet wide at the widest. The highest part of the valley is at the east end; here the hills approach closest, being only 200 feet apart, and across this gap are built two lines of massive walls of dry stone. There appear to be some springs in the vicinity. Near the walls are collected a number of fragments consisting of chaityas and remnants of Buddhist figures. At the eastern foot of the southern range is a stone 2½ feet high and 1 foot square, with a Buddha rudely carved in a niche on one side; this stone is now worshipped, and is covered with vermilion. Within the valley and to the west of the lines of walls are numerous mounds; one is 300 feet to the west of the walls. On some stones in the vicinity are cut

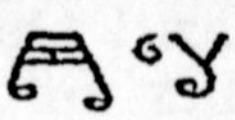

masons' marks of these shapes. 300 feet further back are numerous mounds;* F I J K appear to have been temples, as the square, or at least rectilinear forms of the structures which once existed, are yet traceable. On K is a moulding and the pedestal of a statue inscribed with the Buddhist formula "*Ye Dharmma.*" The mound F is the largest; L is a small mound. G H are other mounds. On G is a large mutilated figure of Buddha. On the spur of the hill adjacent there appears to have been

* See plate.

some kind of structure M; the stones are quite rough; perhaps it is only the quarry whence materials for the temples were obtained. The mounds appear to be the ruins of temples, built, not of stone, but of brick picked with stone. A and B are two mounds, A being the largest in the place. On A lie some plain granite pillars of the size and form shown in plate XVI. C D E are long low mounds which, having been lately excavated for bricks, are shown to have consisted of cells or rooms 10 × 8, evidently the remains of the cloisters of the great monastery at A. I could not find a single entire brick, but from the fragments it is evident that the bricks were more than 10 inches long and more than 6 inches wide. From these mounds have been exhumed numerous statues, of large size and in excellent preservation; they have been carried off to the adjacent village of Bishanpur Tandwa, about a mile to the south by a little west from this place. The whole of the ruins here appear to be of Buddhist monasteries and temples; there are no traces of any Brahmanical temples here.

The ground all over to the west of the hills is for some distance strewn with brickbats, but I could see no distinct mounds marking the sites of any structures outside the valley.

There are two tanks, one a large one between this place and Bishanpur.

BISHANPUR TANDWA.

Of the statues at Bishanpur carried off from this valley, the principal ones are a fine statue of Buddha of large size seated, and two smaller ones, one of Padma Pâni, as shown by the lotus symbol, and the other with a symbol which looks like a stem of Indian-corn.

These three statues are among the finest in Magadha and well deserving of preservation; they are in black basalt, and the execution and design are both good.

On a small bas-relief representing a figure seated cross-legged in Buddha fashion is inscribed *Ye Dharmma Râsi Maha Kasyapa;* this statue is clearly therefore one, of the venerable president of the first synod, and is the only one I have seen or heard of, of one of Buddha's disciples. The existence of this statue is a proof that in the later days of Buddhism the great disciples of Buddha may have come in for a share of the devotions of the Buddhist congregation.

The great statue of Buddha stood on a pedestal, which is now placed near it, the statue itself being set on the ground; the pedestal is inscribed in Kutila characters with the usual Buddhist formula.

A small inscribed female figure of Akshobhya is among the collection; the inscription is mutilated; the terminal letters are perfectly distinct.

The chaityas represented in these sculptures are in height twice the width of base, exclusive of the umbrella on top, which consists of seven diminishing discs, measuring in the aggregate height one diameter of the base of the chaitya, the total height to the top of the umbrella being three diameters.

There are numerous other statues, many Buddhist, but a few also Brahmanical. Of these last, the principal one is a fragment of Ganeça, but greatly inferior to the Buddhist sculptures in execution and design.

To the south-east of and just outside the village is a high rocky eminence which must once have been crowned by buildings, as the remains of floors and foundations yet exist; they were built of brick, as shown by the existing remains and by the numerous brickbats strewn about; tradition says it was a garh built by a Rajput Raja named Sobh Nâth, after whom the eminence is named Sobhnâthia.

Regarding the ruins at Hasra in the Kol valley, tradition gives no information beyond this, that the ruins there are the remains of the palace and garh of the same Raja who built the temples of Punâwa; his name is variously given as Tiloknâth and as Banauti Raja.

SITAMARHI.

About 12 miles east from Punâwa and a mile and a half south of the road from Gaya to Nowâda is a curious isolated boulder standing by itself known as Sitamarhi. This boulder has been hollowed to form a chamber 15 feet 9 inches long by 11 feet 3 inches wide, the doorway being 2 feet 1 inch wide at bottom and 1 foot 11 inches wide at top, with a height of 4 feet 4 inches. The roof of the chamber consists of a semi-ellipse with its major axis vertical and the minor axis at the level of the floor; the semi-major axis is 6 feet 7 inches, being the height of the roof at the apex above the floor; details are given in the plate accompanying. The interior is highly polished, and is fully equal in this respect to the finest of the polished caves in the Barâbar and Nâgârjuni hills; the interior, however, now is of a dirty colour from the effects of smoke; portions of the flat wall at the further end opposite the doorway appear either to have escaped polish, or what is more likely, to have lost the polish by peeling off of the stone. I have described the roof as semi-elliptical, but more correctly it is formed of two curves meeting each other at so great an angle as to leave no sharp line of junction. There is at present inside the cave a miserable statue, through which a couple of sleek and insolent Brahmans obtain their livelihood. The boulder is near a small mango tope and far from any village. Tradition makes it the residence of Sita during her exile; it was here that her son Lava was born, and Kuça manufactured by the sage Valmiki; the sculpture inside representing what I strongly suspect to be Buddha with two attendants on two sides, as in the much larger and fine sculpture at Kispa, which is said to represent Sita and her two sons, although the statue is not female; a second piece of sculpture is said to be Lachman; there is besides a Devi on a lion, Pârvati no doubt; and a long wavy mark on the wall is confidently asserted to represent Hanuman's tail.

It was in the wide high tanr near this boulder that Lava and Kuça are said to have fought with Rama's army led by his nephew.

About one mile to the east of this curious boulder is a group of bare, rocky and picturesque hills. On one of these near Rasulpura is a tomb, said to be of a local saint, Sheikh Muhammad; the building is a plain square-domed structure of unplastered brick; the building dates to a very early period if we judge from the style of the dome, which is without a neck and is surmounted by a very small top knot; the building stands within what once was a court-yard with towers at the corners. Facing the east entrance of the dargah is a lingam doing duty as a lamp post. The foundations of the building are of rubble, the bricks used are of various sizes; there is no doubt it occupies the site of some older Hindu shrine.

About 500 feet north of this is another similar but smaller hill with ruins of tombs. About 1,000 feet to north-east is another similar hill crowned with the ruins of a dargah.

BARAT.

Barat is a largish village on the north of, and close to, the road; this place is said to have been the residence of the Saint Valmiki when Sita was sent into exile. At his orders

Viswakarman constructed the rock cave noticed above for Sita's residence. At present the only object of notice here is an old mud fort standing on a high mound; the fort is said to have been the garh of Durinarayan Chaudhari Hartakya Brahman; it is 300 feet long by 250 feet wide, rectangular; its interior is about 20 feet above the level of the fields adjacent; above this the earthen parapets tower another 20 feet or so; the parapets are built entirely of mud, precisely like the mud walls of the large huts of the present day; but these walls appear to have been baked or in some way submitted superficially to the action of fire after being built; the fort is a plain oblong with a round tower at each corner.

GHOSRAWAN AND TITRAWAN.

Ghosrawan and Titrawan possess numerous remains, but they have been so fully noticed by General Cunningham, Captain Kittoe and Mr. Broadley, that I need only refer to their writings.

PÁRVATI.

Párvati, or rather more correctly Daryâpur Párvati, contains numerous ancient remains, mostly on and about the Párvati Hill or Garh Parávat as it is also called. General Cunningham has suggested that this may be the site of Hwen-Thsang's Parvata, or pigeon monastery, and if coincidence of name, and the occurrence of undoubted Buddhist remains, can compensate for its want of coincidence in position with recorded bearings and distances, it is certainly entitled to be considered as the site of the ancient pigeon monastery.

The hill rises with a very steep slope, almost vertical on the west, where the river Sakri during floods washes its base. On the south-east it sends out a long gentle spur with plenty of level ground on it. On the top of the hill is a small space of tolerably even ground. The easiest ascent is up the long spur. On this, at various spots of level ground, are the ruins, or rather traces, of ancient buildings; these appear to have been built, not of stone alone, as fragments of bricks are scattered profusely all over the place. There are altogether 13 mounds of a large size, and 5 or 6 of a smaller size; of these, that on the northernmost peak is the ruin of a tope 15 or 18 feet in diameter; it had been dug into before, and the poor laborer that dug into it was rewarded by finding some coral beads and a few coins; the man had left the village, and my efforts to obtain a sight of the coins failed. I dug down to the rock below, but without finding anything. The tope was built of brick and was covered with strong lime plaster; a part of the lower circumference was still intact, and I left it undisturbed.

To the west of it another and a larger mound appears, also said to be the ruins of a tope. It was dug into by the Executive and Assistant Engineers when the head-quarters of the Bihár Local Roads Division was at Giriyak; it is said to have yielded only some ashes, so that this was clearly a tope built on the ashes of some Rahat. Two other mounds, one at the south-east end of the hill (not of the spur), and one to north-west of it, are also said to have yielded coins; the coins were found only a few years ago, and the result was that every one began actively to dig in search of treasure; the last find was, as I have related, from the small tope on the extreme north peak, but the whole of the ruins were in the meanwhile dug up; and as the result of the diggings, brick-bats, could be easily disposed of as road metal (of which large quantities are here stacked,) there was no fear of the labor of the diggers going entirely to waste, even if they found no treasure.

The two mounds which are said to have yielded coins are clearly the remains of buildings, monasteries or temples, not of topes, as the straight walls can yet be traced, though for the most part dug up by the depressed line of hollows thus left; they are traditionally said to have been respectively the Baithak and the Kachari of Báwan Subáh. On the largest piece of level ground on the hill; which, however, is not in the highest part, are the ruins of extensive buildings, traditionally said to have been the palace of Báwan Subáh; the building really appears to have been a large monastery, with rows of cells round a court-yard; perhaps a temple, now dug up, existed in the middle; at present there is, just where it ought to have been, a suspicious-looking depression.

There are no statues on the hill; one solitary mutilated block exists to show that statues were not wanting, but the demand for stone metal for roads is said to have operated very effectually in bringing about the destruction of all conveniently movable stone blocks. At the foot of the hill on the north side are a few statues in fair preservation; a remarkably fine one lies in the mango tope near the well at the foot of the hill, and two or three others lie further off; these last are, however, mutilated considerably. I could see no remains of structures about the foot of the hill; any that existed on the west, north-west and south-west sides must have long ago been washed away by the river Sakri, which began flowing down this, its present, bed not very long ago, its original course having been far to the west about 3 miles off; the old bed is still distinctly traceable all the way to its point of separation; the channel which is now the bed of the river was a small irrigation channel, but, as I have before remarked, the universal tendency of rivers here and hereabouts is to run east of their present beds. Already a great portion of the waters of the Sakri goes down an irrigation channel, which was taken from its east bank about 6 miles above Wahari, near Roh, east of Nowâdah, and but for the circumstance that constant efforts are made to keep the flow within bounds, this channel would before now have become the main river; as it is, it has become 100 feet wide, while it originally was barely 8.

About two miles due north of Párvati, the Sakri, in cutting away its banks, is said to have laid open a deposit of coins; these are said to have been in an earthen pot, and were of gold; some boys, playing about, found the pot, and each ran with a handful to his parents, who, of course, lost no time in securing the prize; but so ignorant were they, that they imagined the coins to have been of brass, and sold them as such; the place was probably the site of an old monastery or stûpa; it has now been entirely cut away by the river, but the high banks there show that the site was a small eminence.

One of the statues at the foot of the hill has the usual Buddhist formula, *Ye Dharmma*, &c., inscribed on it in Kutila characters; the statues are all of black basalt.

Besides these Buddhist ruins, there is a small Muhammadan dargâh. Tradition says that an old Hindu fakir was once living here, when a corpse came floating down the Sakri, and the fakir dreamt that the corpse told him its name was Chán Haji, and that it wanted a decent burial in a grave to be dug on a spot near the south-east end of the hill, which he described, and as a reward, he promised the Raj (sovereignty) of the district to the fakir. The fakir did as directed, and became king afterwards. The dargâh that now stands was the one built by him. It is no way interesting, except for some Hindu stones used in it. Chán Haji is a saint of wide celebrity in Bengal; he is known universally as Chán Saudágar, and many are the spots where this benevolent saint is said to have kept silver and gold vessels, &c., for the use of travellers. A traveller, on arriving at one of these fortunate spots, which was generally either a well or the banks of a tank, had only to make known his wants, when Chán Saudágar's vessels of gold and silver would float up and allow themselves to be used by the traveller, who had, however, scrupulously to return them when done with; but men are covetous, and at each of the places where I have heard the legend, some unlucky man was too weak to resist the temptation of appropriating them, and since then the miracle has ceased.

The legend of Kunwar Bijaya Mall is so intimately connected with this place, that it will be interesting to give a brief sketch of the story; it is generally sung, and is a universal favorite.

Kunwar Bijaya Mall used to live in Jhuṅjhunwá Garh; he came here to be married to Báwan Subáh's daughter; he was accompanied by his father and his elder brothers, he himself being then a child. Báwan Subáh treacherously seized his father and brothers and put them into prison. Kunwar Bijaya Mall's horse, however, fled with his rider and carried him safe back to Jhunjhunwá Garh. Here he grew up in ignorance of the fate of his father and brothers, and there being no male relatives of the boy to avenge his wrongs or take his part, his female relatives, of whom his sister-in-law was chief, kept him in ignorance of the fate of his father and brothers lest he should rashly venture to fight and lose his life. This sister-in-law, named Sonmat Rani, took great care of him, had him taught all arts, and intended, when he should grow up, to live with him as his wife. When Bijaya Mall grew up, he wanted bows and arrows and the gili and danda to play with. Sonmat Rani gave him the ordinary wooden ones, but he broke them, and wanted stronger ones, till finally he got manufactured for his special use an iron danda of 84 maunds weight and an iron gili of 80 maunds. Kunwar Bijaya Mall took them and went to play with his companions, but they refused, saying they could not use his danda, so it was agreed that each was to use his own danda and gili. When Kunwar Bijaya Mall's turn came, he hit his iron gili so forcibly that it flew to Garh Paravat, and smashed in a part of Báwan Subáh's palace. His companions searched for the gili for seven days, but not finding it, they came disgusted to Kunwar Bijaya Mall and asked him why, when he was so strong, he did not go and release his father and brothers from confinement. Hearing this he went to his sister-in-law and demanded to be told the circumstances of their confinement; she long tried to evade, but finding him persist, she went and adorned herself superbly and radiant with gems and beauty and came out; he asked her why she had adorned herself, she said—"Your brother and father went west to fight, and I expect them back to-night;" he would not believe but drew his sword, threatening to kill her; then she told him the whole truth. The groom of the horse Jingna Khawas was called and confirmed her story, and Bijaya Mall ordered the horse and arms to be brought, and prepared to go. Sonmat Rani begged him to eat before going; he sat down and finished his supper; then she beseeched him to lie down and rest a while; he did so and fell asleep; she then went and laid herself beside him; on waking and seeing her he said—"I consider you as my mother; don't be uneasy, I will go and rescue your husband and my father in four days;" she then left him and he went to Garh Paravat.

At that time a covered passage led from the palace of Báwan Subáh to the tank at Afsand. Kunwar Bijaya Mall, on arriving, alighted near that tank; a female servant of Báwan Subáh's daughter soon arrived at the tank to carry water, and seeing him there, asked him who he was, and how he dared to walk about near that tank; this led to hot words between them, and the young man, having very ungallantly seized the damsel and torn her clothes, she beat a hasty retreat, and went and informed her mistress Rani Tilko; meanwhile Rani Tilko, the wife of Kunwar Bijaya Mall, had seen the young man from the roof of her house, and had taken a fancy to him, and when the maid complained of his conduct, she pacified her and desired her not to let her father hear of it; she then went with her companions, all dressed exactly like her, to the tank on pretence of bathing, but really to see the audacious young man. On reaching the place she saw the young man still there, and went up to him to ask him his name, and whence he came. On hearing his name she immediately covered her face, as she saw she had met her husband, and on being asked in her turn who she was, her reply showed Kunwar Bijaya Mall that he had met his wife. There was then a very tender scene between them, she beseeching him to take her and fly, and he refusing to run away with her like a thief, but expressing his determination to win her with his sword. Tilko Rani returned sorrowful to her apartments, and prayed for her husband's success against her father. Kunwar Bijaya Mall on the other hand went to the prison where his father and brothers were confined; but finding the walls and gate of adamant (Bajr) he despaired; here his horse seeing his grief came forward and smashed in the gates, so that he got in and released the prisoners; he then went and pillaged the favorite bazar of Báwan Subáh. News of these events having now reached Báwan Subáh, he sent the chief of his forces to fight Kunwar Bijaya Mall, and on his defeat, he sent his son with fresh troops; these shared the same fate. Báwan Subáh then went out himself. Long the battle raged, Kunwar Bijaya Mall not wishing to kill but to capture his enemy; in this he at last succeeded, and he cut off one of Báwan Subáh's hands, and put out one eye of his son; he then set them free, and demanded that his wife, Báwan Subáh's daughter, should be sent to his house with due pomp and ceremony as she was now of age. There was no alternative for Báwan Subáh, so he sent his daughter to her husband's house with due ceremony and pomp, and Kunwar Bijaya Mall returned to his own house accompanied by his brother, Sonmat Râni's husband, his father and his own wife.

This legend serves the important purpose of shewing that the ancient name of the hill was Garh Parávat, or rather this was the name of the fort on the hill. The origin of the name is not difficult to ascertain. The hill has an almost perpendicular face to the west and portions of the south, and in the vertical cliffs, wild pigeons in great numbers habitually build their nests, as they are safe from man or beast. Three years ago, when employed as an Engineer in this district, I had often occasion to travel past this hill, and could count with certainty on finding wild pigeons here; this year, consequent, I am told, on the famine which visited the district, all the pigeons were caught and eaten up by the people; there are now, therefore, very few left, but the convenience for nest-building and security are so great, that it must always have been a favorite resort of pigeons. The name Parávata is thus accounted for.

But whether this be or be not the true origin of the name, there can be no doubt that it was named Parávata in ancient times, and as, besides the identity of names, it contained numerous and important Buddhist structures, I think we may safely regard it as the site of Hwen Thsang's pigeon monastery, although its bearing and distance from Giriyak do not agree with his account.

Párvati retained some importance even so late as Akbar. There is mention of Dariyâpur* in Stewart's Bengal, page 155, where it is described as situated 50 miles from Patna, which is very near the actual distance *viâ* Bihár. Since then the place has lost its importance, and is now only a second-rate village.

There is another legend which makes Párvati a place of importance in the age of the Pandus. According to it, when the sacrificial horse was let loose, Rájá Sankhadhwaj of this place seized the horse and prepared to fight. Before joining battle, however, he performed a jug. The Rájá's Guru demanded that orders be given for every one to be ready and present at a given spot by a certain hour. The Rájá's son Surat Dhwaj was newly married, and his bride happened to arrive that very day, and at her entreaty Surat Dhwaj delayed a short time. The Brahman demanded the punishment of the young man, and accordingly he was thrown into a caldron of boiling oil, but he came out unhurt. The Guru suspected the oil was not hot enough, so he heated it well, and to try the heat threw in a piece of the husk of a cocoanut; the violence of the heat caused the husk to be thrown up against the Guru's face, blinding his right eye and burning away the right half of his face. The Rájá's son, it was found, had escaped because he had prayed to Mahadeo and had held a tulsi leaf in his mouth when jumping into the caldron!

AFSAND.

Afsand is a very small village 3 miles to the south by a little east of Párvati; here are several ancient remains, the principal of which is a high conical mound, the ruin apparently of a temple; there are also several statues, but mostly Brahmanical, among them a large varaha,-the finest in Bengal I have yet seen, and a few, a very few, Buddhist statues. There was once an important inscription here which was removed by Captain Kittoe, and which he sent back to be replaced here, or rather to be let into a pillar or pedestal here, but it now exists no longer. I have been able to trace it to the Magistrate's kachari at Nawâda; beyond this there is no clue; the loss of this inscription is much to be regretted, as it was an important one, and was not so clearly copied and read to render its loss now of no consequence; this

---

* Párvati is known as Dariyâpur Párvati.

should be a warning to officers to be careful in removing inscriptions and statues, &c. That Captain Kittoe gave orders for its being sent back to Afsand, there can be no doubt; but he did not take sufficient care to see his orders obeyed, and this is only too common a fault,—so common as to be almost a national fault. I refer to Captain Kittoe's original paper in the Asiatic Society's Journal for an account of the remains at Afsand, to which I can add little.

SATGAON.

Satgaon is a small village near the Sakri, south of the Kauwa Kal Hills; the place enjoys some local reputation, and is said to possess some old temples. I did not see the place.

EKTÂRA.

Ektâra is a small place of pilgrimage situated in the wild Rajauli Hills at the source of the Dhanarjeh river which flows past Rajauli; here is a very picturesque waterfall and a small rock cell; not far from here I see "rock temples" marked in the Indian Atlas sheet, but my enquiries for them were vain.

RAJAULI.

The wild hills of Rajauli are in their way deserving of mention; the seven Rishis are said to have lived on them, and particular peaks are named after one or other of the saints; of these the most interesting is Singar Peak, so named from Sringi Rishi; there is a rough stone platform on the top with some shapeless boulders as objects of worship; a fair is held annually at the foot, and devotees toil up the steep ascent to the top to pay their devotions.

A fair is held annually also at Ektâra, at the Mahabar hill near Satgaon.

ROH.

Roh is a largish village, which has an old mound; here are several statues, and the mound contains old bricks; close to it is an old well, into which an inscribed slab found here is said to have been thrown. When I heard this, I tried to get the well examined by divers, but there was then too much water in it, and it could not be done. If an inscription is really at the bottom, it is quite safe there, and can be laid hold of at any time.

SHEKPURA.

Shekpura has few ancient remains, besides an old tank and a dargah on its bank. The dargah avowedly stands on the site of an old temple to Kâli, and the tank is still known as Kâli Matokhar's Tâl. The dargah contains the tomb of a saint, of whom the following legend is related :—

At Matokhar lived a Muhammadan Aulia, named Matokhar Khân; he founded the place, and hence its name. Some say it was founded by the uncle of Kunwar Bijaya Mall on the mother's side. Be this at it may, Matokar Khân had a son. Near the dargah was a garden, which was kept in order by a pretty young *malin*, who used daily to present the saint a garland of flowers. One day she went into the house when it was quite empty, and seeing a little rag hanging, from which issued a delicious perfume, she took it and smelt it. Shortly afterwards, the pretty *malin* was in an interesting condition, and the saint's suspicion fell on the son, whom he ordered to be flayed alive. The son, hearing the order, desired that no violence should be used, as he would give over his own skin ; and accordingly he soon went with his skin in his hands to his father; the father was astonished, an explanation followed, and it was finally found that so great was the young man's sanctity and power, that the interesting state of the pretty *malin* was due entirely to her having in ignorance touched and smelt an unmentionable garment of the young man which he had one day left in the room where the *malin* used to bring her flowers! Of course, after this, the young man's fame spread far and wide and eclipsed his father's, and holy men from distant countries came to see him.

SIKANDRA.

Sikandra is a place of much importance, about 24 miles south of Shekpura ; it is said to possess a dargah, but I have not seen the place.

PREMAYA.

Premaya is a place noticed by Buchanan ; it is said to be five kos north of Shekpura, and must be near the old course of the Ganges. I am sorry I was unable to visit this place.

LAKHISARAI, RÁGHOGARH AND BALGUDAR.

The group of villages, Rajjhâna, Rághogarh, Lakhisarai, Jaynagar, Birdaban, Hasanpur, and Nongarh, have already been described by General Cunningham, and I have little to add. At Rághogarh I dug at the site of the singularly beautiful pillar, and was rewarded by finding two bases—one perhaps *in situ;* these bases are quite plain and of granite; they are 10 inches deep; one is 2 feet square, the other 1 foot 7 inches square; they ran due east and west, and were 4 feet 12 inches clear space apart; the smaller one was, however, 1 foot higher than the other.

BALGUDAR.

Balgudar is a small village to the north of the Halohar river, and contains a curious and large four-faced lingam, besides several other statues and fragments.

JAYNAGAR.

There are traces of a small tope on the northern range of hills at Jaynagar; it is on a small flat piece of rock at the eastern end of the range, and just below the peak. Close to it is said to be the treasury of Indradyumna sealed with a magic seal; the spot presents the appearance of plain, smooth rock, perhaps artificially smoothed; but there is no difficulty in the way of popular belief, which flies at once to the supernatural. It is said Indradyumna had a great warrior, whom he trusted greatly and raised to the highest posts; at last the man began to entertain the idea of asking his master's daughter in marriage; the king informed of this became very angry, but the man was too powerful to be easily subdued, so he contrived that a cavern should here be constructed, into which he removed all his treasure, and when all were secured, he invited the warrior to the place; the man unsuspectingly went in, when Indradyumna at once let fall the trap door and sealed it with a magic seal; but it was not long before he suffered for thus killing his best general; the Muhammadans came down on him, drove him from place to place—his last place of refuge, as pointed out, being a natural cavern on the top of the southern range, and he finally was obliged to fly to Katak.

Indradyumna had a queen, so beautiful and of such airy lightness, that she used to bathe seated on a lotus leaf in the tank. When the Muhammadans had not yet come, but were about to do so to attack her husband, one of the premonitory signs vouchsafed was, that the queen could no longer be supported by the lotus. Some say this was the result of Indradyumna's treacherous behaviour to his general; for, as his wife floated on the lotus by force of the good acts of herself and her husband, the commission of a crime by him was at once shewn by the lotus refusing any longer to support his wife.

An annual fair is held here at the Dasahra festival.

For further particulars, I refer to General Cunningham's Report, Vol. III.

Two new inscriptions (short lines) from the pedestals of statues were found—one on a Ganeça at Lakhisarai, the other on the fine female statue of Párvati at Rajjhâna.

NONGARH.

The complete exploration of the tope at Nongarh was entrusted to me by General Cunningham, and the result is detailed below.

Continuing the shaft sunk by General Cunningham downwards, I found the even horizontal layers of bricks to extend to a depth of 8 feet below the floor of the lower chamber laid open by General Cunningham; below this the bricks lay in distorted positions, and the irregularity continued right down. At a depth of 19 feet below the level of General Cunningham's lower chamber, I found an even floor of bricks laid flat in two layers over each other, covered with a thick coat of soorky and lime-plaster; over this was a thin, fine layer of lime-plaster: this floor was clearly the floor of the sanctum of a small temple. At a distance of three feet from the centre of the shaft, which itself was down the centre of the tope, was found a line of wall running east and west, or rather east by a little north; this was apparently the back wall of a room. Opposite to this, on the other side of the shaft, lay the fragments of an arch of bricks, built edge to edge, as already described in the Buddha Gaya temple. This arch appears to have been rather a sort of vaulted roof, springing from a point one foot in advance of the line of walls; this space of one foot appears to have been gained by corbelling out from the wall, as I found a brick with a bevelled edge at a depth of 14 feet below the floor of General Cunningham's chamber, or five feet above the floor of the temple below, so that the vault sprang probably from a height of five feet above the floor of the temple.

The entrance to the temple appears to have been on the north, or rather slightly to the east of north. It was impossible to determine correctly the dimensions of the sanctum from the limited size of the shaft dug, but it appeared to me that it could not have been more than seven or eight feet square; it had a vaulted roof meeting in a ridge as at Buddha Gaya, springing at a height of five feet above the floor of the sanctum. The half span of the vault appears to have been one foot, or at least 9 inches, less on each side than the half width of the sanctum, so that the vault could not have been of a larger span than perhaps 6½ feet. What came over this I had no means of ascertaining with certainty; but, judging from the irregular, loose, and confused position of the bricks above, it appears to me that it was surmounted by the usual hollow tower roof.

The bricks in the lower or confused portion were 14 inches long by 11¾ inches wide, and 3 inches thick, while the bricks in the even layers above, down to a depth of 8 feet below General Cunningham's lower chamber, or 11 feet above the floor of the temple below, were 12 inches long by 9 inches wide, and 2½ inches thick.

It appears, therefore, that there once existed here a small temple facing north; that in course of time this temple fell to ruin and became a low mound above 12 or 13 feet high; and that, subsequently, on this mound a stûpa was built; this stûpa was opened by General Cunningham.

There is nothing to shew the age of the stûpa beyond the small model stûpa found by General Cunningham in the relic chamber. Judging from this, it is not probable that the stûpa is so old as the first century before or after Christ; but the existence of the mutilated red-stone statue, with its inscribed characters, shews that there was some sort of religious building here as early as the beginning of the Christian era.

As it is clear that the stûpa was built on the ruins of the temple below, and as the stûpa is clearly not of the period about the beginning of the Christian era, the temple on whose ruins it stands must be considered of the same age as the inscribed red-stone statue, *viz.*, of the first century before or after Christ.

This is a most important position. I am satisfied in my own mind of the correctness of this conclusion, but I wish it to undergo rigid scrutiny, as on it depends very important deductions.

Having no doubt myself that the temple was certainly as old as the statue which, according to General Cunningham, dates to the first century before or after Christ, it follows —

(1) That the true arch was known and used in India at that time.

(2) That although the principle of the true arch was known, it was, so far as we as yet positively know, built

invariably of bricks edge to edge, and not face to face as our modern arches.

(3) That the use of mortar, lime and soorkey was known.

(4) That fine lime-plastering was known and used at that early period.

From the mutilated statue it appears to me idle to speculate as to the deity to whom the temple was dedicated, whether Buddhist or Brahmanical; the probabilities are in favor of its being Buddhist.

INDAPPE.

The exploration of the old fort of Indappe, pronounced Indpa by the people, was also entrusted to me. Owing to active opposition from the Rájá's people, I was unable to do more than complete a survey of the locality, and the result may be seen in the plate; but I can confidently say that a careful and thorough examination of the mounds, and especially of the great tope here, will prove a great acquisition to our present meagre knowledge of ancient Indian structures. The tope, judging from its dimensions, 125 feet in diameter at base by 35 feet in height, must be very old; for, although the base now is necessarily broader from the accumulation of debris than it was, yet, on examining the dimensions of the mound at a height of 20 feet above the ground, we find it to have been 65 feet in diameter at that height. When I examined the tope, it was almost entire, as the lowest portion of the socket hole for the umbrella existed then; so that the tope which I found 35 feet high could not have been much higher at any time—38 feet, perhaps, is as much as it ever could have been without the umbrella. Assuming this to have been its height (and for the purpose of ascertaining its form in view of its age it is safer to err on the side of excess of height, and consequently lateness of age), we find that at a depth of 18 feet from the crown it had a diameter of 65 feet. From these data, and remembering that the round portion of topes was usually a hemisphere, we find the radius of the hemisphere to have been about 37 feet, so that this tope was probably a plain hemisphere on a very low platform, and therefore must have been built at a very early period.

NAULAKHAGARH.

A few miles south of Indappe is an old fort, known as Naulakhagarh, so named, it is said, because in its construction 9 lacs of each sort of current coin from the rupee down to cowries was used. This, of course, is an idle tale. The fort is ascribed to either Akbar or Sher Shah. It is said that after it was finished, the Emperor ordered a cannon to be taken up to the peak of the adjacent range of hills,—known generally as the Kauwakol hills—and on firing it at the fort with shot, the shot was found to fall within the fort; it was consequently abandoned as untenable! The walls are in fair order; the fort is small, built of rubble and mortar; some few buildings may probably have once stood inside, but none of any consequence, and no remains exist. Details of the fort will be found in plate; the walls are 38 feet high; the fort has four gates, one on each side; the north entrance appears to have been the principal one; it is defended by a weak outwork, which is entered at its east corner; it is apparently an after-thought. The pillars that adorn the jambs of the various gates appear to have been obtained from older Hindu structures, and several have been piled on each other to obtain the necessary height. The outer archway of the gate springs from a height of 10 feet, the inner from a height of 6 feet only; the arches are of the usual Muhammadan pointed style; the towers that adorn the fort are large, and form an important feature of the fort.

This closes my account of the antiquities of Magadha. In conclusion, I wish to offer a few remarks on General Cunningham's supposition that the Son-Bhândâr cave is the Sattapanni cave, and the inference therefrom that stone-cutting was an art known to Indians as early as Buddha's period (p. 143, Vol. III, Reports).

I believe I have been able to shew that General Cunningham has erred in considering the Son-Bhândâr cave to be the Sattapanni cave, and his argument, based on this supposition, consequently falls to the ground; but as the cave, although not the Sattapanni cave, is nevertheless one in which Fa-hian says Buddha used to meditate, the bearing of General Cunningham's argument, though based differently, would be the same as regards the knowledge of the art of stone-cutting in India.

With every deference for his experience and judgment, I cannot allow this position to pass unchallenged. I submit that, although there is no doubt Buddha used to meditate in the Son-Bhândâr cave, it by no means follows that the cave *as we see it* is the same as *Buddha used it*. I maintain it as highly probable that after Buddha's death, and probably when Asoka reigned, the original rude natural cavern was chiselled into an elegant, or at least a regularly smoothed cave. If we assume that the cave as we see it now is as Buddha used it, then we must be prepared to grant an indefinite extension of time to the introduction of the art of stone-cutting in India; for as existing records do not make any mention of the cave having been especially prepared for Buddha, the chisel-cut cave must have been in existence before, and must have been simply appropriated by Buddha, so that it may have been cut in the time of the first of the 24 Buddhas, for all that we can prove to the contrary. But, independently of this consideration, if the cave existed ready cut in Buddha's time, it must have had an owner, and could not have been going a begging for the first beggar that chose to squat in it. If it had an owner, Buddha could not have taken possession of it without the owner giving it to him; and as we have detailed records of various gifts, even trifling ones, that Buddha received, we should expect to find a record of the gift of this cave. No such record has yet been found, and so far then we are justified in considering, not that Buddha appropriated a ready-cut cave, but that the cave which he appropriated was a natural cavern which no one cared to own.

So far I have kept quite clear of the argument derivable from my proposed identification of the Sattapanni cave; with its aid the argument is even more strongly in my favor. The Sattapanni is the one cave which of all others would have been artificially smoothed if the art of stone-cutting were known in Buddha's period, but we find no trace of stone-cutting in or about it; it is highly improbable that the less important cave should have been cut and smoothed, while the one in which the synod was held was left in its natural ugliness.

That the art of stone-cutting was known in Asoka's time I have no desire to dispute; but it does not necessarily follow, because we see the art carried to great perfection then, that therefore the Indians must have been practising it for a long time. There are two modes by which they may have attained to the high state of improvement: (1) by a slow and gradual process of improvement, (2) by learning the art from artists of another nation, who had already attained excellence in it (by whatever means does not now concern us). If they learnt it by the first mode, we should expect to see the remains of a period when the art was in its rude infancy, and we should expect that the energy which brought the art so high would advance it further. I need not add that we have not a single authentic example of Indian stone-cutting in its earlier stages of progress, nor have we any material improvement in the art over what it was in Asoka's period. But if they learnt it from artists of another nation, we should expect no remains shewing the ruder stages of development of the art; we should, on the contrary, expect the sudden appearance of the art in a highly advanced state; and we should further expect that a people who had been unable or unwilling to use its energies in discovering the art themselves, should, even when it was communicated to them from outside, remain stationary or retrograde. The history of Indian sculpture is one of retrogression; not a single step forward have the Indians made since Asoka's time, but backwards they have been only too readily moved.

It is my conviction—a conviction I have been forced to regretfully—that the Indians knew nothing of stone-cutting or stone sculpture till the Greeks under Alexander, or perhaps Darius, invaded India, and communicated the art to its people. In support of this, I point to the vast difference in the art of sculpture between the remains found in and near the Punjab, where Greek influence was strongly felt, and those of the same age found further east; more than this, there is positively an appearance of a graduated deterioration, proportioned in some measure to the distance of the locality from Greek influence; and finally, as Greek power and influence declined, a corresponding decline affected the art of Indian sculpture.*

Before passing on to other places, it may be interesting to give what appears to me to have been the ancient names of the ranges of hills at the extremity of which the ruins just noticed are situated, and of the rivers issuing from it; the hills are now known locally as the Kawa Kol hills.

HILLS AND RIVERS.

If we consult the Bhagavata Padma and Mârkandeya Purânas, we find among the mountains one range called the Konwa or Kolahala (Vish. Pur., Vol. II, p. 141, Notes, FitzEdw. Hall's edition), and there is every probability that the Kawa Kol hills are meant. I have, however, other evidence of the probability of my identification, which is to be

---

* Since the above was written, the discoveries at Bharhut prove that the earliest temples or buildings (as there sculptured) were wooden; at least the style and constructive features are purely wooden.

found in the Mahábhárat Adi Parvan, Chap. 63, V.V. 29-38, which I translate :—

" Bye and bye to the possessor of boundless power and energy, Vasu (Rájá of Chedi), were born five sons. The paramount sovereign Vasu anointed them sovereigns of various kingdoms. The name of one of Rájá Vasu's sons was Vrihadratha ; this hero was famous in Magadha ; the name of another was Pratyagraha ; another son's name was Kasasva ; many used to call him Manivâhana ; another son's name was Mavella ; and another of the King's son's name was Yadu ; he was never defeated (in battle). Oh Rájá ! these five were the sons of the Rajârshi Vasu of abundant energy, and from each of these five sons of Vasu a separate long-abiding ruling race has been produced.

" The high-souled Rájá Vasu, when dwelling in air in the Indra-bestowed crystal Mindra, used to be served by all the Gandharvas and Apsaras, and from his thus living up above, he became known by a corresponding name. Near his city was a river named Saktimati ; the living mountain Kolahala, moved by desire, arrested her course. Vasu learning of the robbery, kicked the mountain, and through the passage opened by his kick, the grateful river, rendered pregnant by intercourse with the mountain, issued and addressed the King. The Rajârshi Vasu appointed Vasuprada, son of the river, his victorious Sanapati, and married the daughter" Girika, &c., &c., &c.

This valuable passage establishes (1*st*) that the Kolahala range of mountains was not far from the puri of the Rájá, and (2*nd*) that the Saktimati river passes through a gap in the range. As a matter of fact, the Sakri river does pass through a rather large gap in the range of which the portion to the east of the river is still called the Kawa Kol mountains, and these hills are not far from Girivraja or Râjgir ; it therefore appears probable that the river known now as the Sakri is the Saktimati, and the Kolahala or Konwa range is the Kawa Kol range.

But we know from numerous instances that a river took its name from the mountain whence it issued, as for instance, Mekhalanandini, a name of the Narmmada, from the Mekhala hills ; and Mainakaprabha for the Son from the Mainaka mountain ; and the Ganges is well known as the daughter of Himâlaya ; and as the Pauranic lists mention a range of hills as the Saktimat range, there seems little doubt that it is the name of that range which gives rise to the Saktimati river.

As a matter of fact, the Saktimati, or Sakri, river rises in the range to the south of the Kawa Kol range, and passes through, or at least hugs, the foot of the Kawa Kol range for several leagues before emerging into the plains ; hence the legend of her being the daughter of the Saktimat mountains and the wife (by force) of the Kolahala mountains.

But we have other evidence for the probability of my identification of the Saktimat range of hills. The Vishnu Purân says that the Rishikulya Kumâri and others flow from the Saktimat mountains.

This Rishikulya must not be confounded with another Rishikulya, which flows past Ganjam.

As a matter of fact, the Kiyul and the Kaorhari rivers actually do flow down from the range I have identified as the Saktimat range; the Kiyul I take to be the Rishikulya, and the Kaorhari to be the Kumâri of the Vishnu Purân.

I would in passing suggest that the name Giriyak is derived, not as General Cunningham suggests, from *Giri* and *eka*, but from *Girika*, the allegorical daughter of the Saktimati river; this would imply that a branch from the Saktimati river went eastwards close to the place; as a matter of fact, traces of an old channel of the Sakri are still to be seen to the east of Giriyak, starting from the Sakri near Bellari, and Government at the present day expend annually a small sum of money to keep in repair a bund at the spot to prevent the waters of the Sakri flowing down this channel to the injury of the zemindars. The works were under my charge when I officiated as Executive Engineer of the Burhee Division.

The Saktimati is said in the Mahábháratá to flow past the capital of Chedi; this would, if the identification be correct, place the Chedi country about the sources of the Kiyul and Sakri rivers, and its capital somewhere on the Sakri. I have heard of extensive ruins at Dumduma, and near Mahâvar hill and in the vicinity; but the country has hitherto not been examined. I will note, however, that General Cunningham tells me the capital of Chedi was Tripura, modern Tewar, near Jabalpur, and this would be fatal to my identification; but there is no river at all approaching in name or features the Saktimati as described in the Mahábhárat flowing past it, for the Narmmada is evidently not the Saktimati. I give my speculation for what it is worth, and only note from personal knowledge that, in the district indicated by me, and also in the vicinity, the name Chedia is a very common one among the lower classes. I also append a description of the Chedi country from the Mahábháratá, Chap. 63, sl. 8:—

"Oh, King of Chedi! the Chedi country abounds in wealth and grain, and is suited for the habitation of animals, very clean, deserving of being cherished like heaven, very beautiful; the land possessed of fertility, possessed of various gems of value—the land of that country is full of wealth; therefore go and live there: the people of this country are pious, always happy and learned,* to say nothing of other occasions no one here, even in jest, utters a falsehood; the sons do not separate from the fathers, and always remain devoted in obedience to their religious preceptors. In this country no cultivator subjects oxen to carrying loads or dragging the plough, or gives them any kind of pain."

There is, however, one theory which reconciles the apparently conflicting conclusions arrived at by General Cunningham and myself regarding the Chedi country. The Mahábhárat distinctly states (*vide supra*) that each of the five sons of Vasu, Rájá of Chedi, became the founder of a distinct dynasty of kings; it is evident that Vasu could not have given to his sons kingdoms which he himself did not possess. One of them we find to have been Vrihadratha, Jarâsandha's father, King of Magadha; so that it is perfectly certain that Magadha formed a part of the Chedi Raj of Vasu Rájá. Inscriptions from Tewar shew that Tewar (ancient Tripura) was in the Chedi Raj; hence we have the Chedi Raj extending from Magadha in the east to at least Jabalpur in the west; the northern limits must have been the Ganges, for we know that to the north of the Ganges were the dominions of Rájás not of Vasu's lineage. We know further that at Mânikpur, which must have been somewhere near the present Ratanpur, reigned kings not of Vasu's lineage, nor in Odra, Anga, Kalinga; hence the southern limits appear to have been the present southern limits of the Chutia Ñagpur commissionership and the southern limits of Riwa. We have accordingly the large tract of country, including the present districts of Patna, Gaya, the Chutia Nagpur commissionership, Riwa, Jabalpur, and possibly Ara and Mirzapur, as comprising the kingdom of Vasu Rájá, which after him became divided into five separate kingdoms, of which Magadha was certainly one, and Chedi Proper with capital at Tripura, or Tewar, another.

This being admitted as highly probable, if not rigidly accurate, it is no longer difficult to suppose that the capital of Vasu Rájá on the Saktimati (modern Sakri river), on the break-up of the old king's kingdom, became deserted or comparatively neglected, each of his sons naturally selecting a city more centrally placed in his own territory; and hence there is really no discrepancy or contradiction in

* Contrast this with the notorious saying regarding the people of Bundelkhand.

supposing the ancient capital of Vasu Rájá to have been at or near Dumduma, and the capital of Chedi Proper (one division only of Vasu's empire) to have been at Tripura or Tewar. I have not the time now to wade through the Mahábhárat for positive evidence on this point; but I trust that this statement of the question will induce others, who may be in a position to contradict my views, to bring forward their evidence, and thus throw light on this knotty point. I shall, without regret, abandon my theory in favor of a better supported one.*

That the empire of Vasu Rájá did include Magadha is placed beyond doubt by the passage which relates the births of Matsya Rájá and Satyavati. The passage is too broadly obscene for reproduction; but from it, it is evident that a Jamna river flowed between the forest where Vasu Rájá went hunting and the city where his wife Girika lived. Even supposing that his wife did not live in the city or village now known (and as I conjecture named after her) as Giriyak, yet the Yamuna river could not obviously have been the well-known river which flows past Mathura; we must look for another Jamna south of the Ganges and below Allahabad, and the only river which answers our requirements is the small stream known as Jamna, which flows from the Barabar hills and crosses the present Patna-Gaya road about 8 miles south of Jahânâbâd. The passage referred to is in continuation of the passage from the Ádiparvan already quoted, and the capital of the Rájá and the forest where he went to hunt must have been within a reasonable distance of each other, on opposite sides of the river, say a three or four days' journey.

On the east side of the Kiyul river, about 6 miles east by a little north from Nongarh, is a place of pilgrimage and some springs; they are situated among the wild Singhol hills. The places of interest here are a small temple at the base of the hill which runs east and west, a waterfall and a spring, and to west of temple a kund. A fair is held annually on the Sivaratri festival in Falgun and in Kartik; people carry their children there to shave off the hair. The kunds and the temple are situated in a plain. Tradition says that here was the residence of Rishyasringa, who was enticed away from his retreat by the gay women sent there by the King of Champa for the purpose. The story is to be found in the Râmâyana, Griff.,

---

* Since this was written I have found that the Sakri river flowed down the bed of the present Khuri river, and consequently that Rajagriha was on the river Sakri. I now hold therefore that Râjgir was the capital of Vasu and was situated on the Saktimati—see reports for 1877-78.

pp. 51-59, vol. I. A little rivulet, which is now almost dry, is said to have been the channel up which the raft with the maidens was floated to near the hermit's residence; it is believed by the people that pilgrims who go to the shrine there with firm faith are not molested *en route* by wild beasts, while others are. To west of the temple, which is Saivic, is the site of the Tapasya of Dastratha (?), and the remains of a natural cave; to the east of the temple is a sculptured slab, evidently a sati pillar. The sculpture is in three compartments: the first represents a lingam, showing the religion of the man; the second has two elephants—he was, therefore, probably a great man who rode an elephant in the fight; the last compartment shews three women, being probably the number of his wives who were burnt with him.

There are three inscribed statues or fragments near the temple, one known as Hara Gauri, one of a four-armed female, and one a fragment; all three inscriptions contain merely the Buddhist creed *Ye Dharmma*, &c., in Kutila characters; they evidently date to the later days of Buddhism, judging from the characters.

KHERHI.

The hill at Kherhi, 10 miles south-west of Bhagalpur, contains numerous remains; these are to be found both on the hill and in the village below; in the latter, all that now remains are brickbats and low mounds. I saw three of these, but found nothing of interest; perhaps excavation will yield interesting remains. Numerous low mounds also occur at the foot of the hill, along the northern foot of which an old road appears once to have existed; there are also numerous low mounds further west; over most of these the plough has been driven for a long time, and their artificial character is inferred solely from the numerous fragments of brick which have been, and still are, constantly being turned up by the plough.

The principal existing object of interest is, however, the fort on the hill. This is an irregular enclosure, of rough large blocks of stone laid on each other without cement, occupying the whole of the tolerably level top of the eastmost hill, which, though only one of a long series of hills, is quite isolated, being connected with the western range by a low pass. The hill is saddle-backed, the highest portion being an elevated piece of table-land at the extreme west end; this portion was formed into a citadel opening into the fort by one gate and steps, and having a small postern opening outwards, but without any paved approach to it. The outer fort had two gates, each reached by a long, easy, paved approach ; the easiest and largest is in about the middle of the south long wall ; the other leads down from the peak at the east end ; in both these ascents, as well as on numerous stones within the fort, and on the steps or paved approach leading from the fort to the citadel, are numerous detached inscriptions of one or two words, and almost all in the shell characters ; some of these are evidently derived from the old Gupta characters, as the disguise of flourish is not in all cases sufficient to mask the characters. I found twenty-two of these curious detached records, among which one was clearly in old Gupta characters curiously flourished : in one of the inscriptions the word *Dharmma* occurs, but the mere occurrence of the single word *Dharmma* is not enough to justify its being considered Buddhist. The other remains on the hill consist of a remarkably large and fine well, very deep, built of brick, and evidently very old, a smaller one similar to it, and several lingams, both in the fort and in the citadel : there are no traces of any Buddhist statues or other Buddhist remains. The temples that enshrined the lingams were of stone and of brick, and have long ago disappeared entirely.

There are remains of extensive buildings in the citadel; but what they were it is impossible now to tell without extensive excavations; one was most probably a large Saivic temple.

Below the hill, near the pass to the west, is a stone known as Vagheswari Sthan ; the stone is a large black slab ; it is inscribed, the inscription consisting of four lines in mediæval characters ; it opens with Swaste Pratâpa Râmânuya; the mention of Râmânuj fixes a superior limit to its age.

BHÂGALPUR.

Kherhi, or Purani Kherhi, has been noticed by Buchanan, who also notices the caves at Bhâgalpur. As there is nothing of interest about these caves, I need say nothing about them. There are, of course, wonderful stories of their extent and ramifications, but all except one that I examined were small, and the one I could not examine was probably similar to, or a little longer than, the others.

The remains of dargâhs, masjids, and temples in and about Bhâgalpur and over these caves are all modern and of no interest.

JETHUR.

On the west bank of the Chándan river, the ancient Champavati, and about 20 miles south of Bhâgalpur, is a hill with a small temple; here was found a single line of inscription on what was called the Charana of Narayana, dated Samvat 1053. The place, therefore, must have been of some importance as early as the tenth century of our era; the place and hill are named Jethur.

MANDĀR.

The famous hill of Mandár stands about 1½ miles off the present road from Bhâgalpur to Seuri, near the village of Oureya; the antiquities here have been noticed by several writers, the last of whom is Babu Rashvihâri Bose, whose paper is to be found in the first volume, Indian Antiquary.

At the foot of the hill on the south side, near the south-east end, is a tank named the Pâpaharani, which, as its name implies, purifies from sin. This tank is used to throw in the dead, and for this purpose corpses are brought from several miles distance all round. The bodies before being thrown in are supposed to have been burnt, but this operation is only nominally performed in many cases, and I saw numerous entire bodies, which could have been but slightly scorched by fire, lying and floating on the tank waters.

This tank once had temples on its banks; there lie numerous moulded or cut-bricks and stone, and several statues, or rather fragments, on its eastern banks; among these is a mutilated figure of Garud, which was once surmounted by Vishnu, but which is now broken off, leaving the legs across Garud's neck alone visible. At the north-east corner of the tank are the ruins of a small temple, which appears to have been Saivic, judging from a fragment of Nandi. Judging from the style of sculpture, and from the shallowness of the mouldings of the temple shewn by the loose carved stones, I should ascribe it to a post-Muhammadan period.

On the north banks of the tank the rock shelves down to the water; it is covered with fragments of stones—cut, rough, and sculptured; the carvings are more elaborate and carved stones are more numerous; the ruins are of more than one temple; one large temple certainly occupied a wide, flat space on the spur, but there must have been others and smaller ones in the vicinity. The temples were Saivic, judging from a fragment of Nandi; the temple, or at least the principal one, was of the style of the brick temples of Mânbhum, to be described further on, and appear certainly older than the Muhammadan conquest; the temple was evidently richly sculptured, I found a corner stone carved into statues on two faces, each being a female in the usual attitude; the hair of each is represented as tied into a knot on the left side of her head.

Besides this old temple, there stood more recent temples also, about the middle of the north bank, and on the rocky spur; these appear to have been of the style of the Barâkar temples, but with far shallower lines and of coarser execution. These temples I ascribe to a post-Muhammadan period, and, for reasons to be detailed subsequently, to the time of Akbar and his general Mân Singh. These temples were also Saivic, and several coarsely executed lingams lie to attest their purpose.

At the north-west corner are the ruins of a temple which appears to have been similar to that on the north-east corner.

There are some ruins on the west banks also, and these appear to be the remains of a single small group of temples. These temples appear from their carvings to belong to an older period than those described on the north-east and north-west corners and in the middle of the north bank, and to belong to the same age as the single large temple which stood on the north bank as noticed above.

To the north-east of this tank is another, now dry; on its west banks stood an old temple with numerous statues, and ornamented with deep mouldings.

At the eastern foot of the hill is a tank, on the southern banks of which stands a large irregular stone structure with numerous rooms enclosed within a courtyard. The pillars employed are plain, but with elegant octagonal shafts; they are used to support the verandahs in front. The stones employed in building this structure are of various sizes and various workmanship, and are set in mortar; they were clearly obtained from older structures. There are several small windows secured by stone lattices of plain and heavy patterns, which let in just light enough into the obscure interior chambers to render "darkness visible." The enclosure wall is in keeping with the building inside, having, however, in addition to stones of various sizes and qualities, bricks also. The structure belongs to the Srâwaks or Jains, and one of the rooms contains a charan, or sacred foot-print, sculptured in stone and set up on a platform.

The only other remains near the east foot of the hill are a number of nondescript tombs, or rather chhatris, built of brick and stone; some of these are inscribed, and from them we learn that they date to only the seventeenth century; one gives the name of a petty local Raja, and is dated Sake 1621.

The eastern face of the hill. is peculiarly impressive in appearance; it rises sheer up, a mass of smooth stone without a single blade of grass all the way up in the central portion; the form in outline is a graceful curve somewhat resembling a parabola with its vertex upwards. When within about 30 feet of the ground, vegetation begins to shew itself, and thence the slope is a gentle one in the reverse direction till it meets the plain; the outline, therefore, of the entire hill here is a curve of a double flexure, and is singularly beautiful.

The ascent to the hill is up a series of rude steps cut along a spur on its south face. There is another minor series of steps also on the south face cut on another spur, the ascent up which is much steeper, and it appears that, eventually, the attempt to carry the steps all the way up by this route was abandoned.

Following, however, the principal ascent, which is cut on a spur, that starting from the main hill on its west side curves round to the south, and ascending up the slippery steps a short way, one comes upon a large rock-sculpture to the right. The sculpture represents a ten-armed, three-headed figure (male or female it is impossible to tell from its rudeness) cut on a large boulder lying on the hill-side; the right hand holds a sword, a gada, a vajra, a spear and an hour-glass-shaped article. The left holds a chain, a shield, a spear, a chakra and a bow: the figure which has only two legs is represented trampling on a squat prostrate figure with large ears and large earrings in them; he has a short sword in his right hand, and over his head appears a canopy as of the spreading branches of a tree similar to the canopies of tree branches sometimes seen in sculptures of Buddha and of Mâyâ Devi. The ten-armed figure wears crowns; it has long ears but small earrings; it has anklets on the feet and bracelets on the arms, and also wears the sacrificial thread.

I have been thus particular in describing this rude sculpture, which, as a work of art, is of no value on account of its curiosity. It appears to me to represent nothing less than the triumph of Brahmanism over Buddhism, for the prostrate figure with a canopy of what I conceive was meant to represent the Bó tree, is most probably intended for either Buddha, or as a type of Buddhism; it is a singular piece of sculpture.

Close to it is a figure of Ganeça sculptured on the rock, and close to these are two rude rock-inscriptions, close to, and almost touching, the steps on their right side; the inscriptions appear to be in modern Nâgari characters, but are so rough as to be illegible.

Continuing to ascend, there stands to the left the remains of a small temple, and to the right, but on another spur separated from this by a ravine, the remains of two others. This spur is the eastmost of the southern spurs of the hill; from that spur to this extends a shallow double line cut on the rock; it appears to have been meant to mark out an intended line of wall, as on the other spur near its ridge, the line is interrupted to form a chamber or gateway; the line of walls was, however, never built. On this spur the line meets a line of walls of brick (now in ruins) which ran down along the left or west side of the ridge on which the steps of the main ascent are cut.

A little distance further up are the remains of two small and one larger temple. Among the ruins of the larger temple lie the fragments of a three-headed figure similar to the rock-sculpture already described. The mouldings of this temple were remarkably bold but perfectly plain. Just beyond the large temple are the remains of two other small temples. The small temples mentioned are not of any particular interest. No portion of any of the temples noticed is now standing. The smaller ones may or may not be old; there is no means of judging with certainty; but the larger temple just mentioned, to judge from its bold mouldings, belongs to the better days of Indian art, and before the Muhammadan conquest; and although the sculpture, both here and that described before, is very rude, this may rather be due to the refractory nature of the material of the rock than to a degeneracy of art; I would ascribe this temple to the period when Brahmanism finally prevailed over Buddhism.

Beyond this, the ridge up which the ascent is carried divides into two; one higher, and the main one leading up to the peak of the main hill; the other, a lower and subordinate one, leading to one of the minor peaks to the west of, and considerably lower than, the main peak; on this last are two temples, one large and one small.

There is necessarily inclosed between these two branches of the ridge and the main range of hills, which at its eastern end culminates in the Mandar peak, a hollow basin which has no outlet, but it is remarkable that though it has no outlet, there is no water in it.

A short way up is another large inscription to right of and touching the steps; it is in late Gupta characters, but very roughly cut, so much so that is was found impracticable to take impressions; but two eye-copies were made by me by hand under varying aspects of light. Near it, a little way higher, is a female figure sculptured on the rock. A short way further, the ridge again divides into two, which inclose a deep, narrow basin containing dirty water; the basin has steps on its south banks, which is raised artificially, and helps to keep in a large volume of water and at a higher level than the unaided height of the ridge alone would. On the sides the rock shelves down to the bottom, which is considerably below the crests of the inclosing ridges. The embankment appears to have been built, or perhaps only repaired, with stones from the ruins of temples that once stood here; the temples had mouldings not very bold, but quite deep enough to make them rank among the temples which were built before the Muhammadan conquest.

It appears to me that there stood four temples on the western ridge of this basin, one by itself, and three in a group; these last appear to have been at the south-west corner of the present embanked basin; the solitary one was on the same side, but higher up. In style the temples appear to have been like the Mânbhum ones.

The two ridges inclosing the basin meet higher up. Between their point of meeting and the north edge of the basin, is a tolerably level piece of ground, on which stand the huts of some jogis; this piece of ground is naturally inclosed on three sides by the ridges. To the west the ridge slopes gently down to it, but on the north and east there is an abrupt descent. On the north side is a cave, partly natural and partly artificial. I was not permitted to approach it, but it is said to enshrine a statue of Narasingha; on the east (*i.e.*) on the west face of the rocky wall which bounds this low bit of level ground on the east, is cut a gigantic human head; the sculpture is evidently unfinished, as the rock below the head is cut into preparatory steps for completing the sculpture; the extent of these preparatory steps being just such as would suffice to take in a figure corresponding in size to the gigantic head already cut; even this head is not finished; it is only roughly cut, and the lines and angles have not yet been rounded off; the head is now known as Madhu, and is said to represent the demon whose death at Vishnu's hands obtained for him his title of Madhusudana.

Close to this sculpture is a cleft high up in the face of the rock and approached by a ladder; this cleft communicates with a small basin to be described further on, and contains water; it is approached by a wooden ladder, up which even my Hindu servant was not permitted to ascend; this is the famous Akâs Ganga, and is perhaps the holiest spot in the whole hill. It is said that the volume of water in this cleft never enlarges or diminishes, but this must be untrue, as I could see traces on the rocky face below the cleft, which proved that the water overflowed at times, and it is evidently connected with the external basin to be presently noticed.

Close to the holy Akâs Ganga is sculptured on the rock a representation of the Vaman avátar of Vishnu.

Of the two ridges which inclose the basin, the western one has already been noticed as having had four temples, three near the south-west end of the basin; the eastern ridge also had temples, the largest being at the north-east end. Beyond this point, this eastern ridge again divides into two, of which the west face of the west, or the left one, has already been noticed as containing the cleft of the Akâs Ganga and the great face of Madhu; the two ridges necessarily inclose a small basin; this basin is triangular, one of whose angles is in the direction of the cleft known as Akâs Ganga; the water in the basin is remarkably transparent, and one can see that at the bottom of the basin, but especially at the corner on the west, lie cut-stones that once belonged to temples. So far as I could judge, the level of the water of the Akâs Ganga and of the basin is the same; and I have no doubt that the two communicate by a hole at the angle, which, whether accidentally or designedly, is encumbered with cut-stone from ruined temples.

The ascent is along the right, or eastern one of the two ridges just noticed. On it, close to this place, are the ruins of a small temple occupying the north-east end of the depression, in which is the basin that communicates with the Akâs Ganga. A short way higher up, the ridge again divides into two, inclosing a longish depression, across which two cut-stone walls were built, dividing and forming it into tanks; the walls or embankments are now in ruins and the tanks dry.

On the spur overlooking the lower tank was a small temple of coarsely cut-stone. Stone from it and from elsewhere has subsequently been used to build a modern shrine overlooking the upper tank (also dry now); it is a small, square, flat-roofed house of no interest; it is dedicated to Sivá, and a lingam stands in the sanctum.

The ascent is up the western or left-hand ridge of the two which inclose the depression just noticed; it goes up northwards, and at the first secondary peak, to the west of the great main one, it meets the other spur, which was noticed before as having, cut across it, a shallow double line to mark an intended line of walls and a gateway; from this peak the ascent goes eastwards up the slope of the great main peak.

The highest peak is crowned by a Jain or Sarawaki temple with a bulbous conical dome built of older materials. To the west of this and immediately under its walls, at the summit of the hill, is a deep chasm or hollow. I did not attempt to descend and ascertain its depth; it is overgrown with jangal which rendered a descent unsafe. The Jain temple stands to the east of and immediately on the brink of this chasm. On the rock is cut a figure of the Varaha incarnation, from which it appears probable that originally a Brahmanical temple stood on this spot.

Close to this Jain temple, which is of no interest, stands another small pyramidal-roofed temple and some other buildings, none of any interest.

I have omitted to notice a single line of inscription in characters of, perhaps, the 1st century of our era, which is cut on the rock on the ascent.

This closes my account of Mandar Hill. For a sketch of the peaks and lines of principal ridges, I refer to the plate; it is merely a sketch. I could not spare the time necessary to make a survey of the hill and of its offshoots. The hill is not encircled by a spiral mark of any kind; there is a little bit of a slanting line towards the base, and a little towards the summit, formed by the jagged end of a broken shell or outer layer of rocks, and imagination probably continues the line all round, forming a connected spiral from top to toe; the hill was probably volcanic, as suggested by General Cunningham.

About twelve miles from Naya Dumka, and three off the road between it and Mandar, is the shrine of Bhaski Nath; the temple there is apparently modern, and there is nothing of interest except the legend.

The legend relates that in ancient times some Parihar Rajputs used to live in these jangals, feeding on roots and fruit. One of them, Vasu Patr, in digging for roots, came upon a lingam, and continuing his excavations, found an entire lingam and argha; these he cleaned and went home; there he dreamt that he was ordered to worship it; he wanted to know where he could get water for libations, when he was told that in a copse, to the north of the lingam, he would find water in a hollow. On waking, Vasu Patr did as ordered, found the water, and began to worship the lingam, making offerings once a week, every Monday. The lingam, after Vasu Patr, came to be known as Bháskinâth. Bye-and-bye Vasu Patr dug a tank; for his zeal, the god appeared to him in his dream and ordered him to make and keep ready ropes, as he would send him many buffaloes. Vasu Patr, however, had not this time much faith in the dream, he nevertheless made a small length of rope. At midnight he was ordered to go to the tank and to tie as many buffaloes as he could; he went to the tank, but not having ropes enough, he could tie only a few; he tied some with his pagri and his dhoti, but these were found too weak to resist the attempts of the animals to get away.

Subsequently, Rupá Manji, a gwallá, was ordered to build a temple; he began it, but could not finish it; it was then taken up by Babu Gopál Sing, Raja of Negawán, and on his death, by his brother, who finished it. The proceeds of the temple are now divided between the Pandás and the Raja of Negawán.

BAIJNÂTH.

About 30 miles west by a little north of Bháskinâth is Baijnâth; this place is famed for its sanctity all over Northern, Central and Eastern India, and thousands of pilgrims flock here from all parts, even from the Dakhin. The remains here are numerous and extensive, but little of great antiquity, and almost all of no interest, apart from what attaches to them as the objects of reverence to thousands of pilgrims.

The objects of reverence here may be divided into three groups :—

(1) The group of temples in Baijnâth.
(2) „ „ „ at Harlajhuri.
(3) The caves, &c., at Tapoban.

The remains at Baijnâth consist of several detached temples in various parts of the city, and of the great group of temples within an enclosure near the east end of the city.

The former consist generally of single cells of various, but none of ancient, periods; they are of various styles and built of a variety of materials, among which the materials of former temples make a prominent figure. There is nothing of interest in or about them, and they may be dismissed without further notice.

There is, however, one object that must be excepted: this is a great gateway consisting of two pillars spanned by an architrave; this is clearly the remains of some great ancient temple, which has entirely disappeared, leaving its outer gateway alone standing. I infer it to have been an outer gateway from its resemblance in all essentials to the great outer gateway of the temple at Pathâri in Central India; like it, it stands entirely isolated, and although the pillars are plain rectangular ones, and have not the elaborate sculpture and the graceful statues that adorn the example at Pathâri, there is nevertheless about it an air of impressiveness that takes it out of the common place. I could not obtain access to it, but was obliged to content myself with a distant view; it is situated in a small raised spot entirely surrounded by private huts; at present it is known as the hindola, or swing, and at a certain festival the statue of Krishna is brought and made to swing beneath it.

The great group of temples is enclosed within a paved courtyard by high walls. There are four entrances to it; the principal one is to the west, and a similar one is on the north. Of the two minor ones, one is on the north and one on the east. Within the enclosure, which is an irregular quadrilateral, is a fine octagonal wall. The number and disposition of the various temples may be seen from the plate.

From a study of the plans of the temples (*vide* plate) it will be evident that of all the temples that now exist, there is not a single one which can be considered as old, or if old, in its original condition. The irregular grouping of the pillars that support the mandapas, and the clumsy way in which the mandapas are joined on to the sanctums, are proofs that these are subsequent additions; the sanctums may be ancient (I was not allowed to go in), but if so, the tower roofs that surmount them appear to have been added on afterwards. The finest of all the temples is the unfinished temple D; this from the plan is seen to be a single cell, once surrounded on all sides, now on three sides only, by pillars, which supported the roof of a verandah all round. From an examination of the pillars, however, it is clear that they formed no part of the original design, as they differ among each other in form, in size, in execution, and in position with reference to the central building, the pillars being not at a uniform but at varying distances from the walls on the various sides; these pillars further shew that the enclosure wall is a later addition even than themselves, as one of the pillars is imbedded in the eastern enclosure wall.

Divested of its pillars, this temple is seen to be a single cell, surmounted by a tower roof; it is ornamented externally by plain raised bands of mouldings; these are neither elegant nor bold, and are situated so high up, leaving such a height of bare blankness below, as to look quite out of place. Below, the corners are indented and sculptured into plain rectilinear mouldings by way of ornament; this process has the effect of making the corners look particularly weak, and, but for the verandah which now acts a friendly part, by breaking up the height, and shutting off as it were the main tower from the basement portion, the error of the proceeding would become painfully evident.

A general idea of this temple may be obtained from the photograph. The tower does not diminish with a graceful curve, but slopes upwards from above a certain point in almost a straight line. The knee or point of intersection of the vertical lower portion and the inclined upper tower portion is so little rounded as to be painfully prominent, and prominent too in such a way, as to shew that the architects really did not know how to deal with it; they had not the courage to leave the line sharp, and bring it out by a bold moulding, and they had not the taste to round it gracefully.

The form appears to be a compromise between the Muhammadan dome of the early type, *i.e.*, without a bulge, and the Hindu spire; if a semicircle be described on the top of the vertical portion of the tower, and if on the semicircle so described a triangle, whose base is less in width than the diameter of the semicircle, be slipped till the lower extremities of its sides rest on the curve of the semicircle, we shall get a form that nearly approaches that of these towers.

Judging, therefore, from the form of the towers, they cannot be ascribed to a period anterior to the Muhammadan conquest, and this inference of their late age is confirmed by the painful want of relief and variety both in plan and in elevation. The insipid flatness of design of these temples, whether we regard the plan or the profile, is indeed their most essential characteristic, and this want of relief is a strong argument against any great antiquity being ascribed to them. For these reasons, combined with the evident want of proportion and beauty, I ascribe the first erection of these temples to the earlier periods of the Muhammadan conquest.

But as intolerance was a characteristic of the early Muhammadan conquerors, and as we have no record of any event which could render it probable that Hindu temples had been built at any time after the Muhammadan conquest and before the reign of Akbar, and as, lastly, we have distinct record of a Hindu General, Mân Singh, exercising supreme authority in these parts during Akbar's reign, I consider it most probable that to Mân Singh's period these temples owe their construction.

The inference thus arrived at becomes a certainty when we examine the inscriptions; there are altogether thirteen of these, distributed as follows:—

1. Inscription on the outer entrance to the great temple S; it consists of thirteen long lines, and two small ones written sideways; it is in Bengali, and is divided into slokas; it records the erection, or rather I consider the repair, of a temple by one Sri Bydyanatha Mahamyáma. This name and also the name of one Raghunatha recurs in the last line.

2. Inscription from the inner entrance or the real entrance of the original temple, divested of its verandah and vestibule, which are evident after-additions; this consists of five lines in modern Nâgari; it mentions the name of some king with the title of Nripati. Raghunatha's name also occurs in the last line.

3. One from outside of the great temple; this is in seven lines, and is in Bengali; it records the name of some local Raja in the second line.

4. One from the temple of Káli Mái, temple C; this is cut in relief in modern Nagri characters in two compartments of five lines each; it was dated, but the date has been purposely chiselled out, having the word Samvat followed by a rough space; this again followed by Mâgh Sudi, then a blank, and lastly "tisa;" the record is clearly one of the building of the temple; the builder's name occurs in the second compartment.

5. One from the same temple in Sanskrit slokas in nine lines; it is a record of the construction of the "Sundara Mandirâm."

6. One from the temple of Anna Purna, temple F; this is in Bengali in 10½ lines, and is a record of the dedication of the temple to "Anna Purna" Devi.

7. One from the temple to Ganeça, temple R; this is in eight lines, Bengali; it mentions a Tikarâm Dvijendra.

8. One from the temple of Sanjhyá Mai; this is in eleven lines in Bengali; it records the construction of the temple by several people.

9. One from the temple of Surya, M, in six lines, Bengali; this is dated in the 17th century Sake; it is in bad order.

10. One from Anand Bhairon, temple J; this in in nine lines in modern Nagri, and is dated in Sake 1745.

11. One from the statue of Anand Bhairon in three lines; this is apparently an ancient inscription, dating to, perhaps, the 9th or 10th century.

12. One from the statue of "Surya" in two lines, is also old; it is the usual Buddhist formula, *Ye Dharmma*, &c., &c.

From all these inscriptions it is evident that not a single one of the temples dates to the pre-Muhammadan period, while several are very recent.

Among those which I consider as likely to be more ancient, dating, however, at the furthest only to Mân Singh's time, are temples S B D; but even these I should not be surprised to find dating to a later period.

It now remains to ascertain, if possible, why these temples were built here, and not rather at any other place; this is accounted for by the existence of the two ancient inscribed statues, one of which is clearly Buddhist; and of a third figure, not inscribed, but clearly Buddhist, being a fine seated statue of Buddha himself, beautifully polished, and equal in execution to the finest statues to be met with in Bihar. These statues prove beyond a doubt that here was at one time a large Buddhist establishment.

What this establishment was named it is, perhaps, impossible now to determine with certainty; but if I may be permitted to speculate, I should think it to have been the site of the famous Uttániya monastery of Winjjha. Winjjha is the Páli equivalent of Vindhya; the passages in Turnour referring to it are—p. 115—"the monarch departing out of his capital and preceding the river procession with his army through the wilderness of Winjjha, reached Tamalitta on the 7th day," and in p. 171 "From various foreign countries many priests repaired hither" * * * * "There Uttaro attended accompanied by sixty thousand priests from the Uttaniya temple in the wilderness of Winjjha."

It is evident that the wilderness of Winjjha lay on the route from Pátaliputra to Tamluk. I have indicated some of the routes from Tamluk to various places. The principal route would, it appears to me, have to pass through, or close to, modern Bankurah; from here there was a choice of several routes. Clearly the route to Bhâgalpur would branch off northwards from there, passing through Seuri, under Mandar, close past Bhaskinâth; it is remarkable that an old track yet exists from Bhaskinâth to Deoghar Byjnâth, whence it goes on skirting the eastern spurs of the Kawalkol range, past Afsand, Parvati, Bihar to Patna. I should consider that this was the route taken by the king when he passed through the wilderness of Winjjha, for it appears to me pretty certain that the wilderness of Winjjha can only refer to the wild country now known in part as the Santál Parganas.

If this be admitted, we have but one place in the Winjjha forests where Buddhist temples existed, as testified by existing Buddhist relics, and this place is Deoghar Baijnâth.

It is remarkable that close to the city of Deoghar and still closer to the temples is a small village named Utmuria; this may be a corruption of the original of the Páli Uttama. I put forward this suggestion merely in the absence of any more positive; it is possible that an examination of the 3-line inscription from the Buddhist statue noticed before may throw new light on the subject.

I have described but one of the temples in the enclosure, as that is the best of the group, and may be regarded as the type of the others; it is needless to describe each of the uninteresting edifices in detail. I shall now give the legends and stories connected with the place.

The great temple is the chief of the group, and enshrines a lingam; this is said to have a small depression at its summit, and I am assured by Hindus that the cavity feels soft to the touch. Tradition says that it is the mark of Râvana's thumb, when in his rage he pressed down the lingam, intending to send it to Pâtâla; the legend will be given presently. Facing it is the temple of Pârvati. At certain times the two spires are connected together by a thin, long cotton sheet, and this is done to shew that Sivá and Pârvati are enjoying each other's society. Comment on the gross indelicacy of the idea is needless.

The legend about the lingam is as follows :—

Ravana used daily to go to Uttara Khanda to worship Sivá. One day he went there, and in the exuberance of physical strength he shook the mountain, disturbing Pârvati. Having done this, he went towards Sivá's abode to worship; when he approached, Nandi forbad his advance, as Sivá and Pârvati were asleep together. Râvana, however, was not to be denied; he told Nandi that he being in the place of a son to Sivá, there was no harm in his going in at any time. Saying this and pitching away Nandi to a distance, he entered. Sivá was much pleased at his courage and firm faith, and desired him to ask a gift. Râvana said, "It is a long distance for me to come daily from Lanka to worship you here; be pleased to go to Lanka and abide there." Sivá consented on the condition that Râvana was to carry him all the way, without for a moment setting him down. Râvana gladly took up the lingam, and proceeded; when he arrived at Lájhuri village, near the place where the temples stand (the village is now known as Harlájhuri), he felt it necessary to go to the fields; he could not carry the lingam with him and pollute it, and he was cogitating what to do. In this emergency Vishnu, who saw that if Râvana succeeded in carrying Sivá to his kingdom he would become invincible, assumed the guise of a poor Brahman, and being accosted by Râvana and requested to hold the lingam for a few minutes, while he went a short way, the pretended Brahman agreed. Râvana now made over the lingam to the Brahman and went aside. While Râvana was engaged, the Brahman quietly walked away with the lingam, arriving finally at the spot where the great temple stands; here he set the lingam down and vanished. Râvana on returning at the expiration of the whole day (for Varuna had entered into him and occupied him all that time in letting out the sea of waters within him) found the Brahman gone. After some search he found the lingam, but on attempting to lift it up,

Sivá reminded him of the agreement between them and refused to stir. Râvana enraged, pressed the lingam down, saying, "Since you wont go to Lanka, go to Pâtâla instead." This is the mark which exists on the summit of the lingam to this day. Finding at last threats and entreaties vain, Râvana set about to worship the lingam in its new location, and brought water from the adjacent tank, which he had constructed and filled with water from the Patalapuri Ganga for libations; but Mahadeo refused to receive that water, as it had been contaminated by Râvana's urine, when Varuna, having entered into him, had issued out as a sea of waters. Rávana then dug a well to obtain water for libations, and to this day water from the tank just outside of the sacred enclosure is not used for libations. To console Râvana, however, for his trouble in digging the tank, Sivâ ordained that all his votaries must bathe in the tank before approaching him. At present thousands of pilgrims of both sexes are continually bathing in that tank, a constant stream of bathers always going to or from the tank to the temple; the scene is gay—I cannot say much for its decency, nor for the wholesomeness of the water, which is a thick liquid more resembling pea-soup than water.

The lingam thus established became known as Mahadeo Râvaneswara. In course of time the site of the lingam was overgrown with jangal, and no one but a poor gwâla knew of its existence. This man, Baiju by name, used to dwell in the vicinity, living on roots and fruit; he was ordered by Mahadeo in a vision to worship him; the poor man accordingly used to bring Bel leaves for the worship daily, but having no vessel to bring water, used to bring water for the libations in his mouth. This strange libation, however, did not please Sivá, who, after much patient endurance, complained to Râvana of the gwala's treatment. Râvana came, washed the lingam with water from Haridwâr, and ordained that thenceforth none but Ganges water from the Trithas of Haridwâr, Gangotri and Dasâsumedh (Ajodhya) was to be poured on the lingam, and to ensure its being done, he brought the waters from the Pancha Trithas, the five holy trithas on the Ganges, *viz.*, Haridwâr, Gangotri, Dasâsumedh, Prayâg, Kâsi, Trivini (here are six named however) and put it into the well he had dug.

Subsequently Râma, pursuing Râvana, passed that way and worshipped the lingam.

Siva at last was pleased with the untiring devotion of Baiju Gwâla, and offered to give him any gift he should ask. The independent gwala replied—"What can you give me? I have enough to eat and drink. I want nothing, but if you are determined to grant me a gift, grant that henceforth my name should precede yours." From that day, the lingam known as Râvaneswara came to be known as Baijnâth.

A few miles to the north-east of Baijnâth is Harlájhuri; here are a few modern temples and fragments of statues; two have inscribed on them a jogi's name. Sri Chintâman Das is said to have lived here and built these temples 50 years ago. There is nothing of interest in the place, but an inscription which I found here in late mediæval characters of the Bengali type is of interest as showing that the Krimila Desa, mentioned in the Mongir plate, was here, or hereabouts; the entire inscription is in the margin. This place is the spot where Râvana is said to have made over the lingam to Vishnu disguised as a Brahman; it is incumbent on pilgrims to visit the place.

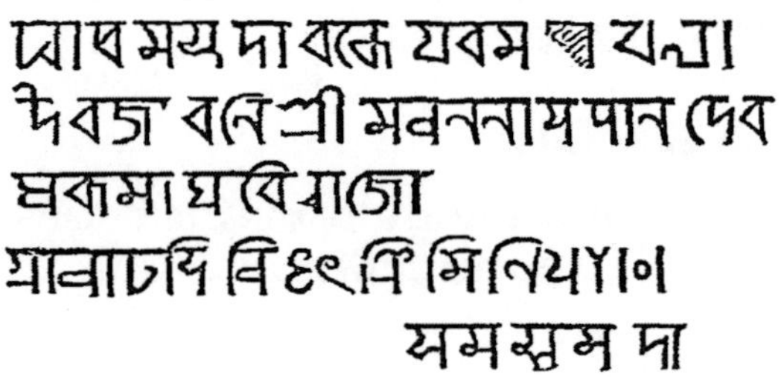

About 6 miles south-east of Deoghar Baijnâth is a solitary hill known as Tapoban; in this hill is a natural cavern, enshrining a lingam which is worshipped; it is said to have been the residence of a Tapasya of ancient times; there is also a kund known as Sul Kund, in which pilgrims bathe. On the rock near the cave are two inscriptions; one, a single line, reads Sri Deva Râmapâla; the other in two lines is quite illegible.

Eight miles north-west from Baijnâth is a group of hills with three curious peaks; it is known as the Trikuta hill, and is marked in the Ind. atlas sheet as Teeor or Tirpahar. Here is a natural cavern, empty, and in the plains below, which is low-lying and said to be marshy in the rains, a small, old, uninteresting deserted fort; there is a lingam here known as Trikutanâth Mahâdeva.

In concluding my account of the remains at Baijnâth and its vicinity, I must express my acknowledgments to the Public Works Overseer at Deoghar, without whose assistance it would have been impossible for me to have obtained the plan of the interior of the great temple.

SHÂDIPUR, RÂMGAON, AND SEURI.

Returning to the road Bhâgalpur to Seuri; near the crossing of the Moa river, are some temples in the villages Shâdipur and Râmgaon; they do not appear to be of any interest. Seuri itself contains numerous old tanks with enormously high embankments; besides these I could see nothing of interest to the archæologist in the place, or near it.

LÁBHPUR.

A few miles to the north-east of the Railway Station of Mallárpur is a small village named Lábhpur, or Phullára. Old temples are said to exist here, and it is said to have been the ancient seat of the Malla Rájás, after whom the districts Mallárpur and the various parganas known as the Malleswar parganas are named. I did not visit the places.

JAMUA KANDI.

Jamua Kandi also is said to have ancient remains; these, however, are said to be chiefly Muhammadan. I did not see the place.

NAGOR.

To the west of Seuri is the great fort, if fort it can be called, of Nagor. The whole pargana is enclosed by a low earthen rampart overgrown with dense scrub and bambu jangal; the ramparts, have a shallow ditch in front, about 20 feet wide now in places, but which once must have been both wider and deeper. The line of ramparts is very irregular both in plan and in profile. As a general rule, however, the height is about 15 feet above the ditch, and the width at base about 80; the top has been naturally rounded by the weather.

The space within the inclosure comprises the entire pargana of Haripur; it is a low, unhealthy, flat piece of land, resembling more some parts of Lower Bengal than the adjacent districts; there is a tirtha here near the village of Tántipâra known as the Tirtha of Bakeswar. The objects of interest are a number of temples grouped near a number of dirty tanks. There is but one large temple, and this is of the style of the Baijnâth ones; it had a line of inscription over the doorway in modern characters, but the characters are now too worn to be at all legible. Close to the temple is a pakka kund, ablution in which cleanses from sin. However this may be, I am quite certain that ablution in it must be particularly disagreeable, the stench its waters exhale being strongly perceptible 50 yards off, and in color and consistence it more resembles the contents of sewers than any other semi-fluid substance I can think of. Pilgrims after bathing in the larger tanks, which themselves are not particularly sweet, are, as a final measure, to bathe in this; there are hot springs in the kund, and the water is warm; there are also cold springs in the kund close to the hot, which is seen bubbling up; the hot springs are sulphurous, and give off freely sulphuretted hydrogen.

The other temples are all very small and very numerous; they are avowedly modern.

Outside, to the left of the long line of temples which line the road, leading straight to the principal shrine, are numerous hot springs; the waters have a sulphurous smell, and evidently contain sulphuretted hydrogen; they enjoy some reputation in curing diseases, and I have no doubt they deserve it; they all empty into a small rivulet, which runs past them, and discharges itself in a small stream about 200 yards from the group of temples.

The temples are built of a variety of materials, brick and stone, both cut and rough; the cut stone is roughly dressed, not smoothed; there are traces of an old brick inclosure about the principal temple, which is situated on a high mound.

There are numerous fragments of statues of no special interest. Lingams innumerable are to be seen at every step. The long lane or road leading from the tank to the temple is lined by semi-nude jogis, and the tanks are crowded by pilgrims, male and female, in gay dresses, busy washing away old sins and clearing the way for fresh ones. The morality, both of jogis and of pilgrims here, is not of a very strict type; this is, indeed, the chronic state of things at most other tiraths that I have seen, but here there is less of even outward appearances preserved than elsewhere generally.

The place is fabled to have been the residence of Bakra Muni, and the lingam in the principal temple having been established by him, is known as Bakeswa[illegible]

I obtained a list of tirthas here, which I append; it is of interest, as giving the names of numerous well-known as well as of some obscure tirthas.

When Parvati in her anger destroyed herself at Daksha's sacrifice and flung her members abroad, they fell at various places, each of which has become a tirtha in consequence; there are 48 of these I was told—

1. Hingulâz—the occiput.
2. Sarkara—the eye (netra).
3. Sugandhya—the nose.
4. Kashmir—the throat.
5. Jwâlamukhi—the tongue.
6. Janukur—the "sthul."
7. Manasarovar—the right hand.
8. Bahula—the left hand.
9. Chattagrama (Chittagong)—the right arm.
10. Ujain.
11. Kandaki—the back of the neck.
12. Vrindavana—the hair.
13. Jayanta—the left thigh.
14. Prayága—the fingers.
15. Mithila—the left shoulder.
16. Kânchipur—the bones.
17. Ratnavali—the right shoulder.
18. Kángaon—the back.
19. Godâvari—the cheek.
20. Kirit Kona.
21. Sri Saila hill—the neck.
22. Prabhâsa—the lips.
23. Chandrabhâga—the canine tooth.
24. Panchaságar—the incisors.
25. Kálamadhava—the right waist.
26. Narmmada—the left waist.
27. Sri Parvat, near the Karatoya river, received the left chin.
28. Kurukhetra.
29. Benares—the earrings.
30. Manikarnika (in Benares)—the breast jewel (brooch).
31. Baijnâth—the heart.
32. Nepâla (Pasupatinatha)—the palate.
33. Tri[illegible]ra—the right hand.
34. Kh[illegible]aon—the left breast.
35. Bhairava Hill
36. Jagannath—the navel.
37. Mâyâpura.

38. Mahendra.
39. Gokarna.
40. Chatramáyá.
41. Bhasmajál.
42. Râmagiri (Râmtek).
43. Bakini.
44. Mâlaya.
45. Kâmakhya—the generative organs.
46.
47.
48. Kâlighât (in Calcutta)—the toes fell here.

I give the list as I got it, without comment or remark.

MANGALPUR.

At Mangalpur, about two miles west of Dubrâjpur, and nine miles south of Bakeswar or Tantipâra, is a tank known as Dántiwara,—so called, legend says, after the teeth of Parvati, of which one fell into it. Close to it, Khágra is said to have been so named after Khagâditya Muni.

BHIMGARH.

The road from Raniganj to Seuri crosses the Ajaya river near Bhimgarh. This is an old fort, with low earthen ramparts, now beaten by the weather into low gentle mounds. The place is attributed to the five Pândus, who, during their exile, are said to have stayed here some time. Some hollows in the vicinity,—the remains, no doubt, of old tanks,—are said to have been caused by the daily pouring out at those spots of the water from boiled rice, and the surplus ghi and sugarcane juice. A tank in the vicinity is named Sona Chál Dighi, and is said to have yielded gold, which the Pândus washed here: hence the name. The interior of the fort is now cultivated, and people say they occasionally come upon sál timber buried underground. I accept this statement as correct, and as an indication of the comparatively small age of the fort.

On the south banks of the river, opposite the fort, are a number of small, uninteresting temples, which are ascribed to the Pândus. The five brothers are said to have established five lingams there, which they worshipped; whence the name of the place Pánchpândeswar. Bhim, however, is said to have set up another lingam on the other side of the river, close to, and west of, the old fort: this is now known as

Bhimeswar, and is enshrined in a small modern temple. All the temples in Pánchpândeswar are modern, and built of brick and stone, without any regularity. Older temples once existed here, but of these, except the materials, there are now no traces. Judging from these, I conclude they were small, plain shrines, somewhat of the style of the Baijnâth temples, and of no great antiquity.

A short distance south of the river Ajaya, and to the east of the road, is a large tank near a village, with the remains of a Muhammadan dargah and of a Hindu temple close to it: they are not very old, but are probably as old as the ruins at Pánchpândeswar.

BARÂKAR.

Barâkar, which is the terminus of the East Indian Railway, Barâkar Branch, and is situated on the Grand Trunk Road, contains several very interesting ancient remains, in excellent preservation. There are four temples, whose towers at least are in entire preservation; besides some ruins. There are two temples together at the eastern end of the group, and one ruined temple not far off. Some few feet off are two other temples.

Temples Nos. 1 and 2 are precisely like each other. As they stand at present, they consist of a simple cell each, surmounted by a tower roof, but there are traces of a mandapa in front, of which all, but the foundations, have disappeared. So far as can now be ascertained, the temple consisted of a cell, with its doorway; an antarala, formed in the thickness of the back walls of the mahamandapa; a mahamandapa, about 13½ feet square (see plate). That there were chambers in front of the mahamandapa I cannot doubt, but no traces now exist of any.

One of the temples is inscribed. The record is engraved on the right jamb of the entrance or doorway of the sanctum. It is in two distinct pieces—one of 11½ lines, the other of 21 lines, both in a variety of the Bengali character. From the style of the characters, the temples do not appear to date to beyond the Muhammadan conquest, or, at the utmost, to just before. The inscriptions are not dated. One of them mentions the erection of the temple by one Harishchandra (Rájá ?) for his beloved; but who Harishchandra was, or when he built the temples, is not mentioned. The temples are particularly interesting, as being the finest existing examples of their type.

The temples face east. In the cell of the inscribed one is a Ganeça on a pedestal, in front of which is an oblong argha, with 3 lingam holes cut into it. It appears to me that only one of the holes was originally cut; the others were subsequently added—why, I cannot imagine. I infer this from the rudeness of execution of the other holes; two nandis and several Vaishnavic sculptures lie outside. A peculiarity of these temples,—and not of these alone, but of the entire series of temples of this type to be found in Mânbhum,—is the sunk position of the floor of the sanctum.

I am inclined to ascribe these temples to a period posterior to the Muhammadan conquest of Northern India, from the circumstance that a temple of this type, existing at Telcupi, to be noticed further on, has had the corners of its mahamandapa cut off (to enable a circular roof to be put on), in the same way as the corners of Iltitmish's tomb at Delhi; but it is to be observed that this mode of construction, although it, undoubtedly, occurs in a post-Muhammadan building in Delhi, is to be regarded as essentially Hindu, especially as we meet no instances of it after the time, when, as is well known, Hindu masons were employed of necessity in the construction of Muhammadan structures; so that, although I am on this ground inclined to attribute these temples to a post-Muhammadan period in the absence of other data, I am by no means satisfied that in doing so, I am right.

The sanctum is roofed by overlapping stones, chamfered at the edges, till the opening is small enough to be slabbed over; but, although the inner roof of the sanctum is thus a pyramidal one, there is space between it and the outer tower roof for a small chamber. I could see no chamber from the outside, and clambering up to ascertain it, was not practicable; but, judging from other examples, it is very unlikely that the entire intervening space is solidly filled in.

The basement mouldings of these temples are not elegant, though they are deeply cut, and rise to a great height. This is due to the circumstance that they do not splay outwards, and thus add to the breadth and solidity of the temple. Constructively, these temples, founded on solid rock, need no splay outwards of the foundations, but, artistically, the very profusion of deep-cut lines, richly sculptured, which do not apparently increase the stability of the temple, is unsatisfactory. In this respect the simple mouldings of the temple at Katrás, similarly founded on rock, will contrast favorably with these, as also those of No. 5 temple here; and even No. 4 has very perceptible advantages over Nos. 1 and 2: see plates.

It is needless to do more than allude to the richly indented towers. As examples of towers richly, yet simply, ornamented, they invite especial attention and study. It is not, however, possible to give a critical account of them till accurate drawings to scale can be made— a work which, as I have before observed, must be undertaken at some future time, not now, when extensive rapid tours are undertaken and accomplished.

Close to and south of these temples stands a raised mound—the ruins of a temple. This temple contained numerous statues of the avatars of Vishnu, several of which still exist in a weather-beaten and broken state. The temple must have been large, and the statues appear to have been ranged along the walls of the mahamandapa, doing duty as pilasters and, perhaps, as pillars, precisely in the style of the temples in the eastern portion of the Central Provinces, which I have since seen. The age of this temple is difficult to ascertain. Judging from the ruins of what its style must have been, and comparing it with the temples in the Central Provinces, to which type it clearly belongs, this temple should be placed at a very early period, perhaps the sixth or seventh century of our era; but as it is found in company with other temples which, apparently, are of a later date, I do not see how any great antiquity can be assigned to it. There is but one solution,—to ascribe all the Barâkar temples to a date prior (but not by much) to the Muhammadan conquest.

Temple No. 4 stands by itself. It, like Nos. 1 and 2, consists at present of a single cell, but, unlike them, it does not appear to have ever had a mahamandapa in front, as the mouldings are carried round to the very entrance of the sanctum. Unlike them, too, it does not face east, but due west. In other particulars it appears to be much like them. The floor of its cell is considerably lower than the sill of the entrance, being 3 feet 7 inches below the level of the entrance sill. Like them, too, it has a pyramidal roof inside, with no chambers visible above, and the tower and the ornamentation of the tower are similar also. The mouldings of the basement are, however, different, both in being unadorned with sculpture, and in being higher and bolder, and altogether more pleasing. A portion of the lower part of the temple is now buried underground.

The object of worship inside is the figure of a fish lying flat, serving as an argha to five lingam holes cut in it. This sculpture is especially interesting, as proving that the fish is essentially a representation of the female power of nature—a character which it bears in the mythology of other nations, but which appears to have been overlooked, or forgotten, in Indian mythology, where it, and a similar symbol, the tortoise, are dissociated from the lingam. Vishnu, as the preserving, and therefore the reproductive, agent, is, by right, entitled to these symbols; but so is he in his masculine aspect to the lingam. The lingam, however, has long, by a strange anomaly, become associated with Siva, the destroying agent, and has lost all connection with its natural pedestal, the yoni, represented by the fish and tortoise, and elsewhere (out of India) by the boat, the ark, &c. It is out of place here to pursue the subject further, but in the history of Indian symbolism, this unique sculpture will occupy a very interesting and important position. The sculpture represents a fish 5 feet 9 inches long from the snout to the tip of the tail, 2 feet 3 inches wide at the swell below the head, and 1 foot 9 inches at the junction of the tail. The tail itself is 9 inches long by 2 feet 1 inch wide at its extremity.

Close to this temple, and facing it, stands temple No. 5. It is now inclosed, or partially inclosed, within a courtyard; but the walls of this inclosure are evidently later additions, as they cover up the mouldings of the temple outside on the sides.

Divested of this wall, the temple consists of a cell and an antarala, or vestibule. It does not appear to have ever had a mahamandapa in front. The object of worship is a lingam, placed in a great argha, 4 feet 7 inches in diameter. Besides this, there are lying, in and out, statues and fragments, among which may be reckoned, Ganeça, a 4-armed female, a 4-armed male holding a sword and a trident in two hands, and some nondescript fragments. The roof is pyramidal inside, as in other temples.

Externally, the tower differs considerably from those of the other temples here, and, though in bad order, surpasses them in beauty and richness, though the sculptured details are not so profuse or minute. The basement mouldings, too, are bold, elegant, and simple, and stand in strong contrast to the richer, more labored, but ineffective, profusion of lines in the other temples. Reference to the plates and photographs will give details both of this and of the other temples.

This temple cannot be classed with the others. In design and in execution it is essentially different, though the same in material; and if style alone be taken as a criterion of age, it should be much older than them. But style is such a vague expression, that it is a vicious system, which presumes from a consideration of that which itself is undefined to deduce the age of any structure. Few, if any, of those who use the expression have any clear idea of its meaning. I certainly have very vague notions about it; and I do not believe it has yet been laid down what, and why, particular features, or what, and why, particular details of features,—whether of plan, of material, of color, of ornamentation, of profile, or of construction,—should be, and what should not be, considered as entering into, and helping to make up, the shadowy thing known (or rather, I should say, not known) as style. Before we can make use of "style" as a test of age, we have, first, to define it; and secondly, to show that style is justly a criterion of age, and of age alone,—not rather of locality, or of a combination of age and locality. I have in several instances been guilty of attempting to judge from "style;" but it has always been done with hesitation, and more because I felt myself somehow bound to give an opinion,—guess it should rather be called,—which will be of use, even if it only succeeds in inviting controversy, and thus helping to throw light from other quarters on the subject.

One interesting feature in these temples must not be passed over unnoticed. The temples are surmounted by urns, and not by cylinders, or spires, or cones. The temple No. 5 had, indeed, once an iron trisul surmounting it, but it appeared to me to have been put in afterwards.

There are no legends in connection with these temples.

KALYÂNESWARI, OR DEVISTHAN.

Six or seven miles north of Barâkar, near the right banks of the Barâkar river, are some temples at a place known as Devisthan. All these appear to me of recent date—perhaps built of older materials. They are interesting, as showing that, even at a very late period, the horizontal arch was used by Hindus, as may be seen from the entrance archway of the enclosure, which is evidently built of the relics of some older structure, of which now no traces remain.

Two of the temples here are inscribed. The inscriptions are in bad order, from having been cut on a soft stone.

They are in Bengali characters, and are cut in relief—an almost certain sign of their recent age. One of them mentions a Rájá's name and Kalyânakot; as the temples are known as the sthana of Devi Kalyâneswari, it appears that formerly a small fort, named Kalyânakot (kot meaning citadel), existed here. The statue of the Devi herself in the principal temple,—a large, plain, massive, pyramidal roofed, dark temple, with balustrade-shaped pillars in front,—is inscribed. The inscription is in Bengali. It reads "Sri Sri Kalyâneswari charana parayan Srijukta Deva Nâtha Deva Sarmma."

Tradition says that a Rohni Deoghar Brahman once saw a jewelled arm rise out of the waters in the nala adjacent; he went and informed Rájá Kalaya Sinha of Kâsipur, Pachet, who came himself to see, and saw the prodigy. At night the goddess herself appeared to him in a dream, and pointing to an irregular stone, somewhat like a rude argha, said, "This is my murtti, worship it;" the Rájá accordingly caused the temple to be erected, and the stone having been duly inscribed, was installed in the temple. As the Rájás of Pachet did not reside at Kasipur till comparatively very recent times, the temples cannot be old.

PÁNDRÁ.

About 9 miles west of Barâkar, and 1½ to the north of the Grand Trunk Road, is the large and important village of Pándrá, the residence of the Chief (now a female) of the district; here are several temples, all in a group, on a high revetted mound enclosed by a low wall; the principal temple is clearly a modern restoration of an older temple, but there are other small single-cell temples, which have not undergone much alteration, though all have received attention and are kept in repair by the Ráni; the place was evidently one of importance in ancient times, and the great terrace on which the temples are built, and the positions of the two existing smaller temples, show that here stood a large temple, surrounded by minor ones; the temples are interesting for the curious moulding (see plate), and the enclosure wall appears to be, in parts, of its original form. It is said that, while repairs were being executed, an inscription was found, and was inserted by the mason into some part of the temple, but where no one knew; and as the temples are well covered with whitewash and plaster, and I was not permitted to go in, I failed to discover it. The temples are ascribed to the Pândus, from whom, also, the place Pándrá is said to derive its name. I need hardly add that this is quite a myth; the temples do not appear older than the mediæval Brahmanical period.

It is said that about half a mile off, in digging near a tank, old steps leading down to it were found, as also a subterranean passage. I accept these statements as correct, and as indicating the former importance of this place.

KATRÁS.

Katrás is an important village, about 6 miles south of the police outpost between Gobindpur and Topçhânchi; there must once have been numerous temples here, but the materials have been used up in building new ones; to the north *of the village is a small temple, perhaps partly old,* but standing on a terrace, which has evidently been restored. As the basement moulding of this terrace are curious, I have inserted it (*vide* plates); close to it, on a small mound, are the ruins of an old temple; here lies an old sculptured doorway and several fragments; in the vicinity are several low mounds, with fragments of statues and cut stone lying about.

To the east of, and separated from, the village by a small rivulet stands a half-ruined old temple known as the Dewal; this temple is especially interesting, as showing the construction of temples of this class—single-cell ones—and for the simplicity of its mouldings; the temple is remarkably plain; it has in front the tall triangular opening, formed of overlapping stones, and divided into two portions by a broad slab let in across; at present I see no remains of any mandapa in front, but the existence of the dividing slab shows that it existed at one time, as otherwise the slab dividing the opening into an entrance proper and an illuminating window becomes meaningless.

The temple is filled up inside to some depth with rubbish; on excavation, I came upon an argha eccentrically placed; judging from this that it was a later addition, I continued the excavation, and came upon an argha centrically placed and *in situ;* the temple was, therefore, Saivic; the exterior of the temple is also buried under about three feet of rubbish, and this may account for my not seeing any traces of the foundations of a mandapa in front.

Close to the temple is a tank, now nearly dry, known as the Ghât Bándhá Tal; it was evidently attached to the temple; its name is said to have been derived from the existence of a stone ghat, which was once found upon digging, but which is now again buried. A fair, lasting one day during the month of Chait, is annually held here. The temple stands on the crest of high undulating ground. The place is known as Jhinjhi Páhári. For details of measurement and construction, I refer to the plates and photograph; description is superfluous. The temple faces west; on the entrance is a human head sculptured on the architrave; the head has matted locks, and is apparently intended for Siva.

I have elsewhere indicated the importance of Katrás; it is even now of some importance, as the Rájá of Jhariá occasionally resides here. There are numerous modern temples and several pakka residences in the village.

From the evident simplicity of the mouldings and the occurrence of the triangular overlapping opening in front, which, however necessary constructively in brick buildings, is not a necessity here, and from this opening being designed in accordance with the proportions that held in brick temples, I infer this temple to be one of the oldest found in Magadha (supposing Magadha to have extended to the Dámudá river southwards). The district of which Katrás is, or was, the capital is known, in Muhammadan history, as Jhárkhand, which appears to have been derived from Jhariágarh; but as Jhariágarh is traditionally said to have risen into importance after the decay of Katrás, or rather as its rise is said to have caused the decay of Katrás, I infer that the temple here must date to a period long anterior to the Muhammadan conquest.

About 8 miles west of Katrás is a temple at Dumra, but which I could not visit.

Two miles south of Katrás are two small and apparently modern temples, one dated in Samvat 1904, 18th Vaisâkh: the village is called Malkará.

About 8 miles south by a little west from Katrás, on the right bank of the Dámudá river, are the ruins of a large religious establishment; the place is now utterly deserted, the nearest village being two miles off; the ruins are known as the ruins of Chechgaongarh.

CHECHGAONGARH.

There are the ruins of a few temples on the north banks of the river also, one faced south, and was built exactly facing a corresponding one on the south, or right bank of the Damuda; the ruins contain several stones, evidently the mouldings of the basement; they are fine, and boldly cut; opposite to this temple, on the right bank of the river and to the south-east and east of it, are other temples, which must have been profusely ornamented; some of the fragments of stones of the basement mouldings resemble the basement mouldings of the superb temple at Udipur in Central India in profusion and delicacy of sculpture; the forms of the mouldings, also, were apparently very beautiful; some of the curves appear to have been parabolic or elliptic—not circular; a remarkably fine one reduced from a facsimile impression is shown in plate.

The temples were certainly adorned internally with pilasters, sculptured as in the examples of Central India; and from the mutilated remains of an elephant statue lying among the ruins, I infer that, like the superb temples of Khajurâha, these temples were also adorned with elephant statues projecting from corners and salient points of the tower; there are also several fragments sculptured with the horseshoe pattern, as in the main body of the towers of the main temples at Khajurâha; of pillars not one exists. Such convenient articles cannot be expected to be left lying about when close to them stands a large flourishing village (one stands within two miles of the ruins on the north side of the river, and has several pakka houses in it, and one on the same side of the river two miles off, also with pakka houses in it); but of statues a few mutilated ones still exist; one is an eight-armed female slaying the buffalo-demon; another is a lingam and its argha; a third, curiously enough, is the architrave of a doorway, with a seated figure, like Buddha, with a halo sculptured round his head; this last is evidently Buddhist, and being on the architrave, proves the existence of a Buddhist temple, side by side with Brahmanical Saivic temples.

The largest temple of the group here was clearly a Saivic temple; the lingam and argha are still *in situ;* the argha is cut on a square large stone, ornamented with mouldings on its vertical faces: this temple faced east, as the spout of the argha, which is usually on the right hand side, points north; to the west of the great temple, about 100 feet off, are the ruins of a small temple, with the mutilated figure of a large nandi, and of others to the north and south of the large temple, as well as to the north-east and north-west, and to the east; of these all appear to have been small ones, and probably subordinate to the great central Saivic one; there ought properly to have been temples to the south-east and south-west also, but I noticed no ruins in those parts ; possibly they have been quite removed.

The temple to the north appears to have been larger than the others ; among its ruins is a slab, the spandrel apparently of a false arch representing a horse or a donkey saddled ; this is probably meant to represent the Kâlkiavatâr ; the existence of an arched spandrel does not bring down the age of the temple to post-Muhammadan times, as the temples at Khajurâha and at Pathari and elsewhere have false arch-ribs to give apparent support to the centre of the great entrance architrave. The mouldings of this temple were particularly old, judging from the fragments ; for there is literally in the whole place not one single stone left standing on another *in situ*, and most of the squared blocks have got carried off long ago.

About 200 feet east of the great temple are the ruins of the second largest temple in the place. All the temples here appear to have been profusely ornamented with sculpture, and the number of amalakas and half-amalakas lying about, with their variety of sizes, shews that each tower rose up majestically out of a cluster of attached flat towers, as at Khajurâha and elsewhere ; the large temple had also mahamandapas and antaralas and porticos ; in short, were complete temples, as at Khajurâha. There were altogether 16 mounds, large and small, all within a space of about quarter of a mile wide by half-mile in length.

To the east and west of the great collection of temples, and half a mile off on either side, on the banks of the river, are other mounds of ruins of temples ; further east, are some few more ; further west, immediately on the edge of the river, a long line of bare rocks juts out ; on these are sculptured numerous arghas, lingams, and figures. The river eddies have cut the rocks here into curious holes.

Near to, and east of, the largest temple on the vertical face of a ledge of rock on the west bank of the little rivulet that murmurs down, are cut two lines of inscription, mediæval nagiri ; in the first line mention is made of Chichitagara, which I take to be the original of modern Chechgaongarh, or Chichinga, and in the second line is mention of Srayaki Rachhabansidra, shewing clearly that there were Jain or Srâwaki temples here ; the carved architrave representing seated a figure with the halo is therefore probably a relic of the Jain temple. On the flat rock alone are cut numerous arghas, lingams, charanas, and figures, male, female, &c., all rather rudely.

Tradition ascribes the temples here, and indeed in the vicinity generally, to one Maheswar Raja. This Raja is said to have been of the same caste as the Ghatwâls of this day of Katrás.

BILONJA.

Bilonja is a small, but important and rising, village, about two miles south of the ruins of Chechgaongarh; here are two modern temples, not yet finished, and several old statues; among these, one is a naked Jain statue, one is of a two-armed female, some others are of no interest. These statues are said to have been obtained partly from the ruins of Chechgaongarh, and partly from the ruins of a large temple once existing to the east of, and just outside, the village of Bilonja. This temple is said to have been very large and complete, and to have been known as the Nava Ratna, from having nine pinnacles. Out of its ruins the modern temples are avowedly built; of it no trace but a low mound now remains. Close to it is another large mound, about 400 feet long by 100 feet wide; it is known as the garh or fort; below it, and to the north of it, is a large tank.

In the village are some plain pillars of the form of those at Hasra, near Bishanpur Tandwa, or Kawá Dol.

The temples now being built are to Durga and to Damodara. Durga is worshipped by the people here for the sake of getting children, and Damodara (a form of Vishnu) to obtain mokhsha. As the people of these parts are mostly of the Kol and Sântal families, it appears that the meaning now attached to Damodara by the Brahmans, *viz.*, a form of Vishnu, is not the original meaning under which Damodara was worshipped; I rather consider that it was the river itself that was worshipped, for it is well known that the Sântals do not consider the spirits of their ancestors as at rest till their bones have been thrown into the great river. The word *mokhsha*, too, appears a relic of Buddhist or Jaina doctrines.

Half a mile north-east of Bilonja is a tank, with some statues on its banks; the place is known as Kalyánithan; there are numerous cut stones and statues of Ganeça and of the eight-armed Devi slaying the buffalo, which are worshipped. There evidently once stood on the banks of this tank one or two Saivic temples.

TUGRI.

One mile north-east of Bilonja, in the Tugri village, are numerous cut stones, used as foundations of huts, several of them sculptured.

BHATBINOR.

Three miles east of this is the small village of Bhatbinor; here are the ruins of large Saivic temples of cut stone, but probably plain, as I saw but few sculptured stones.

ALWARA.

At Alwara, a short distance to the north-east, are the ruins of a large Buddhist temple; part of the architrave and door jambs exist, and on the former is sculptured Buddha seated; it is a draped figure; the place is now known as Mahadevasthan, and a small rounded stone partially buried is the object of worship.

There are along the banks of the river between Alwara and Chechgaongarh a few mounds, evidently the ruins of temples.

Annual fairs are held at Bilonja, at Alwara, and at Chechgaongarh, on the full moon of Vaisakha, on the Sangkranta of Chait, and on the Barani festival, respectively.

DARIKA.

Three miles south-west of the ruins at Chechgaongarh is the village of Darika, or Dandika, with several tanks and a few ruins: the principal ruin there is outside the village on a small mound; it is that of a large temple; the cell is still entire internally, but the roof has long ago gone, as also the mouldings outside; the architrave over the entrance is a plain roughish slab, and is apparently not the original one; the door jambs are ornamented with plain, but deep, lines; the ruins of the mahamandapa lie scattered in front. Among the fragments of sculpture is a four-armed goddess, with a high head-dress, holding a sword and trident in two hands, two others being mutilated; she has large earrings. There is also the fragment of a lion, which appears to have projected out into the air from the tower roof, as in the temples at Barâkar.

The tower roof of the temple was surmounted by an urn, the fragment of one of the minor pinnacles shews this: the temple was built of cut stone without any cement, the stones carefully set so as to break joint; the ornamentation consisted exclusively of plain square, or angular mouldings, as there is not a single curved moulding in the ruins: the pillars which supported the roof of the mahamandapa were plain octagonal, somewhat like the octagonal pillars at Baijnâth.

Half a mile to the east of Chandra is a square pillar, carved at the end into the fore part of an elephant, and having a lingam carved on one side; the latter, evidently after its original purpose had been forgotten, and it had become a pillar; it is set up apparently as a boundary mark; it is interesting, as it is clearly a stone from the basement of a richly sculptured temple, where it was inserted in a horizontal position, with the end projecting out of the face of the building and cut into the shape of the forepart of an elephant, as in the examples at Khajurâha; the temple, therefore, to which it belonged must have had at least a row of boldly projecting elephants' heads as one of the ornamental lines of the basement. I could, however, neither see nor hear of any temple in the vicinity from which the stone could have been brought.

At the first village beyond Chandan Kyári is a statue of one of the Jain heriarchs in black basalt; he is represented seated cross-legged in the usual fashion, and on his pedestal is the bull symbol. It is on the banks of a large, now dry, tank, near the old road from Midnapùr to Benares, which passes through Chás and Párá.

PÁRÁ.

Close to Párá, about half mile to the west of the present village, in a field, is a small inscribed statue of a female on a lion; she is six-armed, of which four are now missing; on two sides of the lion are two pigs, and over them two elephants on each side, one large and one small; the inscription reads, "Sri Venábásini Sri Char" * * * * * &c.; the inscription is in bad order; it evidently records the name of the donor, a private individual apparently, and a worshipper of the charana (sacred feet) of the goddess: the fish emblem occupies the centre of the canopy over the head of the statue; I infer it, therefore, to be Vaishnavic; she is dressed in a short boddice and the sári, with the loose end gathered up and left hanging in folds in front, like the dhotis of the better class of people in Bengal at this day.

Párá contains several temples, most of which are comparatively recent; the one at the extreme west end is a curious and not inelegant building; it is clearly post-Muhammadan, but not of recent date; the roofs are all of overlapping courses, although the arches supporting them are true arches. There are also some brick temples, of probably the same age, in the village; these, but especially the Rádhárâman temple, are profusely ornamented with moulded and cut brick; the minute tracery, executed in such a soft material as brick, exposed to the weather, is in wonderful preservation, and shows how much can be done in this material at little cost; photographs of both temples have been taken, and are worth studying.

The most ancient and interesting objects here are, however, two temples, to the east of, and just outside, the village; one is of brick, the other of a soft kind of stone; both are much weather-beaten and partially broken, but such portions as still exist are interesting.

The stone temple was once a large and complete temple; traces of the foundations of the mahamandapa can still be seen, but only the tower portion containing the sanctum is standing now; this portion was once profusely ornamented with mouldings and sculpture, but the weather has worn away the stone (a very soft sandstone) so much, that the correct outline of the mouldings can nowhere be made out. A curious peculiarity of the mouldings of the temple, and indeed of temples of this part of Bengal in general, is, that at intervals the mouldings are interrupted by thin spaces left projecting, showing that the mouldings were cut after the temples were completely built up plain, generally; the septa interrupting the line of mouldings are solid, but in this temple the mouldings were so bold, that they have found it possible to perforate the septa at the back, and thus carry through the mouldings. This sketch shows the appearance of one where the cross shading represents the mouldings in section; the single shading represents the septum in elevation, and the blank B the portion hollowed through. The faces A of the septa, which are wide, were profusely and delicately sculptured into chaityas, statues, processions, battle scenes, &c.; at present only a few half-worn ones exist to show what they were originally.

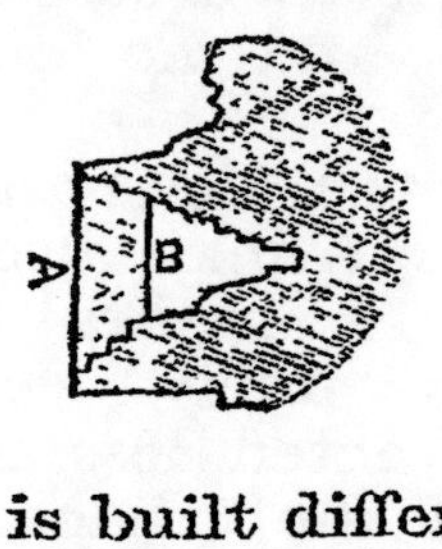

It will be seen from the photograph that the upper portion of the tower of this temple is built differently to the lower, both in material and execution, being of coarse stone (granite probably) plain cut; it will also be seen that the front or entrance is quite plain;

these are clearly due to subsequent repair; in the front portion, not only does the plain portion not fit the ornamental part behind, but there is used, besides stones of various kinds, brick also, to fill in odd spaces; the stone, however, is set dry without any mortar, and this leads me to assign to the repair some antiquity; certainly the repair was not executed within the memory of any living man, nor does tradition say anything about it. I conclude, therefore, as the repair is evidently post-Muhammadan, though of an early period, that it was executed during the time that Mân Singh, as Akbar's General, exercised supreme authority in these parts.

The temple enshrines a statue of fine black stone; it is of Lakshmi, and is two-armed; two elephants are sculptured as holding garlands over her head; she has lost her nose, but is otherwise in excellent preservation, and rivals the fine sculptures of Lakhisarai and its neighbourhood; there is a silly legend to account for the loss of the nose, which appears to me to have really been lost through strokes of Muhammadan axes or sabres before the Hindu General Mân Singh was sent as Chief in these parts.

A coat of plaster once covered the temple; and as the plaster could not have been put on when the temple was in good condition, from the circumstance that in some portions where the plaster still exists the stone underneath is nevertheless weather-worn, I infer that it was put on when the repairs were executed, so as to give a uniform look to the old and new portions; it has, however, long ago disappeared, being now found only in sheltered corners.

The lower portion of the temple is now buried to a depth of probably 3 feet underground.

An inscription was said to have existed in the temple, but had dropped out long ago, and remained uncared for a long time; it is, however, not to be seen now, and no one knows anything about it.

Close to it stands the brick temple; this temple is also old, perhaps older than the stone one; the bricks used measure more than 17 inches long by over 11 inches in width, and are all set in mud; they appear fairly well burnt, and well shaped, and the weather has acted less on them than on the apparently harder stone of the adjacent temple; the temple now stands apparently on a high plinth, but this plinth or basement is a later addition, made most probably to secure the temple from tumbling down, through weakening, by saltpetre or the weather, of the lowest courses; it is, therefore, merely a sort of envelope to the lower portion of the temple, which is, however, by this means completely hidden from view, and it is, therefore, impossible to ascertain the forms of the mouldings of the lower part of the temple without removing it,—a proceeding not to be attempted, as the temple has jealous pujaris in attendance. From an examination of the line of junction of the temple and its outer casing or plinth, it is seen that the lower part of the original temple had become very insecure from the removal or disintegration of the lower courses of bricks; this examination made in front, further shows that the temple did not consist originally of only a cell, but that it had a mandapa in front besides, of which now no traces remain, a huge pipar tree having monopolised the ground which the mandapa once occupied; the plinth or casing is of brick set in mortar, the temple itself being, as stated, of brick set in mud.

The entrance to the lower portion now existing is, as usual, cut up into two portions,—a lower rectangular doorway proper, and an upper pentagonal illuminating window, by a stone door-frame inserted in the opening; the upper portion, when it begins narrowing, does so by the usual expedient of overlapping courses; there is no trace of any arching whatever:—unlike the temples at Buddha Gáyá, and at Konch, the cell has but one roof, being the tall pyramidal roof formed by the tower itself; this is as it should be, for, as I have shown, the inner vaulted roofs of the temples at Buddha Gáyá and at Konch were put in afterwards, and, in the former case, for a special purpose.

The temple enshrines a ten-armed female statue.

The temple was at one time plastered throughout, but the peeling off of the plaster in most places, while it is intact in others, shows that it was put on afterwards; the temple appears to have originally had no coat of plaster, for the bricks forming the facing all round are carefully smoothed, cut and sculptured; and so minutely was the carving done, that a space 1 inch square shows sculptured two tiny bells, their ropes, and the twist of the several strands of the ropes clearly made out,—so that, nothing need have been added in the way of sculpture, in an external coat of plaster; but what conclusively proves the later date of the plaster coat is the circumstance that the sculptured figures, executed in the plaster coat, do not correspond to the underlying sculpture in the brick face itself; the plaster, therefore, is a later addition, and I would attribute it to the same period as the repairs of the stone temple, *i.e.*, to the time of Mân Singh, Akbar's General.

The forms of the towers, both of this and of the adjacent stone one, are very graceful; the upper portion of the tower of this one is broken, and it appears likely to be soon destroyed through the growth of trees, which are allowed to take root and flourish without hindrance.

Close to, and to the south-west of, this temple is a large mound, on which, and about which, lie several tapering plain pillars; this mound was clearly once the site of a large temple, larger than the existing ones. At the east end of the mound still stand two pilasters, with plain square mouldings; they measure 28 inches in width by 16 inches in thickness. Tradition says they are the side supports on which the trunnions of a *dhenki* used to work, the said *dhenki* having been set up by an evil Rankini, who was fond of human flesh, which she used to pound in this *dhenki;* and one of the long stone pillars, lying at the foot of the mound, is pointed out as the *dhenki* beam; it is said that, by agreement with the Raja, she was allowed one human victim daily. One day a poor cowherd, on returning with his cows to his master's house, saw his master and mistress crying bitterly; and ascertaining on inquiry the cause to be that one of them was to be made over to the ogress, he volunteered to go instead, stipulating only that he should be immediately furnished with some gram made of iron and some ordinary gram: armed with these, the man and his two dogs went to the temple and waited; presently in came the Rankini, and was about to seize him, when he said—"Hold, before you eat me, or I eat you, let us make a trial of strength: here is a handful of gram for you, and here is one for me, whichever of us two finishes eating the gram first, shall also eat the other." The Rankini agreed, but vainly tried to masticate the iron gram she had received, while the cowherd soon got through his share, and made as if he would begin on her next: terrified, the Rankini rent the temple and ran out, pursued by the cowherd and his two dogs; the Rankini fled to Dhalbhum, where, seeing a washerman washing at the river, she begged him to hide her, promising him the Káj as recompense; the man hid her under his "pat" (the piece of wood they beat the cloth on), and the cowherd, after a fruitless search, was returning with his two dogs, when, in passing through the

Baghal forest, near the village of Bagháljá, he and his dogs were turned into stone, and exist to this day! In proof of the truth of this legend, they point to the Rajas of Dhalbhum, who are said to be dhobis by caste, and who are notorious for having practised human sacrifices, till very recent times, in honor, it is said, of this very Rankini, who became their tutelary deity and the principal object of worship in the country; her temple is said (and the site is pointed out at Sarangarh, near Ambikanagar) to have existed till within the last few years, and to have been regularly supplied with human victims till it was destroyed by the British authorities.

The petrified cowherd is nothing more or less than a Sati pillar, standing by itself, in the Bagháljá forest (scrub jangal), near the Bagháljá village; it is clear that the name of the village and of the jangal has suggested the identification of the Sati pillar (the real purpose of which was forgotten) with the petrified cowherd; the dogs are said also to be there, but one of them is certainly a lion from some temple, and the other is perhaps another from the same, or some other temple: the Sati pillar is now worshipped, if plenteous libations of milk and ghi be any criterion of worship. The Bagháljá village is a couple or 3 miles off the road, between Kotrá and Jhaprá.

Párá is traditionally said to have been the seat of the Rajas, and is said to have possessed 52 tanks: one version says in Párá there are 6 coris of pokhars and 9 coris (scores) of garhwas (small ponds); there are numerous tanks and hollows to this day, and the temples noticed above stand close to a large one, and not far from several; but they are mostly either dry, or becoming rapidly choked up.

The temple of Rádhárámau in the village noticed before, is said to have been built by one Purshottam Dás from Bindrában; his tomb (chhatri rather) faces the temple; the object of worship is a black two-armed male statue, 3 feet high. The founder having enshrined the statue, and provided for its maintenance, wished to return to his country, and told the statue so, but it replied—"Since you have brought me away, this is your native country; now therefore remain here." The mahant pleaded that he had no sons, and could get none unless he returned home, to perform his funeral obsequies, but the statue at once offered to do it himself; hence of all offerings to the statue the first share is set aside as an offering to the deceased mahant. Purshottam Dás is said to have built the temple during the viceroyalty of Mân

Singh, who is said to have built the curious stone temple noticed at the west end of the village; to him I have also attributed the repairs of the two great temples of brick and stone, and, on the whole, it appears that the later flourishing days of Párá were during or about the period he exercised sway as Akbar's General in these parts.

About 8 miles north by a little east of Párá, near the large village of Chailyámá, is the village of Bándá; here is a stone temple in the middle of some low jangal; in plan, it resembles the temples of Barâkar, and, like them, it consists of a single cell; like them, too, it once had a mandapa, in front of which the fragments, misarranged into a long pillared hall, still exist, but it differs from them in many particulars; the front of the temple has three tiers of openings, first and lowest the entrance of the sanctum, leading as usual into a square chamber, roofed over with a flat roof; over this, a smaller opening leading into a small chamber, whose floor forms the roof of the sanctum; this opening is further surmounted by another opening, which again leads into another chamber, whose floor forms the roof of the next lower one.

As the chambers and their several floors and roofs are not later additions, but form essential, and indeed constructively essential, portions of the original design, the several openings above the doorway of the sanctum cannot be, and never could have been, intended as illuminating windows; this temple, and temples of this class, differ, therefore, in a vital point from the Magadha type of temples, and are not amenable to the laws that govern them in the matter of the openings. This may be perceived at a glance from the photograph, where the three openings are in proportions widely different to the three openings of the Buddha Gáyá temple. Indeed, the Buddha Gáyá temple has three openings, only because later repairs and alterers found it expedient to cut up the two tall upper openings, which properly should not be divided into two portions, as I have shown before. What law, however, governs the size and disposition of the openings in this class of temples, I am unable to state; examples of temples with three tiers of openings are extremely rare, and from one or two examples a law cannot safely be deduced.

The walls of temples of this type being very thin, as may be seen from plans, and more impressively from the photograph of a half-broken temple at Telkupi, and the towers, having these thin walls as sides, being very high, it became a constructive necessity to tie the walls together at intervals, to give the necessary rigidity and stability to the tower; this is most easily, economically, and unobtrusively done by floors extending across, internally cutting up the tall tower into a number of more stable low chambers, and, as may be seen, this has been the expedient universally adopted; constructively, therefore, at least one, and preferably several, floors, extending across the tower, opening internally, is a necessity; the tiers of openings over the entrance are also constructively necessary, to relieve the lowest architrave from the weight of a great mass of superincumbent masonry; and where this expedient has not been adopted, failure has resulted, as may be seen from the temples of Central India and elsewhere; more of which have failed through the single fault of the architrave giving way, than through all other natural causes put together.

But, though constructively correct, it cannot be denied that the front elevation of the temple under discussion is any thing but beautiful; the temple has, it is true, lost the mahamandapa, the roof of which would have been, and was probably designed with a special view to hide away these ugly openings; but how this was effected in this particular temple, where the openings extend a long way up, is doubtful. Remembering, however, that the numerous pillars, now built into a long pillared hall in front, are not likely to have been *brought from elsewhere* for the purpose, but must have been lying on the spot, and *therefore* belonged to the mahamandapa, &c., of the temple, I am inclined to think that the mahamandapa of this temple was of much more than the usual size, and, therefore, had necessarily a larger and higher roof,—high enough to keep the openings out of sight. Whether the temple, as a whole, looked well or ill with this overgrown mahamandapa, is a question which it would be idle to attempt answering, till we can find out the size of the mahamandapa,—a desideratum we do not now possess.

The temple is poor in ornamentation, and the pillars forming the colonnade in front are all quite plain, nor are the mouldings of the basement bold or elegant; it is interesting chiefly as being singular in the elevation of its present façade.

TELKUPI.

About four miles north-east of this place, on the south bank of the Damuda river, is the village of Telkupi, containing, perhaps, the finest and largest number of temples within a small space that is to be found in the Chutia Nâgpur Circle in Bengal. They are in three groups, the largest being to the north by a little east of the village and on the brink of the river; a second group close to the village and somewhat to its west, and a third group within the south-east end of the village. I begin with the first group.

No. 1, or the most northerly temple, consists of a single cell; it faces the south; there is no emblem or figure over the entrance doorway; the object of worship inside is a lingam. The floor of the cell is about two feet below the sill of the entrance, which is itself two feet below the present ground-level. The material is cut stone; workmanship plain, but good; no mortar has been used in bedding the stones, which are carefully set dry; there is not much ornamentation, such as there is consisting of plain lines and mouldings; the upper portion of the temple is nearly entire.

No. 2 faces east. Lakshmi is sculptured over the entrance, with two elephants pouring water over her head. The floor within the cell is buried beneath accumulations of earth and sand, which rise to within six inches of the sill of the entrance; this itself is one and half feet below the present ground-level; the object of worship inside is a lingam; the upper portion of the temple is broken; in material and execution it resembles No. 1.

No. 3, similar to No. 2, but buried deeper under rubbish, the sill of the entrance being buried four feet below accumulated rubbish; the floor is buried deep, nearly six feet in earth and rubbish; object of worship inside a lingam; it faces west; the top is gone.

No. 4 faces east; a lotus is sculptured over the entrance; the object of worship inside is a four-armed statue of Vishnu, in good preservation, with the shell, discus, &c. The temple is much ruined; in material, execution, and other particulars it resembles the others.

No. 5 faces east, and is behind No. 4; Ganeça over doorway; resembles the others in details; the top of the temple has disappeared.

No. 6 is a large temple, facing west; it consists at present of a sanctum, an antarala in the thickness of the front wall of the sanctum and the back wall of the mahamandapa, a mahamandapa, an ardhamandapa, and a portico. The sanctum with its tower roof is entire, but the inner roof of the sanctum, being the floor of the upper chamber, is broken; the chamber above the sanctum has no opening, and therefore is, and always was, inaccessible; the roof proper of the sanctum (now broken) was formed of overlapping stones; the original architrave over the entrance no longer exists, having been replaced at some period by a plain one; this, too, failed, and others were successively put in, till, at this moment, there are four door frames, one within another, thus reducing the original width and height of the entrance considerably; the jambs which were afterwards put in are not all entire pillars, but are made up of miscellaneous fragments, put together so as to make up the required height.

The mahamandapa was roofed also by overlapping courses of stones; the square corners were gradually rounded off by successive small portions, till it formed an octagon, over which the circular roof proper rested; the roof has long ago tumbled in, but the corners are yet intact, and the constructive expedient used may be seen in the photograph; the circular roof was further supported, as is done in several instances elsewhere, by four pillars, placed as a square in the centre of the mahamandapa; these pillars are quite plain; the material and execution of the portion external to the sanctum and antarala differ from those of the sanctum, being of plain, indeed coarsely-dressed, granite, while the sanctum is of finely cut and smoothed sandstone; the line of junction, too, of the mahamandapa and of the sanctum is quite distinct, proving clearly that the mahamandapa is a subsequent addition, the original temple having consisted of the sanctum and its attached vestibule alone; which, far from having the manifestly unfinished appearance of the façades of the Barâkar temples, has, independently of the subsequently added mahamandapa, a finished façade, the portion over the entrance being provided with regular freize, and cornice, and mouldings and sculpture, all which would necessarily be hidden by the roof and architraves of the later added mahamandapa.

Externally, the tower is adorned with sculpture and mouldings, carefully and finely cut in the stone itself. At some subsequent period the tower appears to have received externally a coat of plaster, in which was sculptured devices, ornaments, and figures different to that in the stone below, proving clearly that the original stone tower was not covered with plaster when first built. Over this coat of plaster was put on, at a still later period, a second coat, and on this was sculptured figures, ornaments, and devices differing from either of the previous ones. The ornamentation executed in the plaster coat resembles that used in the plaster coating put on the brick temple at Párá, and therefore presumably of the same age, that is, of the time of Mân Singh, to whom, therefore, I ascribe the extensive repairs and alterations executed in this temple, and in others of this group.

No. 7, a small temple, single cell, faces north; over the entrance Ganeça; the object of worship inside is a two-armed statue, holding a lotus in each hand, being the usual form of statues of Aditya, or the Sun: he has a high head-dress, bound by a fillet, flying horizontally outwards at the sides; four subordinate figures on each side, and two flying figures at the two upper corners, complete the sculpture. The temple, in material and execution, resembles No. 1.

No. 8 is a large temple, facing east: this, like the others, once consisted of the cell alone, but has had a large and very massively built and heavily roofed mahamandapa added on afterwards, the junction being quite distinct. In style, also, the tower and the mahamandapa differ, the tower being plainly, but tastefully, ornamented with sculpture and mouldings, the other being quite plain; the figure of Ganeça is sculptured over the entrances both of the original sanctum and of the later mandapa; the temple therefore was, and has always been, Saivic.

The cell has an inner low roof, as usual, of overlapping stones; the mahamandapa has a roof of overlapping stones also; the object of worship in the cell is a lingam.

The mahamandapa appears somewhat too large for the sanctum behind, and the apparent inequality is increased by the massive heavy style of the former contrasting with the lighter tower behind; altogether, the composition has not been so happily designed as it might have been, though it is probably better than the combination noticed in temple No. 6, the disproportion there being greater.

A wall of plain rough cut granite runs from the back of the temple No. 6 to the façade of No. 8, and is continued beyond the façade on the other side; this wall is pierced with a small true, arched opening; the wall at the opening is raised higher than elsewhere, and the projecting high piece is curved on top, as is often done in buildings in Lower Bengal. The occurrence of the true arch proves the wall to be a post-Muhammadan addition; and as it resembles in details of material and execution the mahamandapa of the temple, I regard both as of the same date, built most probably by, or in the time of, Rájá Mân Singh.

No. 9 is a small temple, facing north; a lotus is sculptured over the entrance; the temple consists of only the cell or sanctum, which enshrines a four-armed Vaishnavic statue; the roof of the temple is very heavy, being plain pyramidal in form, cut up into few and massive steps, and resembling the roof of the temple of Kalyâneswari at Devisthan; the sculpture and lines of the doorway are very shallow, and quite unlike that of the other temples described: the shallowness I take as a proof of its late age. The enshrined statue inside does not face the door, but occupies the eastern side of the cell; either, therefore, the statue has been removed, or the entrance has been changed. As there is a small niche in the west wall, it is not improbable that this niche is the present representative of the old doorway, which once existed on this side; this would make the present entrance on the north a late alteration, an inference justified by its shallow carving; the roof of the temple internally is of overlapping stones.

No. 10 is a large temple, faces west, and consists of the sanctum and its attendant portico, vestibule, mandapa, &c. The mandapa had three entrances, of which the north one is now closed; a lotus is sculptured over the outer entrance, but the object of worship inside is a lingam; the sanctum is surmounted, not by the usual graceful tower, but by an almost straight-sided spire, the native ugliness of which is heightened by its surface being cut up into seven spaces by plain projecting bands. The roof of the mahamandapa is a low pyramid, like that of the Kalyâneswari temple, or of temple No. 9, divided in three steps by bands and recessed mouldings. The temple is apparently much more modern than the other temples here, except perhaps No. 9, and may date at earliest to the same period as the additions and alterations in the other temples noticed before, but is probably still later. The spire resembles the spire of the temples at Baijnâth.

No. 11 is a small temple, facing east; Ganeça sculptured over entrance; within, are an argha without the lingam, and a statue of Aditya, the last being evidently an intruder. In material, ornamentation, and execution the temple resembles No. 1. The upper part of the tower is broken.

No. 12 resembles No. 11; it faces east, and enshrines a lingam and argha; Ganeça over entrance.

No. 13 resembles Nos. 11 and 12; has Ganeça over the doorway, which faces west.

This is the last temple, still in tolerable order. Besides these, which may fairly be considered as standing, there are numerous ones, more or less ruined, some being broken down to the level of the roof of the sanctum, others still more, while of many a confused heap of cut stone is all that remains. There were still others whose only remains are a number of lingams, arghas, and cut stone in the bed of the river. One temple disappeared into the river in the interval between my first and my present visit to the place—a period of little over five years only.

It appears that the banks of the river extended up to, and beyond, a long line of rocks that now jut out in the bed of the river parallel to the line of bank, and a hundred yards off. The builders that chose the site of the temple appear evidently to have done their best in selecting what appeared a safe spot on the river banks, as the line of rocks must then have formed an indestructible natural revetment of the river face, but they did not reckon on the river cutting its way behind the invincible revetment, and rushing through their temples; they erred in not ascertaining, with all possible care, the highest flood-level of the river—an error but too common among the engineers even at this day. In ordinary years, the flood seldom reaches the top of the high banks, and inquiry, unless very carefully made, would fail to show that in certain years the flood rushes with mad fury, four feet deep, through the very court-yards, and into the cells of the temples on the highest spots, while the temples lower down are buried the whole depth of the entrance doorways.

Temple No. 10 is traditionally said to have been thus buried in sand almost up to the eaves of the tower roof, and the heaps now lying outside are pointed out as the identical sand dug out of the mandapa, the cell, and the courtyard of the temple. I made enquiries regarding the flood-level, but found only one man in the village that was of sufficient age when it occurred, to remember it, and willing to inform me. I have heard engineers make disparaging comments on what they consider the excessive waterway given to the bridge over the Barâkar, a tributary of the Damuda, but let them enquire of old people regarding the flood of that year on which the calculations of the waterway of the bridge are based, and they will find that the bridge is none too large.

If the modern pushing batch of young engineers, who have duly served through their "articles," were as particular in ascertaining the highest known floods of the rivers they presume to bridge, as the "old fogies" that designed the Barâkar bridge, we should hear of fewer bridges washed away every year. Throughout the length and breadth of Chutia Nâgpur and Bihâr (the Bihâr old district) I have, from personal enquiry, ascertained that that year (I forget the year now) on records of the flood of which the Barâkar bridge waterway was calculated was a year of such a terrific flood, that even people who remember it will not, when desired to point out the highest flood-level, point to the flood mark of that year, but to the next highest. Let them, however, be asked point-blank about the flood of that year, and the inquirer will then see that his informant did not point out the highest known flood-level, from an impression that it was such a very rare occurrence as to be very unlikely to happen again ; but what *has* happened once may happen again, at however long an interval, and for works intended to be permanent should, if possible, be provided against.

Besides the temples, there are numerous miniature temples, —things that, if Buddhist, would be called votive stupas or votive chaityas, but being Brahmanical, must, I suppose, be called votive sivalas; some are miniature single-cell temples (solid of course), others are pillars, most probably sati monuments, and sculptured on one face with the lingam and argha, or other devices. None are inscribed.

One half-ruined temple now stands on the very brink of the perpendicular wall of clay, which here forms the river bank, and must tumble in next rains. In my last visit I saw some wells exposed by the river cutting away the earth on one face of it; these wells were built of brick set without cement; at intervals bands of bricks set on edge formed the well ring, instead of being set on their beds as usual; in these bands the bricks were set with narrow intervals between them, and not touching at their inner edges. I was inclined to think that they were the foundations of temples, but am now of opinion they were wells, the rings of bricks on edge, set with narrow slits between them, being obviously meant to allow of a free percolation of water into the well; and although *now*, wells in the positions I saw would be superfluous, or rather absurd, they were perhaps not quite unnecessary when the river ran a hundred yards further off, and was difficult of approach by reason of the rocks, which rose from the bed and formed a revetment not easily descended.

Of the other groups of temples, the temple nearest to the group described is almost entire and in excellent order; the top of the tower is crowned as usual by the amalaka, over which rises an urn-shaped stone finial, as in the temples at Barâkar; this temple is deserted. Lakshmi, with elephants pouring water over her, is sculptured over the entrance, and in the interior is a finely executed statue.

To the right and about 1,000 feet south is another temple, also with Lakshmi over the entrance; a four-armed statue of Vishnu is enshrined in the sanctum.

About a quarter mile east of this, another temple, also single-cell, faces north, and has sculptured over the entrance a figure seated, with an elephant raising his trunk over the figure's head; it is difficult to tell whether the figure is male or female; it holds a lotus in one hand; the statue inside is of Vishnu, four-armed, in the Narasinha incarnation.

There is, besides these, a broken temple of Vishnu Chaturbhuj. This temple is valuable, from having lost its front, while the other parts are to a great extent almost uninjured, and therefore capable of illustrating effectually the constructive features of this class of temples. See photograph.

Two temples and several statues stand in the east end of the village, not worth detailed description.

Besides these, there are, further south, several detached temples; one of Vishnu or Siva, and close to it a temple to Buddha, with the ruins of a large monastery, in the shape of a large brick mound, close to it: this is, I believe, the only Buddhist temple in the place; it may, however, be Jain, for the sculpture over the entrance, the only clue now visible as to its purpose, is too small and too weather-beaten to show distinctly whether it is, or is not, Jain.

Near these, but standing by itself, on and near a somewhat large mound, is a temple that appears to have been once larger; the entrance of the temple is profusely ornamented with minute sculpture; there are four lines of figures on each side; the first row or line consists of the incarnations of Vishnu, the next of bearded sages, the third of obscene figures, most probably scenes from Krishna's life; the last row is of fancy animals; the temple was clearly Vaishnavic, and Krishna is sculptured over the entrance; he is represented seated on a throne or seat, one leg resting on the ground, the other tucked up and doubled in front, as in sitting cross-legged.

There are, besides these remains, numerous mounds, both of brick and stone, but more of brick; it appears that such brick temples as once existed have all tumbled down, as not one is now standing; some of the mounds are more than 25 feet high; there are also numerous tanks.

Tradition says that the temples here were all built by mahajans or merchants, not by Rájás, and this confirms my inference that the place, as before suggested, rose to importance because it lay on one of the great traffic lines, and at a principal obstacle, *viz.*, the Damuda river.

There are no inscriptions; only two characters were found after much fruitless search—these probably date to the tenth century.

Telkupi is traditionally said to be so named from the circumstance that Rájá Vikramâditya used to come here to rub oil (tel) on his body previous to bathing in the Chhátá Pokhar at Dulmi; natives of Lower Bengal and of these parts, in short of the whole Bengali-speaking districts, invariably rub oil on their bodies previous to bathing; but though the Chhátá Pokhar at Dulmi is nearly 80 miles distant, that does not seem to have ever been looked upon as any way rendering the story ridiculous; however the name may be derived, the place is now, and probably always has been, considered particularly holy, especially by the aboriginal Sântals.

A favorite national song describes in plain, but obscene, language how young girls come here during the great annual mêla, and permit the improper attentions of unknown young men; Colonel Dalton, in describing the customs of the aboriginal tribes in his province, has noticed the improper freedom permitted to young girls before their marriage, but he has not, I believe, noticed the custom, which I was assured by the Sântals themselves (not alone of the vicinity, but even of districts south of Puralya) prevails; this custom is nothing less than a modification of the Babylonian mylitta; every young Sântal woman *must*, I was told (and I was particular in asking), once in her life before marriage permit the improper intimacy of a man, and this place, "Telkupi ghât," as the song has it, is the great place where such improprieties are especially practised. The people of the vicinity said that it was the only place where a young girl was bound to permit once the impropriety, by whomever attempted, of her own nation; but people living further off did not seem to consider that this was the *only* place, though they admitted that it was one of the places, there being others also on the banks of the Damuda river. The girl may, or may not, afterwards marry the man she consorts with here, but the man is not by any means bound to ask her in marriage; the custom is said to have arisen in this way.

On a certain occasion during the annual mêla, a young girl permitted the improper attentions of a young man, and soon afterwards found herself in an interesting condition; vainly she entreated the young man to marry her, and hide her shame; he would not, and her parents came to find it out, and killed her (some say she was not killed). From that day, girls were allowed to do what they liked during the fair at Telkupi, and that which was originally only a permissive custom, has now petrified into a compulsory observance!

The aboriginal races of India are generally, I believe, admitted as Turanian, and there is good reason to believe that the Turanian races formed the substratum of the population of Babylon: the Sântals of India, and the lower classes of the people of Babylon would, therefore, be branches of the same race, and the prevalence among the former, even at this day, of a custom, however modified, which we know prevailed in Babylon, may be more than an accidental coincidence: the speculation is, however, too wide for me to venture on.

PACHET.

About 10 miles to the south-west of Barâkar stands the high solitary hill of Pachet; at its south-eastern foot is the fort of Pachet, once the residence of the Rájás of Pachet, now deserted and in disrepair; the name of this fort is said to be a contraction of Panchakot, and the explanation of the name now given is, that the Rájás of Pachet reigned over five Rájás, but the word clearly means five forts, and I consider the name to have reference rather to the number of walls that defend the citadel—"kot." There are four sets of walls, each within the other, surrounding the kot on the west, south, and east, the north being defended by the hill itself, at the toe of the slope of which the citadel stands; but, beyond the last line of the walls of the fort, tradition says, ran another line of walls, and the positions ascribed to the parts of this wall show that the so-called outermost rampart was nothing else than the natural ridge-lines of the undulating country round the fort; taking this outer natural line of ramparts—if ramparts they can be called,—we have the five sets of walls necessary to explain the name.

The four sets of artificially built walls of the fort are all of earth, and are each defended by deep and wide moats, now filled up in many places; the moats were so connected with the streams descending the sides of the hill, as to keep them always wet, and to this day they always contain some water; in most places the walls, or earthen ramparts, were also ingeniously led so as to form continuations of natural spurs of the hill itself, thus securing the maximum of defensive power with the minimum of labor in throwing them up. In the walls were numerous gates, now mostly gone, and represented by mere gaps in the walls; four gateways, however, of cut stone, in various stages of decay, still exist, and have names; they are named Ánkh Duár, Bâzâr Mahal Duár, or Desbándh Duár, Khoribári Duár, and Duár Bándh; the last is in the best state of preservation; all of them were built in much the same style, *viz.*, the usual Muhammadan style and with true arches, though overlapping arches were also used: some of these gateways served the double purpose of gateways proper and openings for water, and the Duár Bándh still serves the purpose of allowing water to be taken in from the moat outside, when necessary for irrigating the fields within; the fort is very large, the outermost ramparts having a total length of more than five miles, while the traditional outermost defences, *viz.*, the ridge lines round the fort, inclose a space of about 12 square miles, exclusive of the hill itself.

There are several brick remains within the fort, generally inaccessible, either from being surrounded by water or by dense jangal; they are evidently post-Muhammadan, and of no special interest. Moulded and cut brick and terra cotta sculptured tiles have been used in almost every one of them, which are all of the Lower Bengal type of architecture, *viz.*, with curved instead of straight top lines; the curved top lines appear to me more elegant than the straight ones, and are evidently copied from the curved ridge and eave lines of thatched huts. In the Upper Provinces, where the rainfall is scanty compared to Lower Bengal, curved ridge and eaves are not so necessary as in Lower Bengal; here the rainfall is so heavy that, unless an extraordinary thickness of thatch is put on, water invariably leaks through, especially along the corner beams of a chauchálá (four-thatched). It must be clear that when an oblong or a square room is covered by four thatches meeting either in a ridge or in a point, and the thatches (cháls) have all the same inclination, the slope of the roof at the lines of junction of the four thatches is much gentler than elsewhere, and, as a consequence, leaks are more frequent at these than elsewhere; to give to these lines the same, or nearly the same, inclination as the other portions of the roof, the corners have to be lowered; hence the curved outline of the ridge and eave lines.

Upon the side of the hill, and overlooking the fort below, are a number of temples; they are all massively built, and the occurrence of the true dome and the true arch in them stamps them as of the post-Muhammadan period; the great dome of the mahamandapa of the large temple is of an early date, as it is without bulge, and is crowned, not by a foliated cap, but by a small top knot; I ascribe it, therefore, to the period of Mân Singh; the temple is known as Raghunâth's mandir, having been built by a Rájá of that name; an annual fair, lasting one day, is held here.

The gates of the fort had inscribed slabs let in, which would have fixed the date of their erection and the name of the Rájá that reigned then; they are much injured, but enough remains to fix the date of two of the gates,—the Duár Bándh and the Khoribári gate; each slab consists of 6 lines of Bengali characters, and they appear to be duplicates of each other; there is mention of a Sri Vira Hámira, who, we know from other sources, reigned over a large tract of country, extending in the south-west as far as Chátná near Bánkurá; the date is either Samvat 1657 or 1659, the figure in the units place being alone doubtful through wear, which would bring it to about 1600 A. D., when we know Mân Singh, Akbar's General, was Viceroy of Bengal. The fort having thus been proved to date only to Mân Singh, the temples, both on the hill and at the foot, cannot date earlier, and that on the hill cannot, from its style, be of later date.

The legendary accounts of the origin and establishment of Pachet may be thus related.

Anot Lal, Rájá of Kâsipur, was going, with his wife, on a pilgrimage to Jagannath, when the Ráni gave birth to a child in Aruna Vana (the present Pachet). The Rájá and Ráni, unwilling to delay on account of the child, determined to abandon it, thinking that they could easily get other children, while the fruits of the pilgrimage could not be so easily got, so they proceeded on to Thákurdwárá; the fabulous cow, Kapilá Gai, who used to live in Arunban, seeing the child abandoned, took upon herself to feed it with her milk, and thus the child lived on and grew up, and remained in the jangal.

One day a party of hunters, who were looking for game in the forest, saw the child, and carried him off, notwithstanding the resistance of Kapilá Gai, to Páwápur; when he grew up, the people made him Májhi (chief of a clan or village), and finally, when in want of a king, determined to elect him, and he was accordingly elected king of Pargana Chaurasi (Sikhar bhum); they built him the Pachet fort, and named him Jatá Rájá: on the death of the miraculous cow, her tail was found and carried to the Rájá, who used it as an ensign, tying it to his horse; hence he was also called Chánwar bándhá, and the Rájás of Pachet are said to this day to use the cow's tail, or chánwar, as one of their emblems.

Anot Lal had two other sons by another wife; they were named Nayán and Asmán; they invaded Jatá Rájá's domains, and he was forced to fly, but his conquerors, in seeking for him in the jangal, lost their way and perished, and Jatá Rájá returned and reigned peaceably.

Another version says, the child was not deliberately abandoned, but falling accidentally from the elephant on which he was being carried, the Rájá and Ráni left him for dead; then Kapilá Gai came and fed him; she used to live in Kapilá Páhár (the range of hills south of Puralya), and would come daily to feed the child; when the child grew up, he used to wander in the jangal with the cow, and, eventually, he became king, and built Pancha Kot; as he was made king through election by five Rájás, his fort was named Pancha Kot; he was known as the Gaumukhi Rájá. The Rájá had a cowherd, who one day saw a large snake issue from a hole in the hill-side, and the snake vomited forth a brilliant gem that illuminated the whole forest by its light; it fed and then swallowed the gem; then bands of celestial nymphs and musicians came and performed for some time, and finally all vanished. The cowherd related the particulars to the Rájá, who went to see the wonder, and so great an effect had the sight on him, that he returned bereft of speech, and died in two or three years. During his son's reign, the Rájá of Murshidabad invaded the country, and exterminated the entire race of the Rájás of Pachet, except one child, who was saved by the headman of the village of Suri Lachhiá, hiding him in a drum; the child grew up and regained his kingdom, and he is the ancestor of the present Rájás. The cow, turned into stone, still exists at Jhaldia on the Ayodhya hill. As there are remains of Saivic temples in Jhaldia, the petrified cow is most probably a statue of Nandi. Strange enough, the people of Jhaldia itself know nothing about the wonderful petrified cow, which the people in the vicinity of Pachet insist exists there.

KHELAI CHANDI.

Six miles south of Páchet is a group of bare, rocky hills known as the Khelai Chandi hills; a fair is held here annually on the full moon of the month of Paush, and many people collect there; the object of worship there is a local goddess named Khelai Chandi Devi, who is supposed to live on the hills, but to be invisible; she is said to be eight-armed; at midnight she descends the hill, goes to the sacred tank, washes herself, and returns; hence nothing impure is thrown into it, nor do the people presume to bathe in it themselves; vows are made, and the suppliant vows to dig up with his hands (without any tools) a certain quantity of earth from the bed of the tank and carry it up beyond the tank embankment on his head, in case his (or her) wish is fulfilled; and on the mêla day thousands may be seen with tiny baskets scraping up mud from the bed of the tank and carrying it up the embankments; a small temple (modern) stands at the foot of the hill near the tank; it enshrines a white stone sculpture with hands folded in the attitude of prayer; two lions are sculptured on the pedestal; there is no inscription; the temple faces the hill; this statue is worshipped in place of the invisible goddess Khelai Chandi.

CHHORRÁ.

About four miles before reaching Puralya, on the road from Barâkar, is the large village of Chhorrá; here are some ruins of old temples; two temples, partially ruined, still exist, and the stones of numerous others are to be seen used up in the huts of the village; some of the temples were Jain or Buddhist, as numerous votive chaityas with mutilated figures, either of Buddha or of one of the Jain hierarchs, lie in the village, but the greater number were, judging from the remains of sculpture lying about, Brahmanical, and principally Vaishnavic.

PURALYA.

In Puralya, the head-quarters of the district of Mânbhum, are some old remains; about half a mile to the east of the city, on a high open plateau, are the remnants of two temples: one of these must have been large, and the other close to it was small; a fragment of the amalaka that crowned the larger temple lies on the site; it had a diameter of 7 feet; very few squared stones now remain, the greater portion having naturally been removed to be used up in the now rising city.

BALARÂMPUR.

Four miles to the south-east of Puralya is the village of Balarâmpur; here is a temple of the Baijnâth type, and evidently not very old, but built of the materials of an older temple, as may be seen by examining it carefully, when sculptured stone will be seen used along with plain squared ones in the basement of the temple; the older temple, judging from some very plain mouldings in the stone now built into the more recent one, appears to have been very plain, and of no great size; the present temple is built of cut stone and of bricks, the latter of a variety of sizes, and set in mortar composed of earth and lime, not surkhi and lime; the whole was originally plastered, but is now bare; the cell had a mandapa in front, now no longer existing; the three faces of the temple that have no openings in them are adorned with sculptures of miniature temples, of the tall, straight-lined, ungainly Baijnâth pattern; the roofs of the cell and of the attached antarala are formed of overlapping courses of bricks, in successively diminishing squares; the openings were all spanned by true arches, built *partly* of bricks rubbed to a wedge form, but not sufficiently so to form true voissoirs; one of these wedges has by mistake been inserted in an arch upside down; hidden away behind the entrance, and let into the inner wall of the sanctum, is the architrave of the original temple, but without any emblem sculptured on it to show to whom it was dedicated; the mahamandapa, judging from still existing corners, was domed over, the dome resting on corbelled pendentives; the mouldings used appear to have been tame and flat, and the carvings, which still exist, are all shallow; the spire also, though like the Baijnâth ones in outline, is quite plain, its surface not being broken up by ornamental bands; the pillars, or rather the pilasters, still standing on the sides of the entrance into the sanctum, are so remarkable for their elegant massiveness, that I have, notwithstanding their recent age, given a drawing of one. The temple, judging from the variety in the sizes of bricks used, dates probably to after Mân Singh's period.

BURÁM.

Twelve miles west by a little north from Puralya, on the right bank of the Kasai or Kansai river, is the small village and the ruins of Burám. The ruins are on a knoll at the edge of the river; approaching them after crossing the river from the north, the first ruin is a low mound; on this lies a round-ended flat slab with কাঁ ক inscribed; the characters may belong to the ninth or tenth century; the mound is evidently the site of a temple of brick, faced with stone; there are a few other low small mounds of no special interest.

Of the remains that still stand more or less dilapidated, the first, beginning from the south end, is a large flat-topped temple of brick; it faces east, and stands on a mound 11 or 12 feet high, which evidently formed the basement on which the temple stood; the bricks are $18'' \times 12'' \times 2\frac{4}{5}$ inches and $9'' \times 12'' \times 2\frac{4}{5}$ inches, set close without mortar, but with mud cement; a section and other measurements, &c., are given in plate.

The ornamentation, externally, consists of tiers and rows of niches cut on the face and sides and back walls of the tower. As at Buddha Gáyá, there is not, and does not appear to have been, any plaster coating to the temple, as the bricks are all carefully cut and smoothed; the temple faces east; the entrance is of the usual pattern, a rectangle, surmounted by a tall triangular opening of overlapping courses of bricks; the temple consists, and appears to have always consisted, of no more than a single cell, 11 feet 8 inches square; there is consequently no division of the entrance opening into a door proper and an illuminating window; the figure within is a four-armed female seated on a lion, which, therefore, I assume to represent Parvati.

Near this temple lie the ruins of a stone temple; this was built of stone cut carefully and set without mortar throughout; the stone used was a fine close-grained sandstone; the mouldings are plain, but not bold.

Close to it is the top lintel of an entrance, with a groove in its under-face, extending almost the whole length of the stone; the entrance to which it belonged must have been 3 feet 3 inches wide; there is space for a figure of the object of worship in the centre of the architrave, but the figure, if any existed, has long ago been rubbed away under the treatment of laborers sharpening their field implements;

one of the side posts of the door or entrance is still standing close to the architrave, and apparently in its original position; on it is sculptured the fig. ξ; behind, and to its west, lie the ruins of a large stone temple; this temple, therefore, also faced east, and consisted, like the one described, of a single cell, surmounted by a tower roof; the sculpture, or rather the mouldings of the temple, were, judging from the remains, shallow.

To the north of the first brick temple is a smaller one resembling it; the carving and mouldings are here more elaborate; the temple is now plastered and whitewashed, but I consider the plaster to be a later, and probably a very recent, addition; this inference I draw from the circumstance that the ornamentation executed in the plaster coat does not in all parts correspond to the ornamentation cut in the brick below; this last is plainer, but bolder, and therefore of an earlier age; there is, however, no lack of delicate and minute sculpture, although not so profuse or elaborate as in the plaster-coating: an instance of the discrepancy between the sculpture on the brick face and on the plaster coat is to be seen in a row of lotus, &c., flowers. In the brick the centre of the scroll work is a fine delicately executed eight-leaved lotus, while in the plaster coating the lotus is replaced by a tulip-shaped flower: in front of the remains of the sanctum stand the lower stumps of a number of pillars of plain pattern; these were evidently the supports of the roof of the mahamandapa, which once existed; but though a mahamandapa existed, it is clear, from the façade of the sanctum, that the temple as originally built consisted solely of the cell, the mahamandapa having been subsequently added; and this view is rendered almost certain by the circumstance, that the stumps of the pillars show that they were taken from other stone temples, of which several once existed, and which have left, as proofs of their existence, a number of mounds.

Near this, and to the north of the second ruined stone temple, and in line with it and with the first brick temple, is the ruin of another stone temple; the material and ornamentation are similar to those in the other temple; the cell exists entire and is 8½ feet square. So much of its entrance as still exists shows it to have been of the usual type of a rectangle, surmounted by a triangle, the diminution being effected by overlapping the courses of stones.

To the east of the second brick temple is a figure of Parvati, four-armed, with a small figure of Ganeça to its right, and a female figure to its left; it is half-buried; in execution and style it resembles the sculptures at Dulmi, and I therefore ascribe it to the same age; it formed the object of worship in a small temple, which faced north, and of which the low mound in which the statue, if buried, is all that now remains.

To the east of this are the ruins of a small brick temple, which faced north (the other brick temples face east); there is in the ruins and still *in situ* a life-size sculpture of the eight-armed Durgâ slaying the Maheshâsur; this is the finest piece of sculpture in the place, and fully equals in every respect the similar sculpture at Dulmi, and is a close approach to the sculptures at Lakhisarai; it is in excellent preservation; its age I consider to be the same as of the Dulmi sculptures; it is in better preservation than the sister sculpture at Dulmi.

A few other mounds of no special interest exist; the last brick temple to the north-west of all others resembles them, but is plainer; it was plastered, and the ornamentation on the plaster is profuse and elaborate; the plaster, however, is clearly an after-addition; the temple was Saivic, as evidenced by a lingam and argha in the sanctum.

A few other mounds of no special interest exist.

A remarkable circumstance here is, that *all* the temples without exception, the object of which can now be ascertained, appear to have been Saivic; there is no Vaishnavic or other sculpture at all in the whole place; there must, therefore, have been a large and rich, and probably intolerant, Saivic establishment here.

Four miles south-east of this place, and some distance from the Kasái river, is the village of Ánsá Karandi, said to possess ruins of temples; I heard of them long after I had left the neighbourhood.

DULMI.

Twenty-five miles west of Barâ Bâzâr (which itself is 25 miles south-east of Puralya) on the banks of the Subanrikhá river (the Suvarnarikhsha), is the small village of Dulmi, marked in the lithographed map of 8 miles to the inch as the site of some ruins; the village is known as Dyápar Dulmi, and contains numerous remains. A plan of the place, with the sites of most of the ruins, accompanies, but there are others to the north and north-east of the village.

The ruins consist, with one single exception of low brick and stone mounds, the only standing structure being a small temple of brick on a small isolated hill south of the village and close to the river banks; it is built of brick set in mud, smoothed and ornamented with plain lines of mouldings, the bricks for the purpose being cut to shape; the roof is a semicircular arch internally, of bricks, cut to shape and set edge to edge; the bricks are 14″ × 10″; the entrance is of the usual pattern of bricks in overlapping courses; the temple appears to have been Saivic, but there were probably other temples on the hill; one of the fragments of sculpture represents a female seated on a peacock.

About ¼ mile to north by a little east are the walls of a small fort or citadel; a portion of it has been carried away by the river; the walls were of brick, and were probably strengthened with earth behind; the place was a simple enclosure of no strength.

Of the numerous mounds there is not much to say; some are of stone, others of brick, and are clearly the ruins of temples of the respective materials; the sculptures show that there were Vaishnavic, Saivic, and Buddhist or Jain temples; the last were all exclusively at the extreme north end of what was probably the old city, extending a distance of 3 miles along the river banks; the Hindu ones were in groups; some groups being exclusively Saivic, others as exclusively Vaishnavic. One statue alone of Aditya, on the banks of a small tank, where lie also some fragments of Ganeça, &c., is inscribed, in characters of probably the tenth century; judging from the sculpture, the temples would date to about that period, but it appears that the place continued long in a flourishing condition, for, though some of the sculpture and ornamentation are very good, others are markedly inferior; there is nothing of any special note in the sculpture, but it is almost certain, from the great superiority of the Buddhist or Jain sculpture, that that was the religion which was in the ascendant first, having been succeeded by Hinduism. Some of the sculpture is clearly Jain, and it is not impossible, but on the contrary probable, that the others regarding which there can be any doubt are also Jain; there must accordingly have been a large Jain establishment here in the ninth and tenth centuries, succeeded, say, about the eleventh century, by Hinduism.

The largest tank in the place in known as the Chhátá Pokhar, and is so named from a chhátá or chhátri in the tank. This chhátri is built of stone, in what was once perhaps the middle of the tank; the superstructure consists of a couple of stout pillars, supporting a round slab, ornamented in the usual way, and surmounted by smaller ones in the usual way. This chhátri is traditionally said to be the spot where Vikramâditya used to perform puja before going to bathe. He used, it is said, to rub oil on his body at Telkupi, and perform his puja here; the manifestly absurd story is firmly believed by the people.

The stone used for the sculpture is the soft, dark-colored slate, masses of which crop up in picturesque confusion in the bed of the river. The stone is easily water and weather-worn, and the sculpture has suffered greatly in consequence. A more active agent of destruction is the trade of the place, which consists chiefly of cut-stone cups, plates, &c., cut out of the blocks lying among the ruins; the stone-cutters select such pieces as will give them the least trouble to cut into shape, without any scruple as to whether the piece be a sculpture or not; to this I ascribe the total disappearance of all inscriptions, inscribed slabs answering capitally for large plates.

There are ruins south of the hill on which the temple still existing stands, and they extend to a distance of nearly one mile south, so that a length of four miles must, in all probability, be taken as the length of the city, which, however, was not wide; the extreme width could not have been more than half a mile, as I have seen no ruins further than half a mile from the river banks.

There are numerous kistvaens in the village; these are the graves of the Bhumiyas; they are formed mostly of large slabs of rough stone, set on four rude pieces of stone set upright in the ground. Some of the slabs forming the roof are very large, nearly 15 feet square, and have most probably been used more than once; the bodies are not buried, but burned, and the ashes and bones put into an earthen (or other) vessel, buried, and a slab set up as a roof over the spot; some may even be called family vaults, as the ashes of more than one man are buried in them; the custom is in force among the Bhumiyas, or aborigines; special spots in particular villages are set apart for this sole purpose; they are not to be found in every village, but in most villages of importance.

ICHÂGARH.

About ten miles west by a little south of Dulmi is the large village of Ichâgarh or Patkum; there are ruins of one old temple here, but farther west, about ten miles, and a mile from the south banks of the Kharkhari river, on which Ichâgarh is situated, are numerous remains close to a village named Dewaltand; I did not see the place. Ichâgarh itself is said to contain some old remains, but on examination they appeared to be comparatively recent.

SUFARAN.

Ten miles north-west from Dulmi, on a high swell, immediately on the left bank of the Subanrikhá river, is the small village of Sufaran or Sápharan; here are some low mounds, and the Ind parab is annually held here. From tradition, and from the circumstance of the Ind festival being held here, a festival held only in places which traditionally are said to have been royal residences, there can be no doubt that the village was once a place of importance.

DEOLI.

Close to it, about two miles north-east, is the small village of Deoli, so named from a group of temples still standing under a superb karan tree. The temples appear to have been Jain, as in the sanctum of the largest still exists, *in situ*, a fine Jain figure, now known as Áruánath, and to which offerings are made and pilgrimages performed by Brahmans and other Hindus of the neighbourhood; the deity is especially invoked by females wishing to have children, and offerings are chiefly made to it by them, the conditions of the success of their prayers being that the woman is to visit the spot and creep into the sanctum to make her offerings alone at night. The temple was once a very fine and large one, and had four subordinate temples near the four corners, of which two still exist; the main temple is too far buried in, and surrounded by, rubbish for its plan to be made out without excavation, but it consisted of a sanctum, an antarala, a mahamandapa, an arddhamandapa, and probably a portico; the ruins of the tower have now so shut up the entrance, that the only means of access is by crawling through, much in the manner of snakes; the ornamentation consisted of plain straight lines of mouldings, sparingly used, and the execution, as also the material, is coarse, the last being a coarse-grained sandstone. The statue in the sanctum is three feet high; it is, as usual, on a pedestal, on which the antelope is sculptured, thus clearly indicating the particular Jain hierarch the figure represents; over the trefoil ornament round the head are cut on each side two rows of three naked figures each.

Five hundred feet off are two tanks, touching each other, known as the Jorá-Pokhar; on the banks lies a mutilated bas-relief representing a man on an elephant, possibly meant for Indra on Airâvata; near it lies some stones and the amalaka of a temple, showing that the figure once belonged to a temple on the spot. This figure appears to point to the existence of Brahmanical temples also in the place. In the bed of the small tank to the south of the village lies the side part of a doorway adorned with plain lines.

Some other temples appear to have existed close to the Jain temple, noticed above; these were probably under a large bar tree close to the karan tree; nondescript fragments are collected at its roots and daubed with vermilion.

To south-east of this village at Atma are said to be two pieces of sculpture, one of a lion.

The village and the neighbourhood generally are said to have been covered with jangal till lately.

SUISSÁ.

A mile and a half north-west of this, and about three from Sápharan, is the large village of Suissá. Here, under a bar or bat tree, are collected numerous statues, found, it is said, in the jangal when the place was cleared, but chiefly in a spot 100 yards off, which is, and must long have been, a burialplace of the Bhumij or aborigines; this cemetery is full of tombs, consisting of rude slabs of stone raised from 1 to 4 feet above the ground on four rude, longish blocks of stone, which serve for pillars; people say that when digging for fresh tombs they often come upon the slabs of old tombs now buried; and from the profusion of tombs in all stages of freshness and decay there can be no doubt it has long been a chosen cemetery for the aborigines, the Bhumij or Bhumyas.

The sculptures collected under the tree are Jain and Brahmanical; the principal are known by the names below:—

Monsá, a naked Jain figure with the snake symbol.
Siva, a naked Jain figure with the bull symbol.
Siva, a votive chaitya with four naked figures on the four sides, evidently Jain.

Sankhachakra, a figure of Vishnu Chaturbhuj.

Parvati, a female seated on a lion.

Besides these, there are two small Jain figures naked—a female under a tree which I take to represent Máyá Devi under the sâl tree; another female under a tree, with five Buddhist or Jain figures seated round her head on branches of the tree; on each side are four rows of two each of elephant and horse-faced men. Bunches of flowers and fruit hang round the head of the female figure.

There are a few others of no note; some lingams also form part of the collection.

The Ind parab is celebrated here also.

In his geography, General Cunningham, following the bearings and distances of Hwen-Thsang, places his Kirana Sufalana near Barâ Bâzâr. As there are not many ruins there, while here the remains are numerous, and as the name Sápharan is apparently the original of Sufalana, I think that Hwen-Thsang's Kirana Sufalana may with much probability be identified with the Sápharan near this place; there is not far off a sub-division of Chutia Nâgpur called Karânpur, the Rájás of which place are said traditionally to have once ruled over the greater part of the country, including Dalmi. Admitting the probable correctness of this tradition, the Chinese Kirana Sufalana would be Karna Sápharana: Sápharana means destroyer of curses. In the absence, then, of other data, I propose to identify this place with the capital of Çaçangka Rájá.

DALMI.

Opposite Suissá, on the other side of the river, is Dulmi or Dalmi, said to possess a few fragments of sculpture; and further west, on the Kânchi river, close to Sonahátú, the villages of Jamdi, Burhadi, and Badla are also known as containing ancient remains. Ruins are also said to exist at and near the foot of Chanchalu hill.

BARÂ BÂZÂR.

Barâ Bâzâr or Barâbhum is said to possess one small old temple. I conjecture the name to be a contraction for Varahabhume, but I have nothing to offer for or against my conjecture, beyond the evident similarity of sound.

Six miles south-east of this place is the small village of Bangurda, said to contain ancient remains.

GONDWA.

Sixteen miles south by a little west from Barâ Bâzâr, on the road leading from it to Cháibasá, near the villages of Gonda and close to the Demna Nala, are several rock inscriptions in large characters; the rock is known as Bijak Páhár; the inscriptions are cut on a rock at the foot of a hill to the east of the road. There are no remains of any sort about the place. The inscriptions are four in number, two in the curious shell characters, and two in a transition form of Uriya; these last, knowing that Rájá Mukunda Deva of Orissa at one time held Hugli, must be ascribed to some time near his reign; tradition ascribes the inscriptions to a Banjâra, and it is so far correct that the long inscription in the transition characters reads "Lakshmana prathama Banjara;" this, therefore, is a most curious record, showing that for a long time previous to Mukund Deb's reign no traffic was carried on, at least through this pass; but we cannot allow that this Lakshmana Banjâra was absolutely the first of his tribe who ever used this pass; for the records in the shell characters are undoubtedly older, and must have been written at a period long prior to Mukund Deb's reign, when the pass was used. The second record in the transition characters is worn and of no interest apparently, being a fragment. Of the two inscriptions in shell characters I can make nothing; they are injured to a great extent; whatever of them can now be made out I give here; one is 
the other is 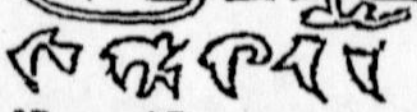
I would ascribe these records to the reign of Sasangka, when we know the country to have been in a highly flourishing state; the form of the characters is certainly as old as the sixth century of our era.

If, then, these records belong to the century when Çaçangka reigned, and the later ones to Mukund Deb, we have a period of about 500 years (ascribing Çaçangka to the seventh century, and Mukund Deva to the sixteenth, and allowing even so much as four centuries after Çaçangka as a period of comparative quiet, if not of actual prosperity), during which traffic through Singbhum appears to have ceased. We know, from the remains of Telkupi and elsewhere in Mânbhum, that the country was flourishing at least in the tenth century, and perhaps even in the eleventh century, but from that time to the time of Rájá Mân Singh not a single temple or sculpture appears to have been executed; the Banjâra's record is, indeed, the very earliest record of the revival of trade in the country. Coupling this with the fact that the fertile country of King Çaçangka appears to have been occupied by the votaries of Brahmanical or Jaina or other Aryan deities, but is now occupied by non-Aryan tribes who reject Brahmanical as well as Jaina deities, the conclusion seems irresistible, that the sudden collapse of all trade and industry was due to the irruption of the Kolarian tribes at some period between the eleventh and the sixteenth centuries. On this point, for further observations, facts and legends, I refer to Colonel Dalton's great work.

PÁḲBIRRÁ.

Twenty miles north-east of Barâ Bâzâr, and a mile east of Ponchá, is the small village of Pákbirrá; here are numerous temples and sculptures, principally Jain; the principal ones are collected within a long shed, which occupies the site of a large temple, of which the foundations still exist; the principal object of attention here is a colossal naked figure, with the lotus as symbol on the pedestal; the figure is 7½ feet high; near it, and along the walls, are ranged numerous others, two small ones with the bull symbol, one smaller with the lotus, a votive chaịtya sculptured on four sides, the symbols of the figures on the four sides being a lion, an antelope, a bull, and what appears to be a lamb; over each principal human figure on the chaitya is represented a duck or a goose, holding a garland; there is, besides this, a second votive chaitya, and there may be others within that I could not see; the temple, which enshrined the colossal figure, must have faced west; it was very large, containing the full complement of preliminary chambers and hall in front of the sanctum.

The colossal figure has a natural crack or flaw diagonally across the thighs and feet, said to have been inflicted by the swords of Muhammadan conquerors of the country when it was first taken! Close to it, I excavated a mound of ruins; the yield consisted of five Buddhist sculptures of a late age; the most remarkable of these is a male and a female figure seated under a tree, which may be meant for a date palm; it has been photographed; the temple where these statues were, was of brick; it faced north; it had a mandapa in front, and must, therefore, have been of a larger size than any that are now standing there.

A large brick temple, the only one now standing, of brick; faces east, and has its doorway of the usual overlapping type, and without the stone sill cutting up its height into a doorway proper and an illuminating window; the temple, externally and internally, is remarkably plain, the only ornamental projections, &c., being at the corners; the bricks are all set in mud; the interior was once plastered, but it is now bare; probably the exterior was also plastered; there is no interior roof to the cell, the pyramidal hollow of the tower being open to the sanctum; there is no object of worship inside.

To the north of this stands a line of four stone temples, three still standing, one broken; these are of the usual single cell-pattern, and the doorway is not cut up into two portions; these then, as well as the brick one just noticed, were single-cell temples, but at some subsequent period mandapas were added to them; they have, however, all got broken, leaving the façades of the temples complete, so that not only is it evident that they were simply added on afterwards, but it is further evident that they were not even bonded into the walls of the original temples; the junctions, where any exist, are quite plain; all these temples face north.

North of this is another, but irregular, line of temples, five in number; of these, two are of stone and three of brick, the latter all ruined; of the stone ones, one is standing.

North of this is another line of four temples, three of stone and one of brick, all in ruins.

Due east of the brick temple, which has been noticed as still standing, are two mounds, evidently the remains of two other brick temples. To the south of this line of temples is another line of three stone temples, all in ruins.

The ornamentation of the stone temples is confined to plain mouldings in the lower part; the façade is quite plain, but entire, showing that they were originally intended for single-cell temples without mandapas in front. A photograph, showing the façade, has been taken; it is probable the temples all stood on a large stone-paved platform, as on excavating near the foot of one I came upon a stone pavement; the whole group occupies the surface of a piece of rising ground 300 to 350 feet square.

There are some tanks close to the temples; one, a large one, had stone ghats and revetments once, now in ruins; there are in the vicinity some few mounds of no special interest.

The material of all the stone temples noticed is a moderately fine sandstone, carefully cut and set without cement; the workmanship is plain, but good; the pillars, that were afterwards added to support the roofs of the mahamandapa, are plain, with square ends and octagonal shafts.

On a low hill or rise named Láthondongri (dongri means small hill) between Pákbirrá and Báramásiá, near Kharkiágarh, is a place known as Khalbir's sthana; here are numerous votive chaityas and round and oblong cut-stone blocks; the place is clearly a cemetery of the Bhumiyas, but why they should have fixed upon a rocky eminence for a site I do not understand; nor am I certain whether the votive chaityas and cut stone lying there, and marking the sites of tombs, were brought from a distance, or were found on the spot; in the latter case, a large temple must have stood on the eminence, of which, however, no traces but these scattered stones remain. The supposition that the stones were brought from the ruins of temples in some other spot is, however, not very probable, as from the known penchant of Hindu architects, and of architects in general, for eminences as sites for their structures, it is extremely probable the eminence here was once crowned by a temple. The hill is densely covered with scrub, and ruins of a temple or temples may exist, unknown to those who acted as my guides.

Tradition calls the votive chaityas, which in form are conoidal frusta, and resemble the native dhole or drums, petrified dhols, and relates that, on a certain occasion, musicians and their instruments, while celebrating a wedding, were converted into stone; what has become of the musicians no one pretends to be able to say.

Half a mile to the east are the ruins of two temples in the sâl jangal; one was Saivic from the lingam *in situ*. Most of the stone has, however, been carried off elsewhere, and only a few remain; the mouldings, judging from the fragments that remain, appear to have been somewhat shallow.

DHÁDKI TANR.

Not far from this, at Dhádki Tanr, near Tulsi Garyá and Asanbani, was a large temple, in an enclosure 120 feet square; the temple faced east, and had a mahamandapa, and the other chambers usual in complete temples; the mahamandapa had windows in the projecting ends of the transept, as in the temples at Khajurâha and elsewhere, but, unlike them, the windows were not open but closed with plain stone lattices. The ornamentation externally consists entirely of plain, shallow recessed lines of mouldings, sparingly used; the temple had other subordinate temples round it, two to the north, two to the south, one in front, and probably there were two at the back, making seven small temples subordinate to the principal one in the middle. From the shallowness of the mouldings and the general appearance, especially of the subordinate temples and of their remains, I ascribe these temples to the period of Mân Singh; and in this opinion I am confirmed by noticing that some of the materials once clearly belonged to another temple, and being supplemented to the necessary extent with fresh materials, have been used in the present one; the difference between the older and the more recent material is quite plain, the latter being much more roughly cut. Odd fragments of mouldings are also seen in places where they have no business, clearly showing that the temple is built of materials from an older temple; the architrave of the outermost entrance lies on the ground, and has a lotus sculptured on its surface; the carving and scroll work of the doorway are all very shallow.

TUISÁMÁ.

At Tuisámá, not far off, is a small temple, which, judging from the architrave lying on the ground, was Saivic, Ganeça being sculptured on it. There are carved and moulded stones also lying about, but as the temple now partially standing is quite plain, I can only suppose the carved stone to have belonged to an older temple, now no longer existing; the fragments of moulding are bold, and there are also fragments of attached corner amalakas lying about, which show that once a richly-ornamented temple stood here; the temple resembles the small ones at Telkupi.

There are traces in the vicinity of two temples, one large and Saivic, and one small, and the ornamented stones noticed above probably belonged to it.

Quarter of a mile to the north-west of this and of the village is a large temple, with mahamandapa and the usual complement of chambers complete; the mouldings and ornamentation are both shallow and few; the temple is now a mass of ruin; near it are numerous votive chaityas, which leads me to infer that the temple was either Jain or Buddhist.

At the east end of the village are two temples, one curiously enveloped in the roots of a bar tree; a few fragments of mouldings lying about show very bold outlines, but the greater portion of the mouldings are shallow; all these temples appear to have been built of the materials of older ones, and, from their shallow ornamentation, I ascribe them to the period of Mân Singh, Akbar's Viceroy.

BUDHHPUR.

Budhhpur is a small village on the left bank of the Kasai river, opposite Madhuárdi and a little below Bangrám, about seven miles south of Pákbirrá; here are numerous ancient remains, the principal of which is a large temple, with its full complement of mandapas, &c., but without the original sanctum, in place of which a modern brick and plaster erection enshrines the object of worship, a huge lingam. The temple is placed on a high plinth, on the topmost point of a low hillock; the temple forms the chief of a group of four subordinate temples, at the four corners, of which two still exist in a ruined condition; of the other two, the foundations alone remain; the whole was enclosed by a low wall, ornamented with projecting pilasters, cornice and footings.

In plan, the temple resembles other temples of the kind, with some petty variations, the principal of which is that at the two sides of the entrance into the antarala are two recesses, like the recesses at the sides of the westernmost temple at Barâkar. The windows in the projecting ends of the transept are closed by plain square-holed lattices cut in the same sandstone of which the temple is built; the windows being projecting, the three open sides of each are thus closed. The entrance into the antarala is similar to the entrance into the temple at Buddha Gáyá, being formed of overlapping courses of stones. The ornamentation externally consists of lines of mouldings of a plain kind, sparingly used; the mouldings resemble those of the temples at Barâkar. The pinnacle that surmounted the original tower roof of the sanctum lies neglected on the ground; it is an urn-shaped vessel, supported by four cobras with expanded hoods and forked tongues, and is graceful in outline and design; there can, I believe, be no doubt that it was, as it now is, a Saivic temple.

Close to it, are the remains of no less than five other temples, all smaller, and none standing. Besides the stones belonging to the temples, there are numerous other slabs sculptured on one face standing and lying about; my guide said they were tombstones, whereat the ministering Brahmans of the temple became very indignant; but there can be no doubt, notwithstanding the head priest's anger, that the stones referred to are sati pillars; none are inscribed, but all are more or less sculptured; the general subjects appear to be a man drawing a bow, sometimes on horseback, but oftener on foot, showing that the husbands of those in whose memories these pillars stand were warriors slain in battle; most of them have animals also sculptured in the topmost compartment.

The lingam in the temple is known as Buddheswar; the people of the place consider it so holy and so well known, as to compare it with the Gadadhar of Gáyá. Gadadhar they say at Gáyá and Buddheswar at Budhhpur are both equally holy and equally well known.

The material of the temples is a tolerably good sandstone, cut to shape and set plain without any cement.

In the village there are a few sati pillars; two of them were inscribed, but the weather has not left the writing legible, and what the weather spared of one appears to have been destroyed purposely by the chisel. I give the inscription in the margin: on the second one, the only word legible is Yuva-râja, in the second, which is also the last line; the first line is illegible.

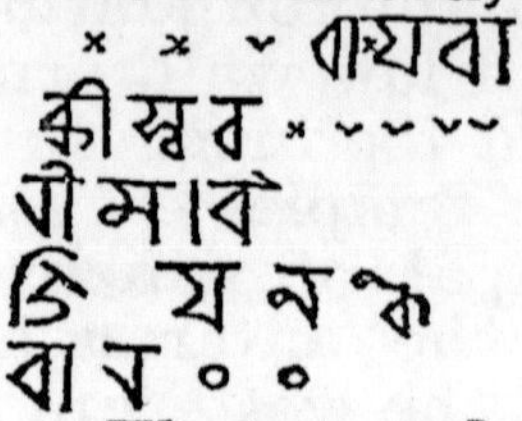

There can be no doubt that Pákbirrá or Ponchá was once a place of great importance. The temples at Pákbirrá appear to have been all Buddhist and Jain, but there is a fair sprinkling of Brahmanical ones in the vicinity. Judging from the sculpture, the older temples cannot probably date earlier than the twelfth or the thirteenth century, and may be somewhat later; while the more recent ones connot go beyond the period of Akbar's General, Mân Singh.

CHÁTNÁ.

About fourteen miles from Bánkurá on the old Grand Trunk Road through Hazaribagh to Shaharghati at the village of Chátná are some ruins; the principal consists of some temples and ruins within a brick enclosure; the enclosure and the brick temples that existed having long become mere mounds, while the laterite temples still stand; the bricks used are mostly inscribed, and the inscription gives a name which I read as Konaha Utara Rájá, while the pandits read it as Hamira Utara Rájá; the date at the end is the same in all, *viz.*, Sake 1476; there are four different varieties of the inscriptions, two engraved and two in relief; the bricks were clearly stamped while still soft and then burnt. Tradition identifies Chátná with Vâsuli or Vâhuli Nagara. At Daksha's sacrifice it is said one of the limbs of Parvati fell here, which thence derived its name of Vâsuli Nagara or Bâhulyá Nagara, a name mentioned in the old Bengali poet Chandi Dás. Its present name Chátná is derived from a grove of Chatim or Chatni trees, which existed here. The Rájás of the country were originally Brahmans, and lived at Bâhulyá Nagara. One of them would not worship Parvati under her form of Vâsuli Devi, and her favor being withdrawn from him, he was killed by the Samontas (Saonts ?) Sântals, who reigned a long time; at last the people rose up and killed all the Saonts they could; one man only escaped by hiding in the house of a low-caste potter (Kumhâr); for this reason to this day the Saonts will eat and drink with the Kumhârs. To this man Vâsuli Devi appeared in a dream, and encouraged him to try his fortune, assuring him of success; the man was filled with profound respect for her, and having undergone various fasts, &c., he gathered together 11 other Saonts and kept wandering in the jangals; one day when very hungry they met a woman with a basket of kendus on her head; she pitying their condition gave them one a piece from her basket; they asked for more, and she gave, but one of them impatiently snatched away one from her; however, the 12 Saonts were refreshed, and the woman was highly pleased; calling them she said—"Go into the jangal and take 12 kend or kendu saplings, and go and fight for your Ráj; Vâsuli Devi and I will restore your Ráj." They accordingly sallied out, killed the Rájá, and obtained possession of the kingdom again; these twelve ruled jointly; the man who had snatched the kend fruit died first, the remaining eleven ruled by turns till, finding it too troublesome, they agreed to give the sole power to one of their number; the descendants of these men are the present Samanta Rájás, who call themselves Chhátris.

The temple is ascribed to Hamira Utara Rájá, and the legend about it is that Vâsuli Devi one night appeared in a dream to the Rájá, and said—"Behold certain cartmen and mahajans are passing through your territory and are at this moment under a particular tree; they have with them a stone in which I have taken up my abode; take it and set it up to be worshipped, for I am pleased with you, and will remain with you." The Rájá accordingly sent men and stopped the mahajans and cartmen, and seized the stone in payment of ground-rent for the ground they had occupied during the night; he then set it up in the temple which we now see.

The temples of laterite are not worth special notice, there being nothing remarkable about them.

EKTESWAR.

Two miles south-east of Bánkurá, on the left bank of the Darikeswara river, is the small village and temple of Ekteswar; the temple is remarkable in its way; the mouldings of the basement are the boldest and finest of any I have seen, though quite plain; the temple was built of laterite, but has had sandstone and brick additions made to it since; there are traces of three different restorations or repairs executed to this temple; the first was a restoration of the upper portion, which had apparently fallen down. In the restoration, the outline of the tower and general appearance of the temple before its dilapidation appears to have been entirely ignored, and a new design adopted. After this, repairs on a small scale were carried out, of which traces are to be seen in various patchy portions of brick and mortar; lastly, a series of brick arches were added in front of the temple. The object of worship inside is a lingam, which is said to have thrust itself up through the ground. Several pieces of sculpture, both broken and sound, and almost all Brahmanical, lie in groups on platforms outside, none of any special interest and none inscribed.

SONÁTAPAN.

Two miles north-east of Ekteswar is the village of Sonátapan; it is situated at the point where the Darikeswara river splits into two, to join again lower down. Of the two channels, the one to the left is the main one now, but, I think, the other one was the principal one before; the sandy bed marking its former extent shows that it was larger than the left channel. Near the junction or fork of the two channels is a tall brick temple, solidly built of bricks measuring 12″ × 8½″; thirty-three courses of bricks with the interposed mud cement make up 7 feet of height. The temple is remarkably solid, the dimensions of the sanctum inside being only 12 feet square, but the great height and the material, brick, need a greater thickness than stone. The roof of the cell begins to contract by overlapping courses at a height of 18 feet; the overlaps are at first of six courses each, then after four such overlaps there are five overlaps of five courses each, after which the overlaps are of four, and subsequently of three and of two courses each. The entrance is of the usual style of overlapping openings; it is 6 feet 1 inch wide; the overlaps are one of six courses, two of five courses each, seven of four courses each, five of three courses each, and one of two courses, there being altogether sixty-one courses disposed in 16 overlaps on each side to the point where the two sides of the triangle approach to within 4 inches of each other, the overlaps being, therefore, of 2 inches each only almost exactly. The temple stands on a high plinth, now a shapeless mound; it does not appear, from the absence of the dividing sill in the opening, that the temple had any mandapa in front, and the façade is indeed complete as it is, there being no part or line where the walls of any chamber or structure in front could touch the present façade without hiding some ornament, or falling upon some moulding or ornamental sculpture; the long platform, therefore, in front of the temple (now a terrace of earth and rubbish), must have been meant for open-air gatherings, as is common to this day, especially in mêlas or fairs, or for a subordinate temple facing the main one.

Close to the temple, and on the low ground which in floods is under water, are several mounds, which still yield bricks; the mounds, as well as the temple, are ascribed to Salivahan, and the mounds near the river are said to be parts of his garh, the other parts having been washed away by the left hand channel when the main stream first took that direction; the old name of the place is said by some to have been Hamiradángá.

The temple was covered with plaster, and richly and profusely ornamented. The plaster, from its ornamentation corresponding in all parts with the cut-brick ornamentation below, I consider to have formed part of the original design, and not, as is too often the case, added afterwards. The plaster has, however, come off in most parts; the top of the temple has disappeared long ago, and is now a shapeless mass of ruin, on which young trees are allowed to take root and flourish undisturbed. It is a pity that a fine temple, as this must have been, should have been allowed to decay.

BAHULÁRÁ.

The finest brick temple in the district, and the finest though not the largest brick temple that I have seen in Bengal, is the one at Bahulárá, on the right bank of the Darikeswara river, 12 miles from Bánkurá; the temple is of brick, plastered; the ornamentation is carefully cut in the brick, and the plaster made to correspond to it. There are, however, ornaments on the plaster alone, but none inconsistent with the brick ornamentation below. I conclude, therefore, that the plaster formed a part of the original design; the mouldings of the basement are to a great extent gone, but from fragments here and there that exist, a close approximation can be made to what it was; some portions are, however, not recoverable; the drawings or photographs give the necessary details.

The present entrance is not the original old one, but is a modern accretion, behind which the real old doorway, with its tall, triangular opening of overlapping courses, is hidden. This old opening is still to be seen internally; it consists of a rectangular opening, 41 courses of bricks in height, over which rise the triangular portion in a series of corbels, each 5 courses in depth; the width of the opening is 4 feet 10 inches; there is no dividing sill, and from the façade of the temple it is evident that the cell, with its attached portico in the thickness of the wall itself, stood alone without any adjuncts in front; there are, however, the remains of a mahamandapa, which was added on in recent times, but it is widely different in construction and in material to the old temple, and is probably not so old as the British rule in India.

The object of worship inside is named Siddheswara, being a large lingam, apparently *in situ*. I conclude, therefore, that the temple was orginally Saivic. Besides the lingam there are inside a naked Jain standing figure, a ten-armed female, and a Ganeça; the Jain figure is clear proof of the existence of the Jain religion in these parts in old times, though I cannot point to the precise temple or spot which was devoted to this sect.

The temple had subordinate temples disposed round it in the usual manner; there were seven round the three sides and four corners, and one in front, the last being most probably a temple to Nandi, the Vâhana of Siva; the whole group was inclosed within a square brick inclosure; subordinate temples and walls are equally in ruins now, forming isolated and long mounds respectively. There is at Dhârapat a small temple, modern, or at least of recent times, but interesting from its dated inscription.*

CHHINPUR.

At Chhinpur is a solitary laterite temple, but of no ancient date.

BISHANPUR.

Bishanpur is famed as an old place, and certainly contains very many temples and other old remains, but their age is not such as to merit detailed notice of them. They are almost all built in the Lower Bengal style, with curved roof lines, and the ornamentation consists generally of sculptured or moulded tile-work. Some of these are very fine, and stand out the weather very well; they consist chiefly of scenes from the lives of Rama or the Pândus, but principally of Krishna, to whom, or to whose mistress, most of the temples are dedicated; the sculpture, as may be readily guessed, is not very chaste. The few photographs will convey a clearer idea of these temples than descriptions. There is also a large old fort, dating evidently to post-Muhammadan times, as evidenced by the remains of gateways which are of the Muhammadan type; in short, the place is full of remains of a certain age, not going beyond the middle of the sixteenth century Sake; they are of interest chiefly for their inscriptions, which I now proceed to notice briefly.

1. The oldest dated temple in Bishanpur is known as the Malleswar temple, *the* temple of Bishanpur, which has long been regarded as the oldest in Bishanpur, and as dating back to near the beginning of the Malla era, chiefly on the strength of the inscription of which Bishanpur enjoys its fame as a very ancient city; the inscription is dated clearly in Sake 928, but this is a mistake, the word Sake having through some oversight been put instead of Mallabda, and the proof of it is to be seen in the next few lines, where the temple is stated to have been built by Vira Sinha in the year Vasu Kara Hara *Malla Sake, i.e.,* the year 928 of the Malla era. The error is so palpable, that I need not say any-

* The inscription consists of five long lines and three compartments of two lines each in Bengali characters. It is not in good order, but the date can be clearly made out as 1626 Sake: the 2 being, however, somewhat doubtful, it may possibly be 1616 Sake, but can be nothing else.

thing further; the date corresponds to Sake 1540, there being a difference of 612 years between the two eras.

2. The next oldest dated temple is that known as Burha Râdha Syam's, which, according to the inscription, was built by Rájá Vira Hambira in the year Malla Sake 949, in the reign or kingdom of Rájá Vira Sinha; there is also mention of Rájá Raghunatha Sinha. The date, 949 Mallabda, is seen from other inscriptions dated both in the Malla and in the Sake eras to correspond to Sake 1561, there being a difference of 612 years between the two eras.

3. The next temple, known as Kista Raya's Jor Bangla, is dated in Malla Sake 960 or 961, the unit figure being somewhat doubtful; the date is also given at length in the Sake era. The Rájás mentioned are Sri Vira Hambira Naresu and Sri Raghunatha Sinha; the date in Sake era corresponds to 1572 or 1573.

4. The next in point of antiquity is the temple known as Kala Chand's; the inscription mentions Sri Vira Hambira Naresha Sunurdá Dana Nripa Sri Raghunâtha Sinha; it is dated in Malla Sake 962, corresponding to 1574 Sake.

5. The next in age is a nameless temple dated in 964 Malla era; it mentions Malladhipa Sri Raghunâtha and Nripa Sri Vira Sinha; the date corresponds to Sake 1576.

6. The next is the temple known as Murali Mohan's; it is stated in the inscription to have been built by the wife of Vira Sinha, the mother of Durjana Sinha, in the year 971 Mallabda; the date is also given at length as Shasti Sapta Sebandhi of Malla Sake, which, from other inscriptions which are dated both in the Malla and in the Sake eras, is seen to correspond to Sake 1583.

7. Contemporaneous with this is a nameless temple, the inscription of which mentions the names of Raghunâtha, Malinâtha, and Rájá Vira Sinha; it is dated the same as the last one, *viz.*, Mallabda 971, or Sake 1583.

8. A dilapidated, nameless temple comes next in order; it is dated in 979 Mallabda, and the date is written at length as Nara Shaila Anka Malla Sake; the date corresponds to Sake 1591. It was built by a Brahman, Sita Ráma Sarmmana, in the reign of Vira Sinha.

9. The next in age as known is Madana Mohan's temple, built by Sri Masvajarna Bhumipati in the year 1000 of Mallabda Kála, the son of Radha Vrija Rajananda (son of king); the date corresponds to Sake 1612.

10. The next is the one known as Dol Govinda's temple; the inscription mentions Sri Gopala Sinha, and another name now illegible; the date is given as Mallabda 1032, corresponding to Sake 1644.

11. Next in order is Máyá Burhiya's temple, near the Ras Mancha, built in Mallabda Muni Veda Khenduganete in Mágha by Sri Radharuja Nayarendra; the date is also given in figures, as 1040 Malla era corresponding to 1652 Sake.

12. Contemporaneous with this is the broken Jor Bangla, built by Gopala Sinha, the son of Chaitanya Chandra, dated Mallabda 1040, corresponding to Sake 1652.

13. Next is the Hijra Párá temple, dated in San 946 and Sake 1661. The San is probably the Bengali San or some local era; the difference is 715 years.

14. The next is Radha Syam's temple. The inscription mentions the famous Chaitanya and a Radha Syama Nripendra; it is dated in 1680 Sake.

15. The next is the one known as Radha Madhava's temple, built by the son of Mahima Sinha, Krishna Sinha's wife, Churamani, in San 1043 Sál, which, adopting the difference (715 years) found from the doubly-dated temple of Hijra Párá noticed above, will correspond to Sake 1758.

16. The next is a nameless dilapidated temple, dated in Sake 1793 and San 1238, the latter evidently an error, if the era be the same as that of the Hijra Párá temple.

The Nanda Lál temple is inscribed, but not dated.

From these temples, and the inscriptions at Pachet and at Chátná, we have the following:—

1476.—Hámira or Konaha Utara Rájá, reigning king, from Chátná inscription.

1540-1561.—Vira Sinha reigning, but in 1561 Vira Hambira and Raghunâtha mentioned as princes.

1572-1574.—Vira Sinha not mentioned, probably dead; Vira Hambira reigning; Raghunâtha mentioned.

1576-1583.—Vira Hambira not mentioned; Raghunâtha probably reigning; Vira Sinha II mentioned.

1583.—Raghunâtha not mentioned, therefore probably died that year; Vira Sinha reigning.

1583-1657.—Long reign of Vira Sinha II, as the Pachet inscription dated 1657 mentions him.

The subsequent names appear to have no order or regularity: probably after the long reign of Vira Sinha, his kingdom got split up among the grown-up members of his family.

Among the remains at Bishanpur I must not omit to notice the very curious pyramidal structure known as the Ras Mancha ; a photograph of it has been taken.

HUGLI.

The remains at Hugli, Hindu and Muhammadan, have been noticed by various writers, but I especially refer to Messrs. Blochmann and Money's papers in the Journal of the Asiatic Society. I need only add to Mr. Money's paper that the temple from the ruins of which the dargah has been built must have been of the style of the beautiful and profusely sculptured temples at Janjgir, which are ornamented internally throughout with scenes from the Ramayana and others. The descriptive labels which still exist in the dargah, as noticed by him, could have been engraved only because the scenes were actually sculptured on the walls and needed the labels to be readily understood.—See my report for season 1873-74.

I visited Jonpur, but as I have nothing to add to the excellent accounts already extant about it, it is needless for me to say anything. Measurements, &c., were made, and the more interesting of such as have not already been published will be found in the plates. I especially recommend to attention the unrivalled profile of the grand corner towers at the back corners of the Jamai Majid. It is strange the great Historian of Architecture does not notice them at all ; for massive, yet elegant, simplicity and boldness they have no rivals in any building I have yet seen.

I examined also several temples near Mirzapur ; among them, the famous one of Vindhyavâsini Devi at Bindhâchal. The building as it stands is modern, but built of old materials ; the pillars are quite plain, and the building altogether of no interest. I am told the figure inside is inscribed, but I was naturally not allowed to examine it. There is, however, nothing of special interest about the temple. The legend about it is to be found in the Native Mahâtmyas and also in the Mahâbhârat, and do not need reproduction here. Tradition says the head of Vindhya lying prostrate in worship of the goddess is near Bindhâchal, while his feet are at Chunâr and Rájmahál, respectively. A different version of the story, which places one foot at Gáyá, is given in the Journal, Asiatic Society, "Account of a tour from Mirzapur to Nâgpur." The name Vindhya has at various times and by various old writers been ascribed to the various ranges from Amarkantak to the Ganges,—see notes, Wilson's Vishnu Purana (edition FitzEdward Hall) ; but the fact of the temple of Vindhyavâsini being at the foot of the northernmost range seems clearly to establish that the name properly applies to the northernmost of the ranges running from Rájmahál in the east to Kathiâwad on the west.

I also examined the temples at Márá near Bairâtganj on the strength of information from a pilgrim ; but though I heard of none of interest, nor saw any at the place, I believe careful search would reveal the existence of some old temples. The temples at Bijayapur are of no interest.

I also visited Chitrkot, but the North-Western Provinces Gazetteer, Vol. I, edited by Mr. Atkinson, gives full information of the temples there ; and as they are neither old nor of any interest, I refrain from needlessly lengthening my report. The Gazetteer omits to note the tiraths of Hanumân and Lachhmân, &c., the first being on a high hill three miles south-east from Chitrkot.

J. D. B.

INDEX.

TOUR OF 1872-73 IN THE BENGAL PROVINCES.

P

R

S

T

U

V

W

Y

PLATE I.

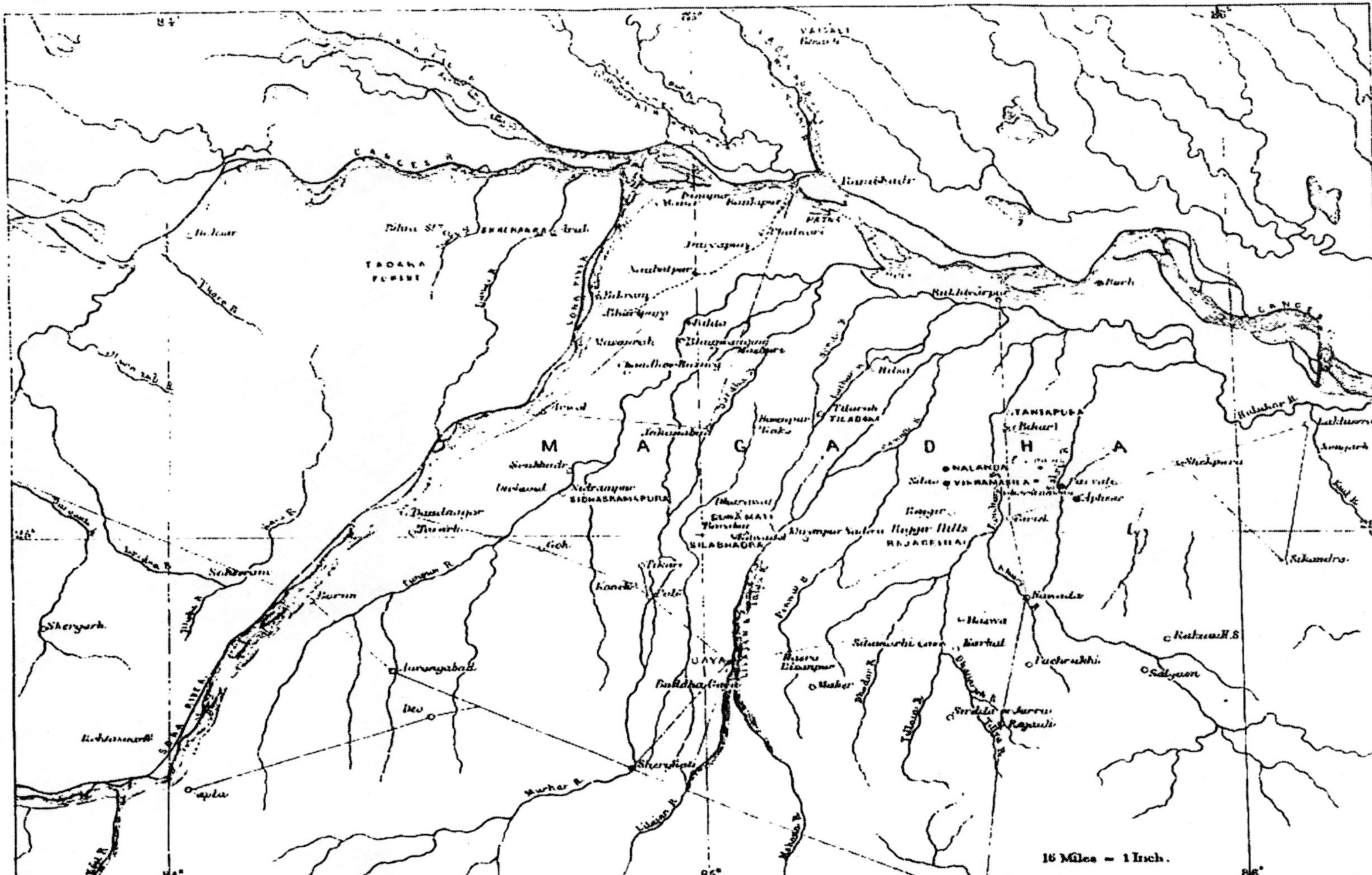

J. E. ...

Lithographed at the Surveyor General's Office, Calcutta, February 187.

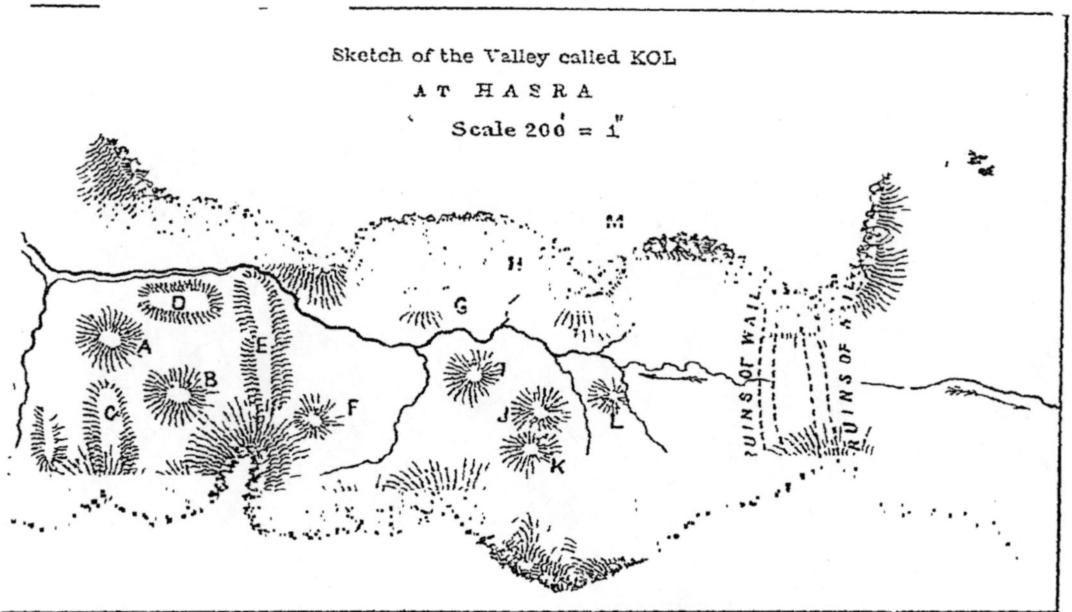

Sketch of the Valley called KOL
AT HASRA
Scale 200' = 1"

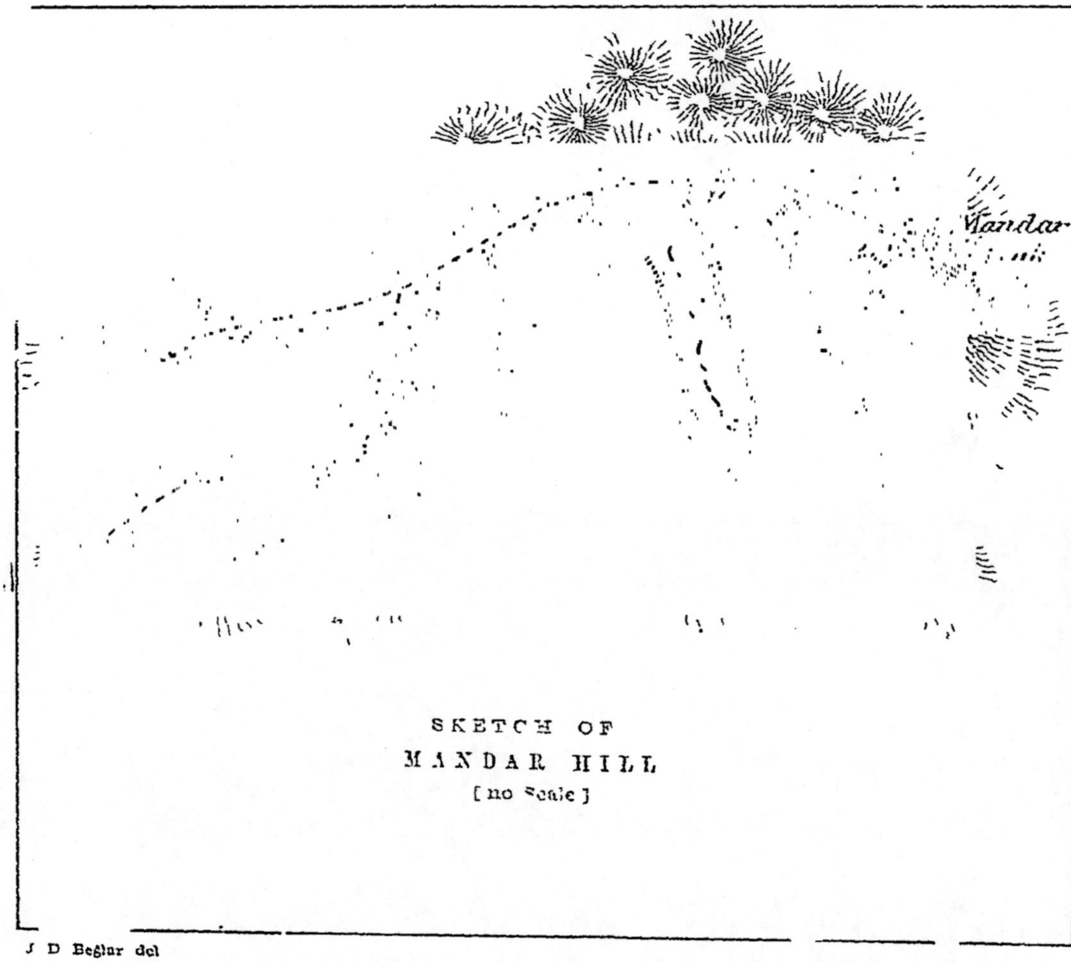

SKETCH OF
MANDAR HILL
[no Scale]

J D Beglar del

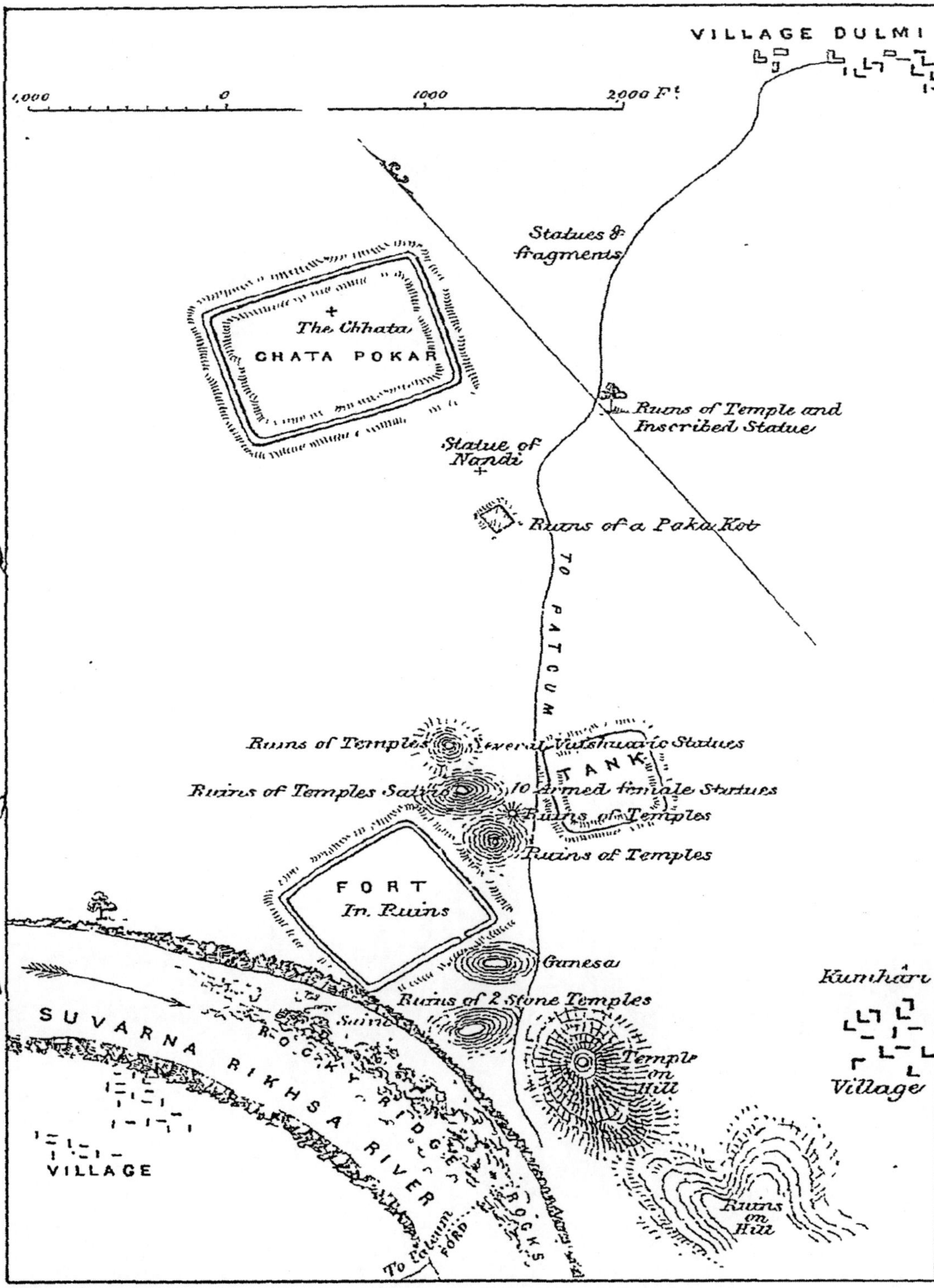

J. D. Beglar, del.

Lithographed at the Surveyor General's Office, Calcutta February 1873

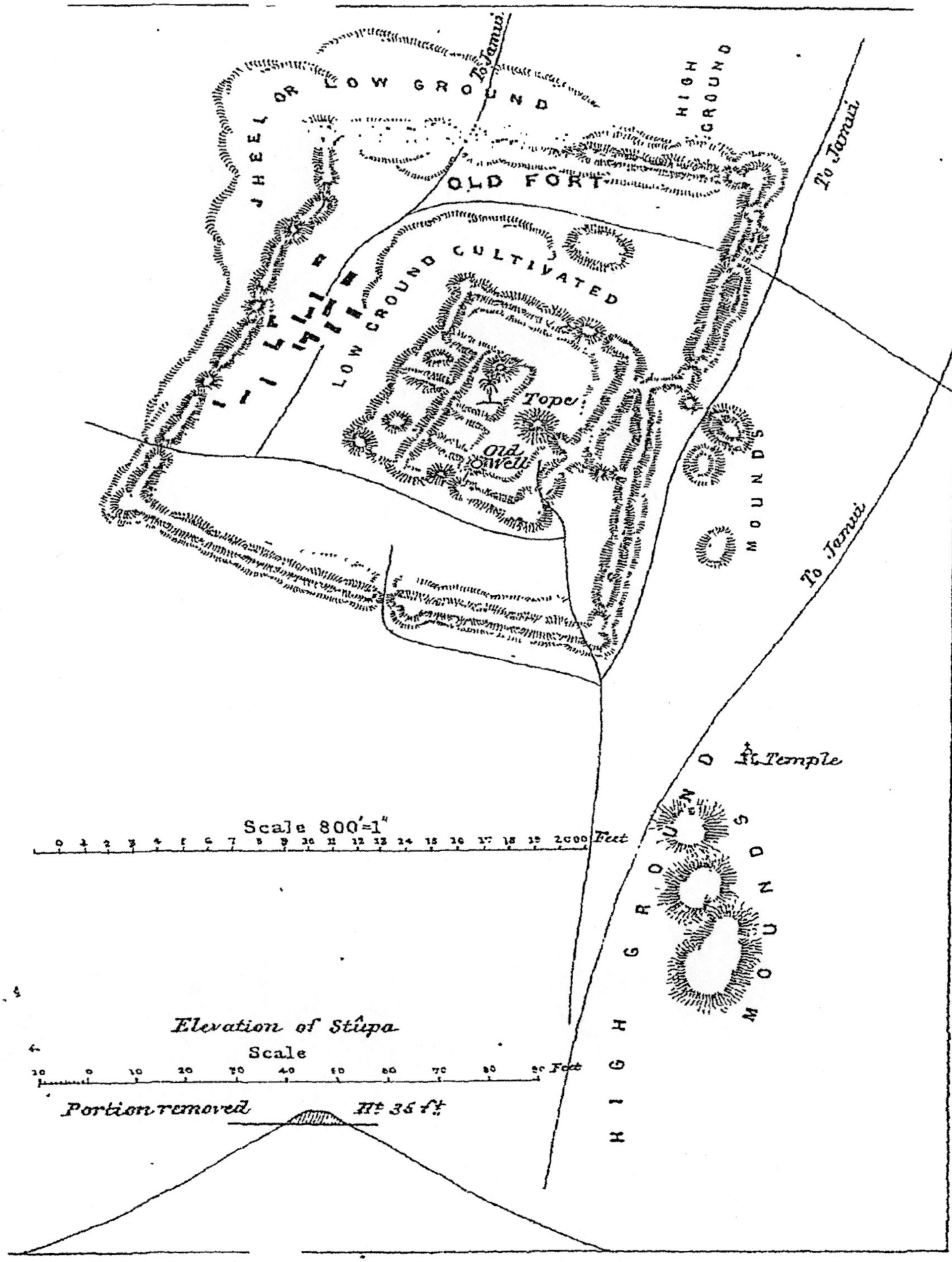

J. D. Beglar, del.

Lithographed at the Surveyor General's Office, Calcutta, February 1876

Plan of a large Bluish Black Stone in the Vageswari Temple at Buddha Gya

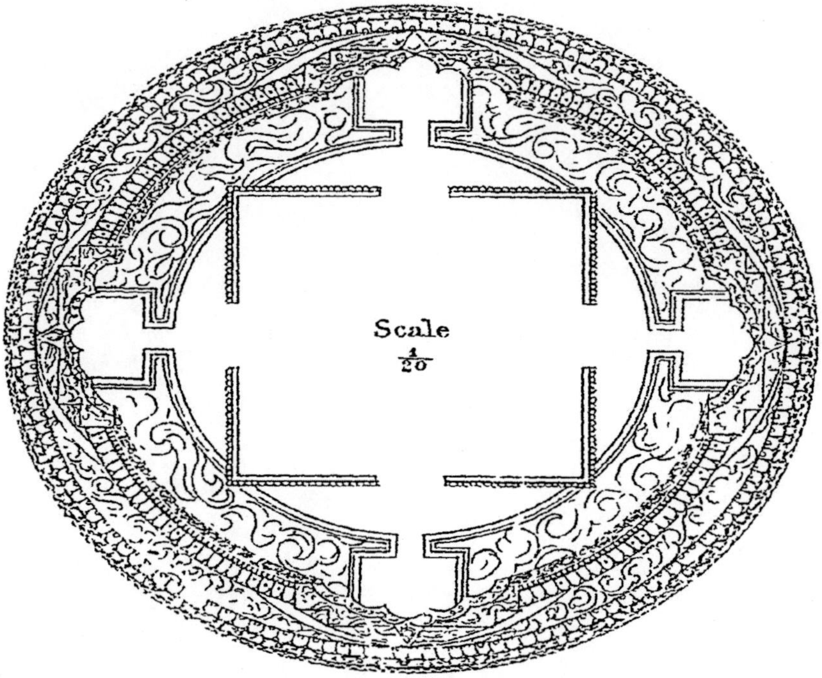

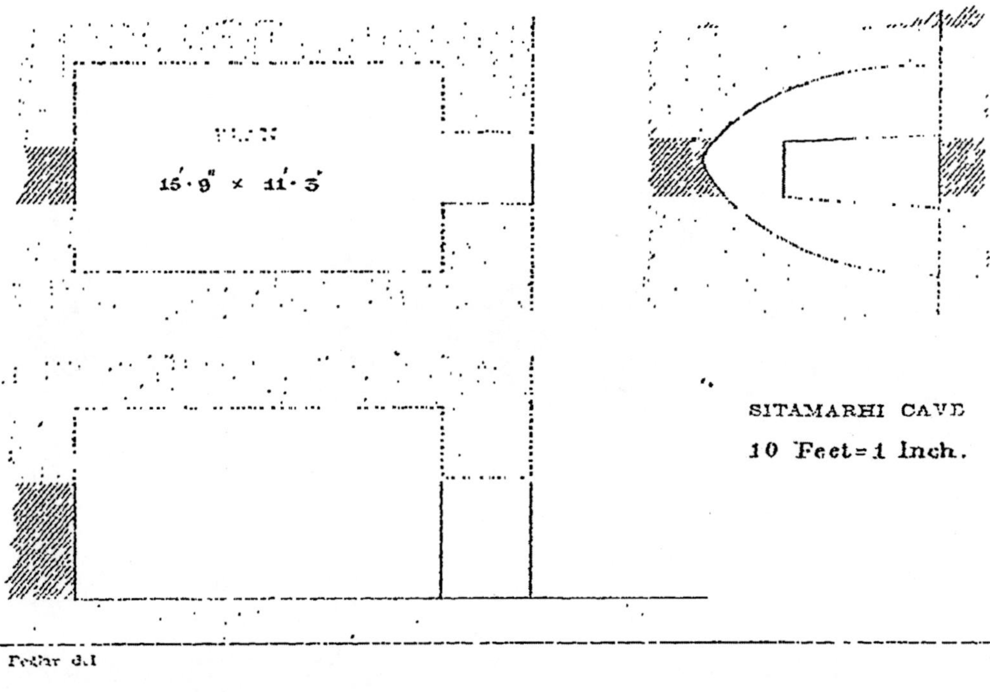

SITAMARHI CAVE
10 Feet=1 Inch.

J. D. Fethr del.

Lithographed at the Surveyor General's Office, Calcutta, February 1878

TEMPLES

PLATE VI.

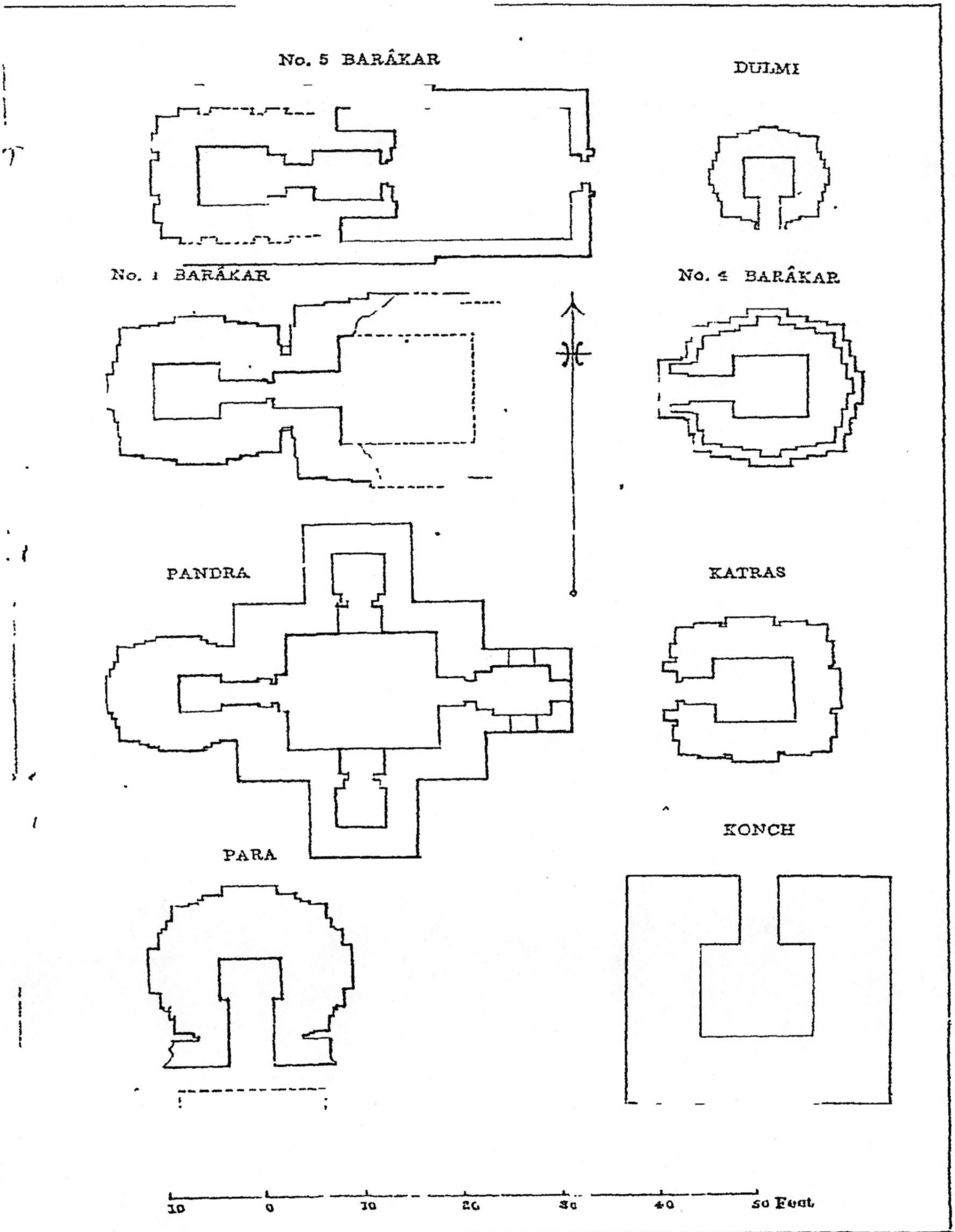

J. D. Beglar, del

Lithographed at the Surveyor General's Office, Calcutta, February 1878

EKTESWAR

Scale 20 = 1"

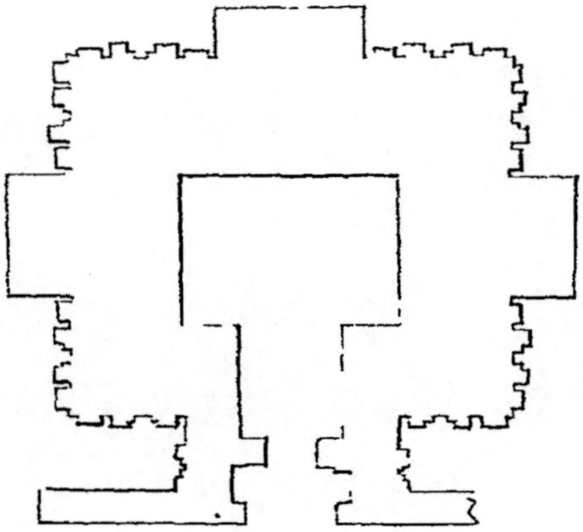

BAHULARA

Scale 6' = 1"

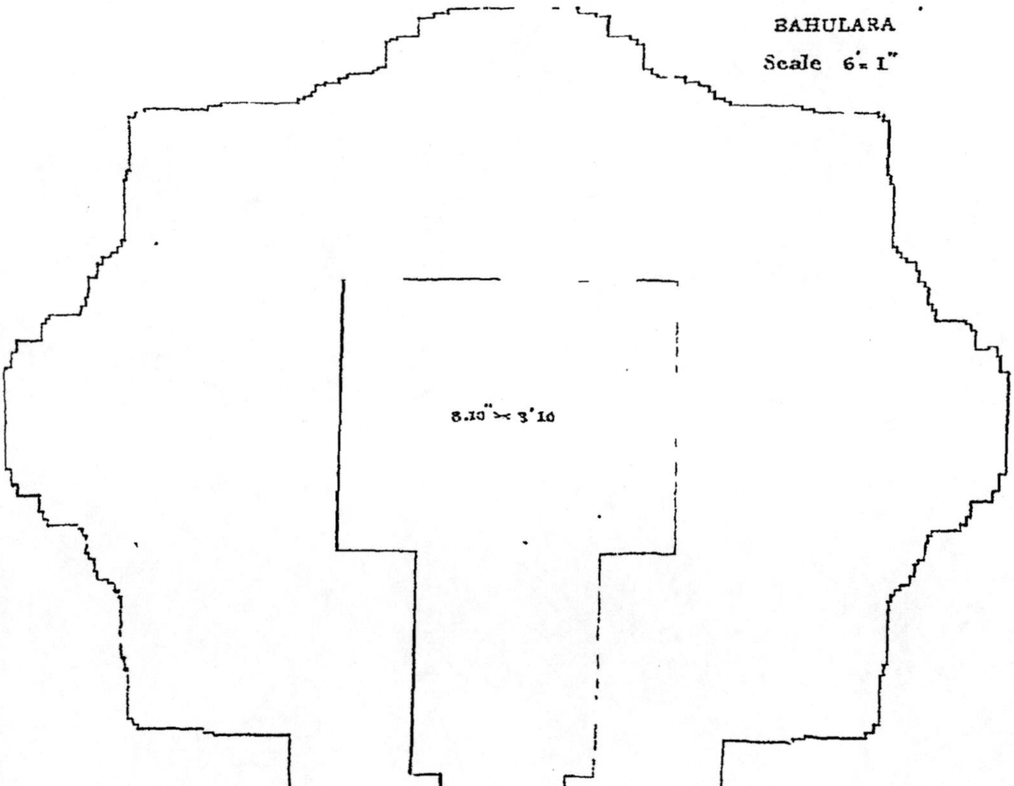

J D. Beglar, del

Lithographed at the Surveyor General's Office Calcutta February 1878

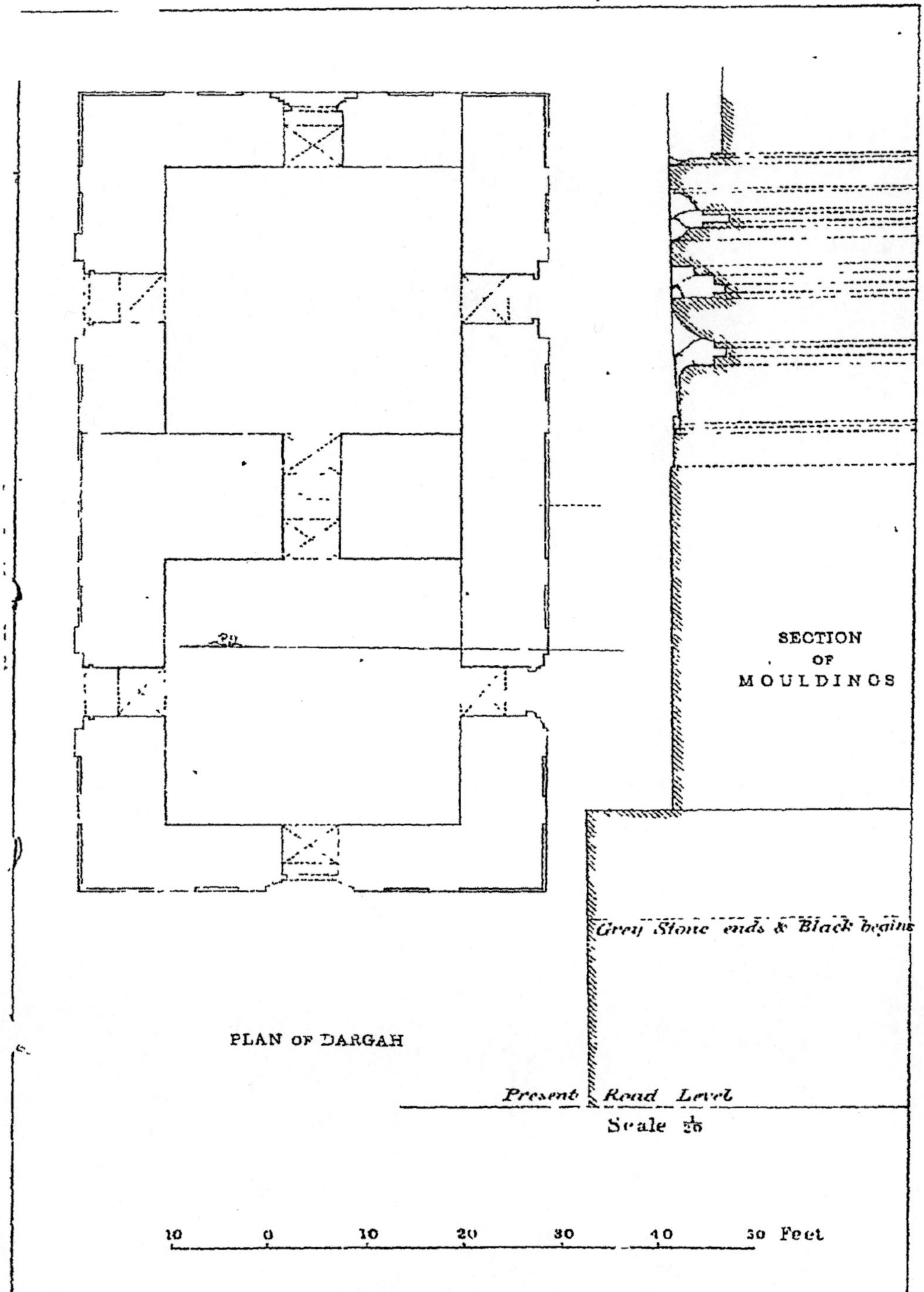

J. D. [illegible] del.

[illegible] Calcutta [illegible]

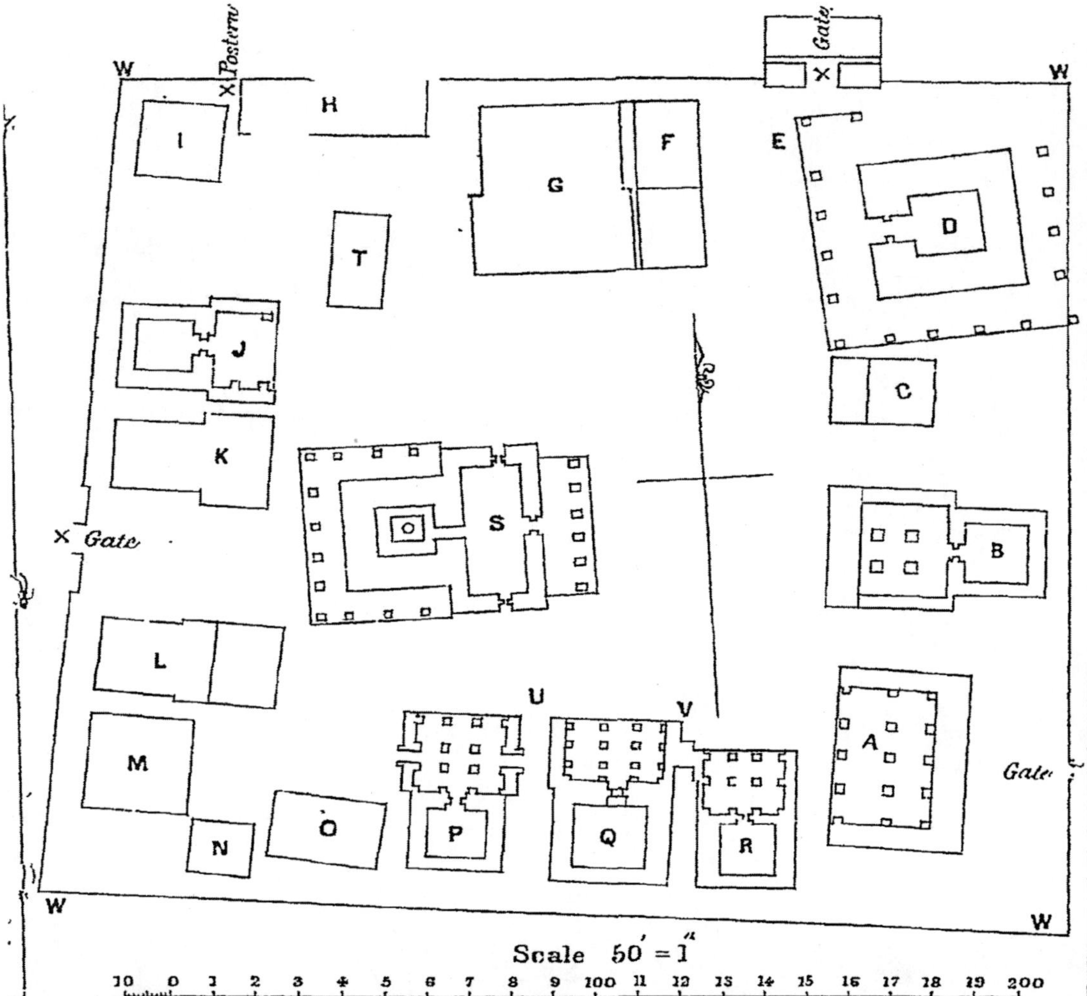

REFERENCES.

- A Temple of Syam Karttik
- B „ „ Parvati
- C „ „ Nilkanth Mahadev
- D „ „ Lakshmi Narayan
- E a Well
- F Temple of Annapurna Devi
- G „ „ Kali
- H The Bhog Mandir (Ruin)
- I A Samadh Platform
- J Temple of Anand Bhairon
- K „ „ Ram Lakshman
- L „ „ Devi Singhavahini
- M Temple of Suraj Narayan
- N „ „ Saraswati
- O „ „ Hanuman and Kuvera
- P „ „ Kal Bhairon
- Q „ „ Sanjhya Mai
- R „ „ Brahma and Ganesa
- S „ „ (Siva) Baidnath Mahadeva Ravaneswara
- T „ „ Ganga
- U Bell presented by Raja of Nepal
- V „ „ „
- WWWW Inclosure Wall
- XXXX are the Entrances.

J. D. Beglar del.

Lithographed at the Surveyor General's Office, Calcutta February 1879

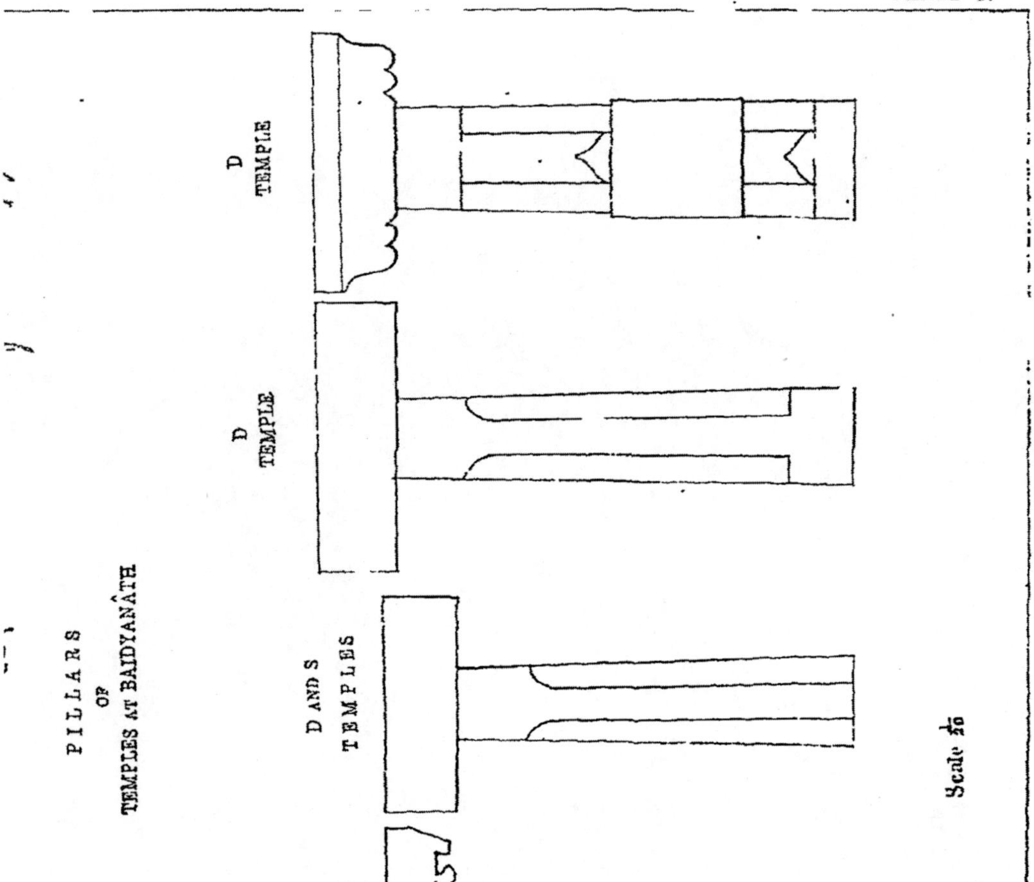

J D Beglar, del

Lithographed at the Surveyor General's Office Calcutta February 1878

PILLARS

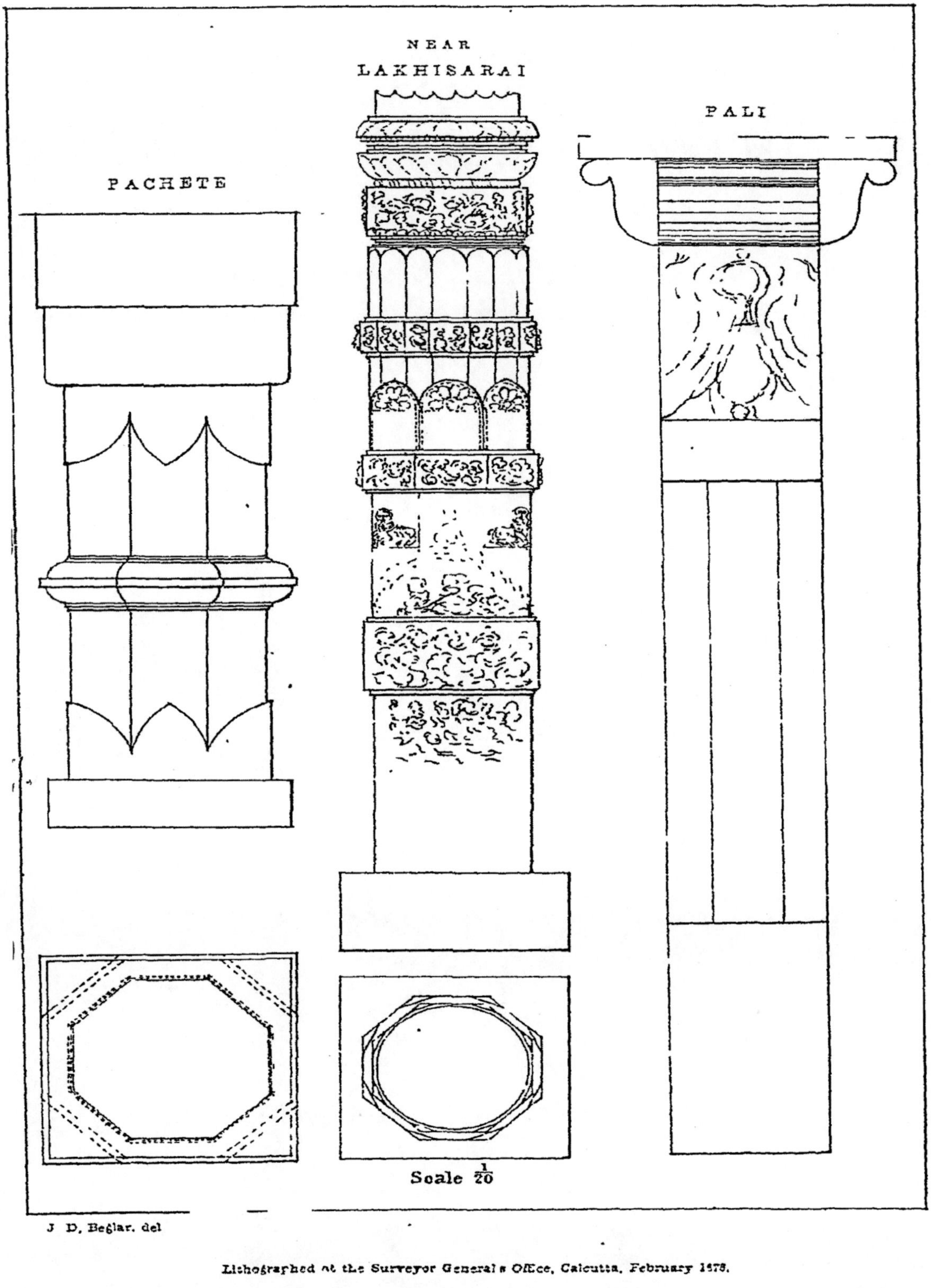

J. D. Beglar, del

Lithographed at the Surveyor General's Office, Calcutta, February 1878.

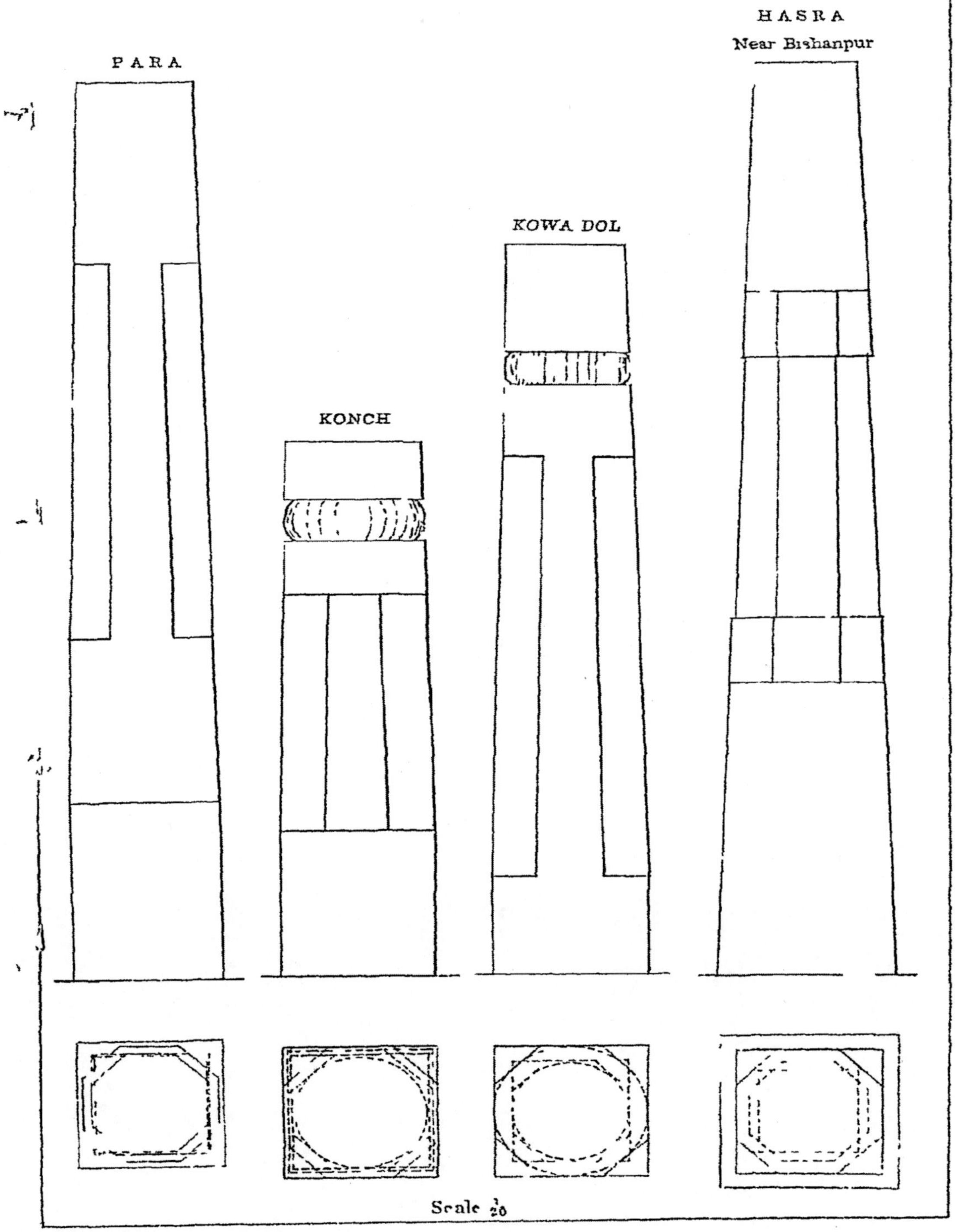

J D Beglar del

Lithographed at the Surveyor General's Office Calcutta February 1878

J. D. Beglar, del.

Lithographed at the Surveyor General's Office, Calcutta, February 1873.

BASEMENT MOULDINGS

PLATE XIV.

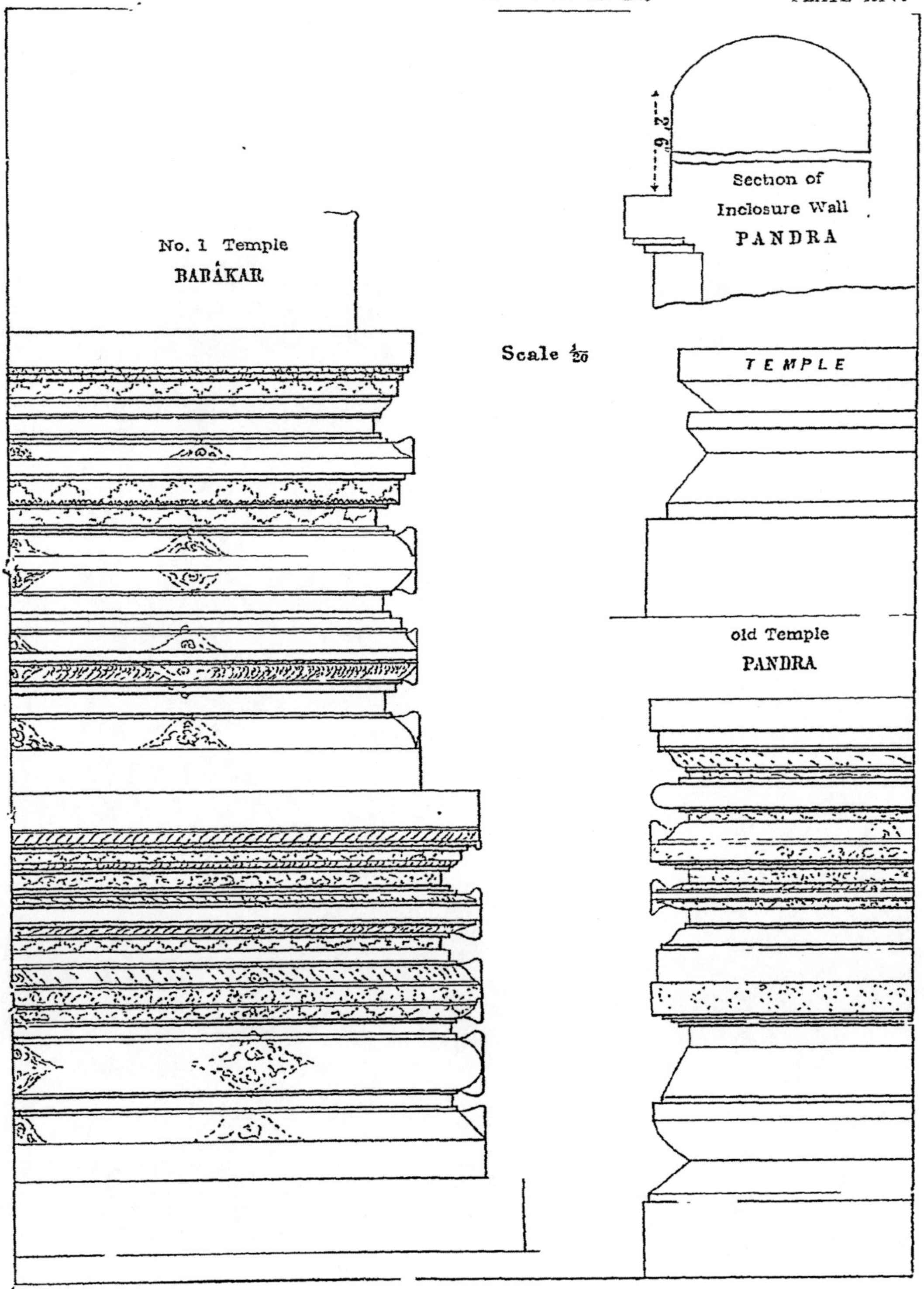

J. D. Beglar, del.

Lithographed at the Surveyor General's Office Calcutta, February 1878

BASEMENT MOULDINGS

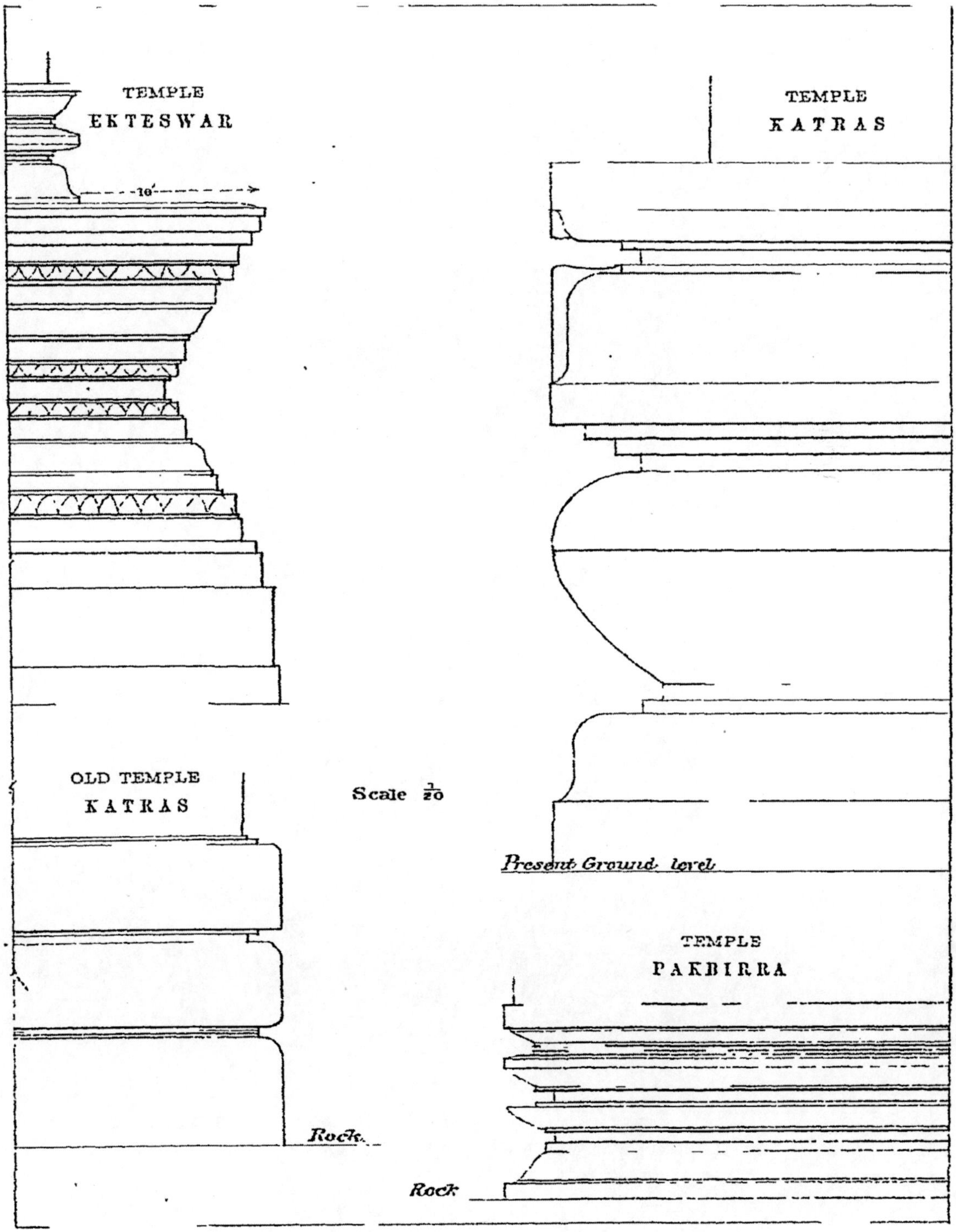

J. D. Beglar, del

Lithographed at the Surveyor General's Office, Calcutta, February 1878

PLATE XVI.

TEMPLE
Sections

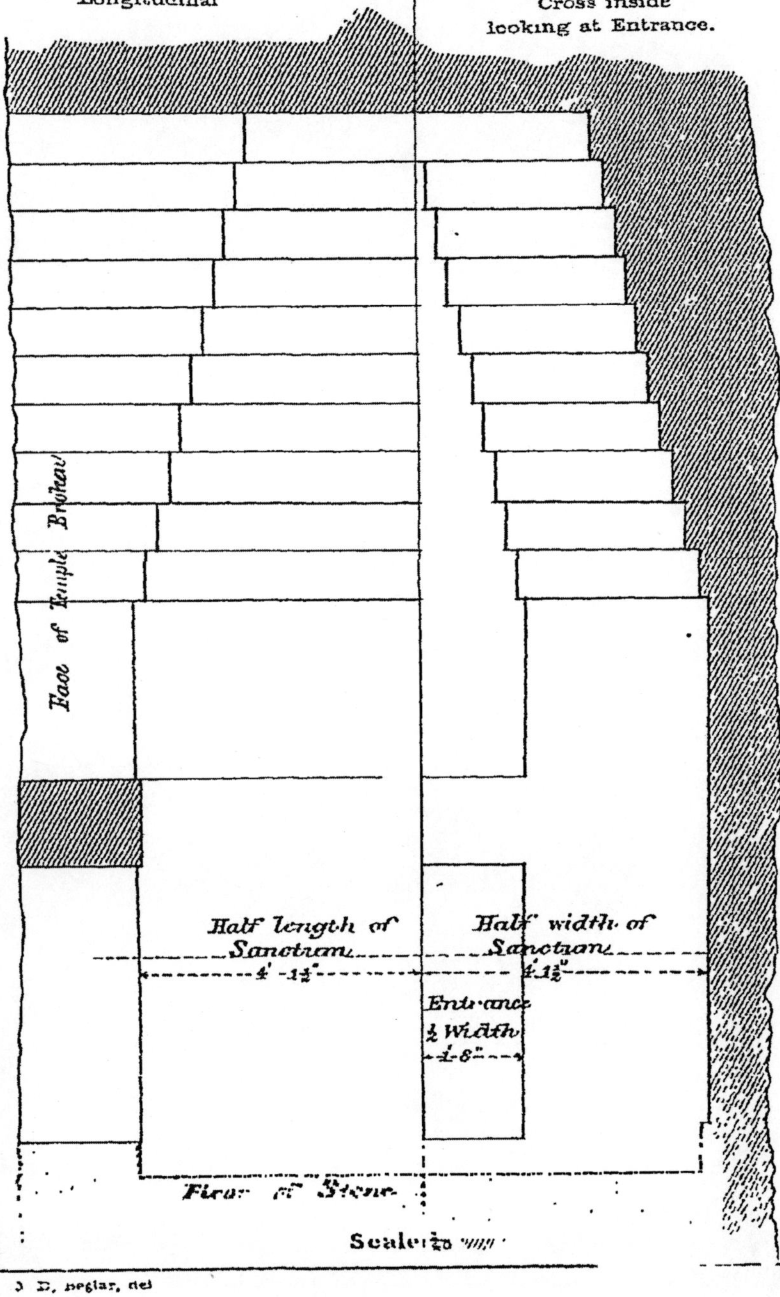

Sections of Mouldings found among the Ruins of CHECHGAON-GARH

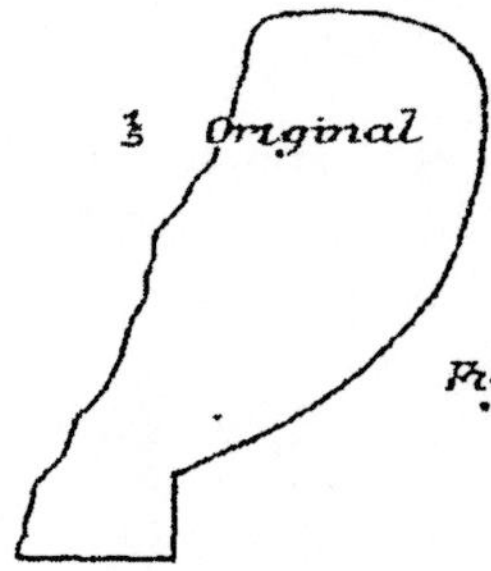

Fig. (1)

Fig. (2)

Papaharani Tank at foot of MANDARA hill

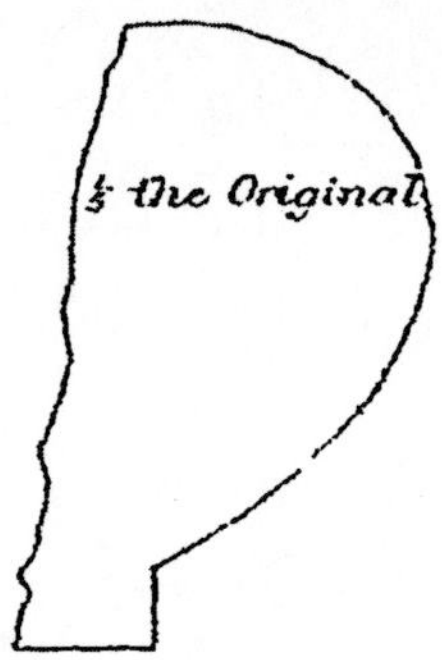

J. D. Beglar, del

DULMI

PLATE XVII

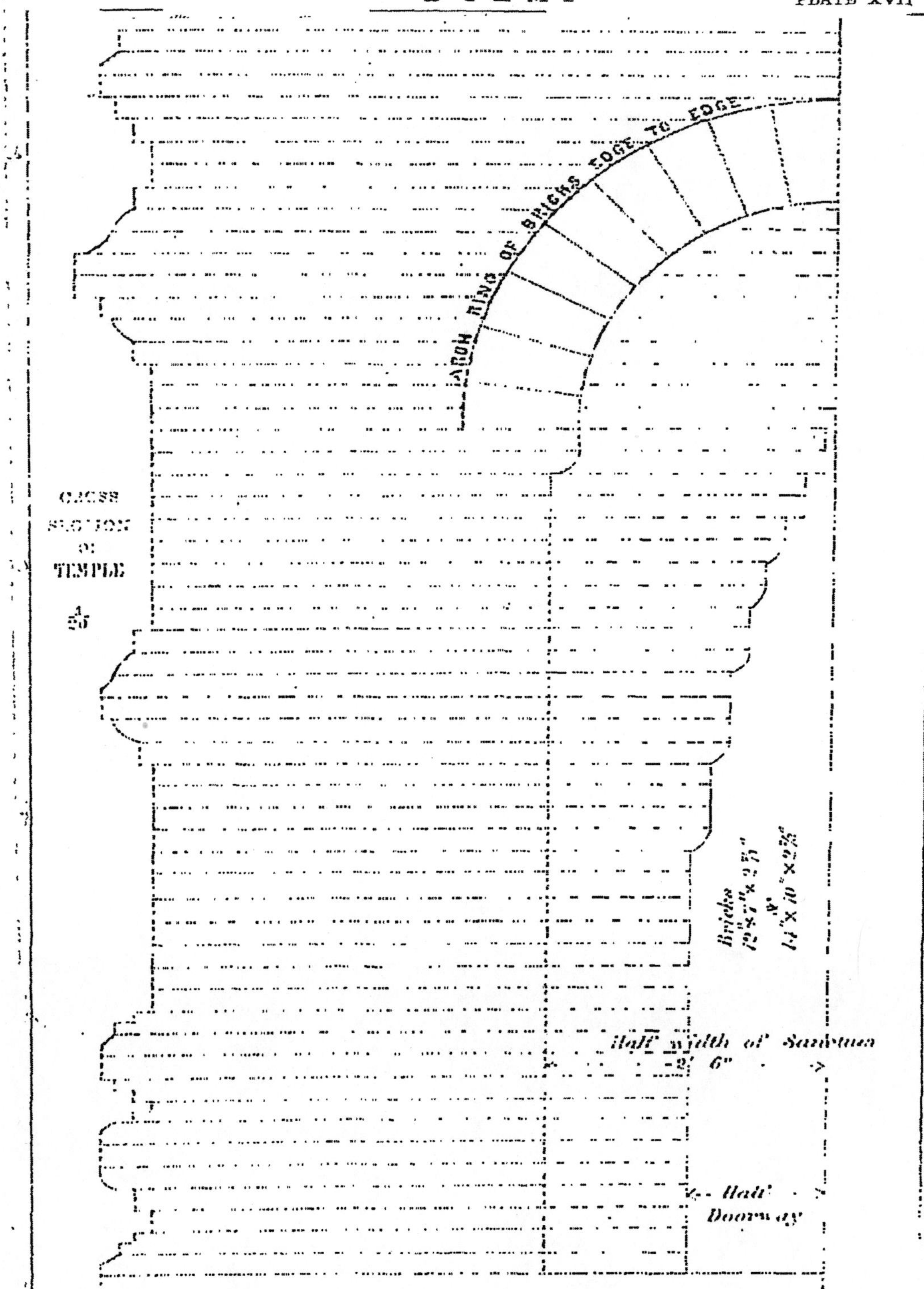

J. D. Beglar, del

Lithographed at the Surveyor General's Office, Calcutta February 1878

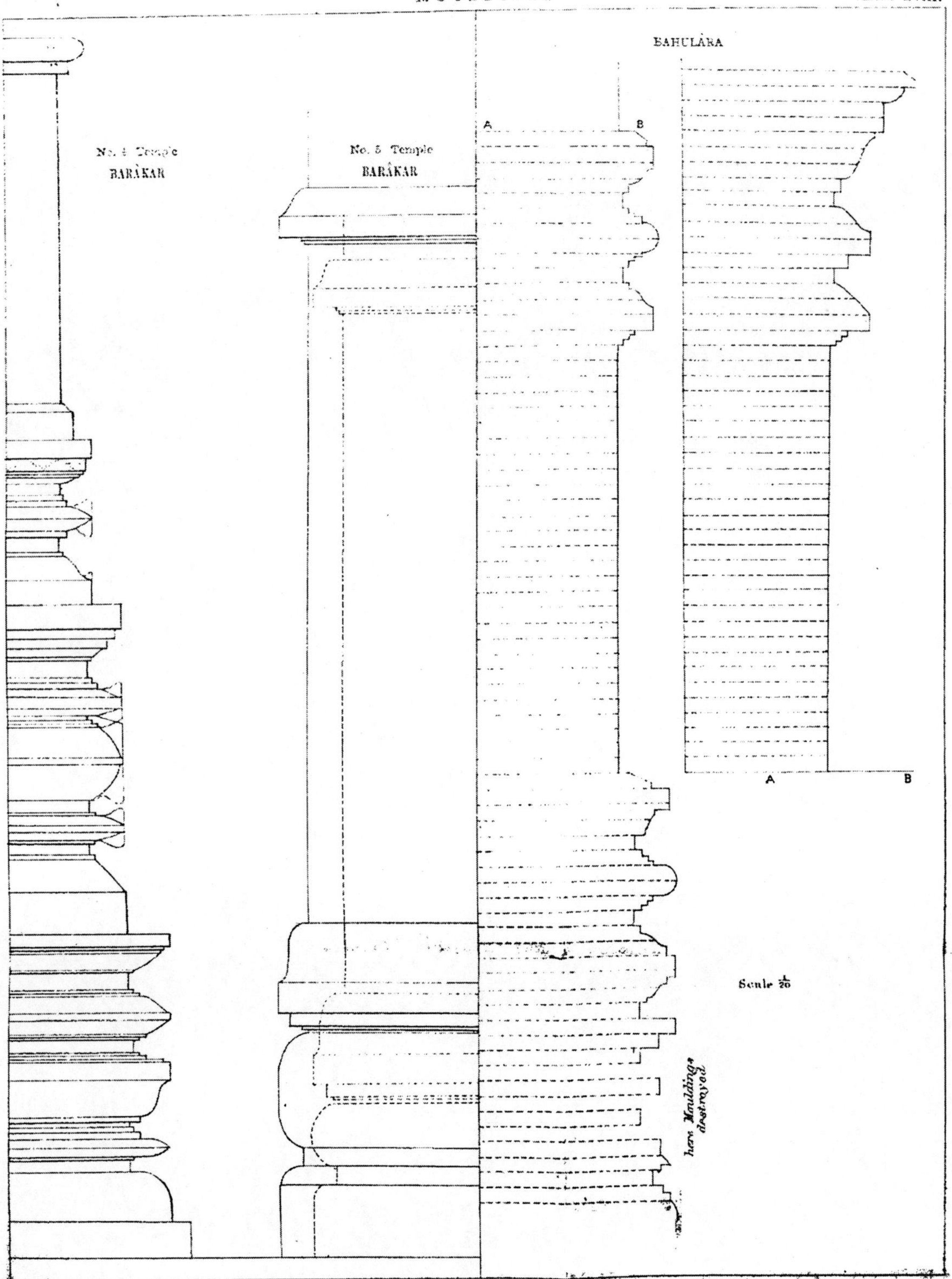

J. D. Beglar, del.

Lithographed at the Surveyor General's Office, Calcutta, February 1878.

Longitudinal (Half) Section of Southern Temple

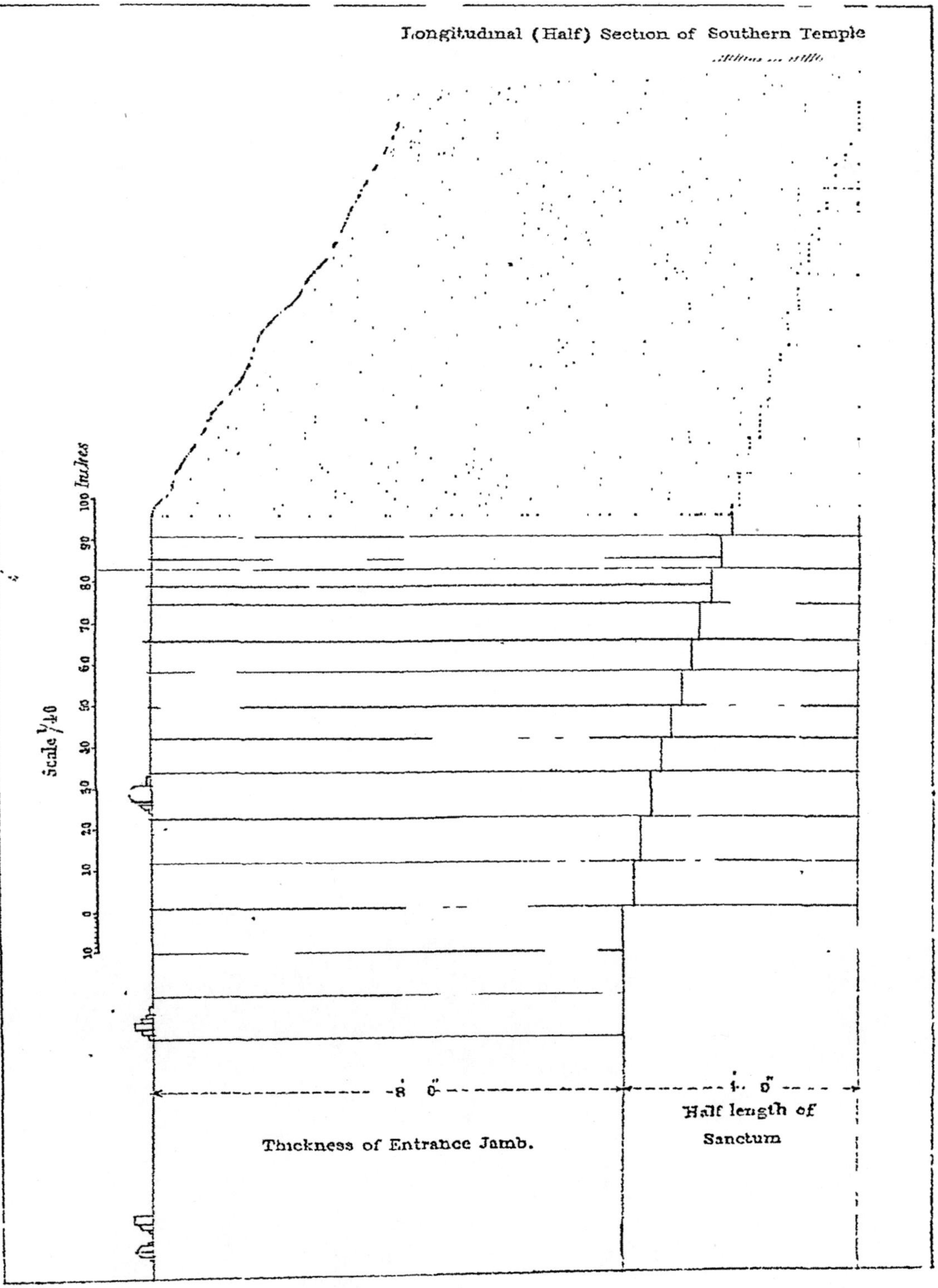

J. D. Beglar, del

Lithographed at the Surveyor General's Office, Calcutta, February 187?.

BASEMENT MOULDINGS

PLATE XX

J. D. Beglar, del

Lithographed at the Surveyor General's Office, Calcutta February 1879

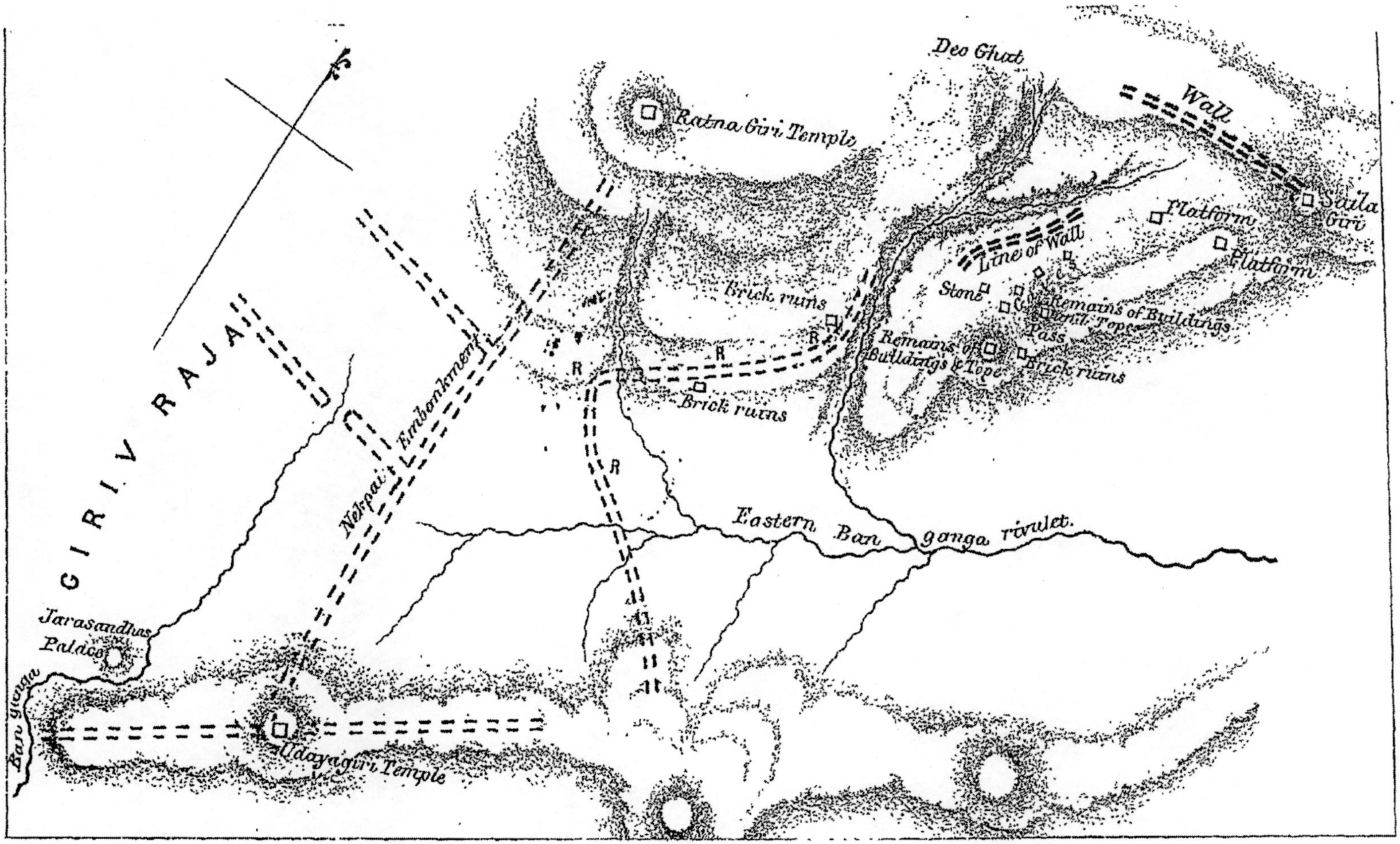

J. D. Beglar, Del,

LITHOGRAPHED FROM AN ORIGINAL SUPPLIED BY THE ARCHÆOLOGICAL SURVEY DEPARTMENT

At the Surveyor General's Office, Calcutta, June 1878